US
MARINE
CORPS
HANDBOOK

1941–5

GEORGE FORTY

SUTTON PUBLISHING

First published in the United Kingdom in 2006 by
Sutton Publishing Limited · Phoenix Mill
Thrupp · Stroud · Gloucestershire · GL5 2BU

ISBN 978-0-7509-4196-9

Typeset in 10/13pt New Baskerville.
Typesetting and origination by
Sutton Publishing Limited.
Printed in the United States of America

CONTENTS

A Marine shares his water with a young island girl. (USMC B-23465A via Real War Photos)

INTRODUCTION AND ACKNOWLEDGEMENTS

When the Second World War began, the United States Marine Corps numbered just under 66,000 officers and men (65,881 to be exact). Of these only 19,432 were on active duty, the rest were reservists. However, by the early summer of 1941, this figure had risen steadily with an ever-increasing number of eager new volunteers joining the Corps, while from 1943 onwards conscripts were inducted into a Corps that had previously been composed solely of volunteers. However, such was the 'gung-ho' (Chinese for 'Work together') spirit of the Marine Corps that some 154,000 of these conscripts rapidly became regular Marines or active Marine reservists. By the end of the war there were over 485,000 men and women in the Corps, the vast majority of whom were serving overseas. This sevenfold increase is of course dwarfed by the massive expansions which took place within the US Army and Navy. However, what makes it so special is the very high proportion of these 'leathernecks' (nicknamed after the high, stiff leather collars on their original eighteenth-century uniforms) who actually took part in combat of the bloodiest kind. During the Second World War, the Corps suffered nearly 87,000 casualties, of which just under 20,000 were killed or missing in action, this figure representing a large percentage of the United States' wartime battle casualty figures and a massive 36 per cent of the total of American soldiers and Marines killed or missing in the Pacific theatre.

The US Marine Corps has always possessed that indefinable aura that invariably surrounds such an elite fighting force, especially one that has taken part in so many battles – namely every conflict in which the USA has been involved since the Marine Corps was first formed in 1775. At the beginning of the twentieth century for example, there were Marines in China during the Boxer Rebellion both as part of the besieged legation garrison in Peking and in the relief force sent to break the siege. They were employed as infantry on the Western Front during the First World War, the Marine Brigade earning glory wherever it fought. After the First World War, they were involved in the Caribbean and in South and Central America – Panama, Cuba, Nicaragua, Haiti and the Dominican Republic – and also in the Philippines; the list is endless. Since the Second World War they have played a major role in Korea, Vietnam, Grenada, the Gulf War and now Iraq. So their fighting prowess is well known; however, much of their wartime organisation, weapons and equipment remains something of a mystery to those outside the Corps, or is assumed to be identical to that of the US Army. They have certainly always intrigued me, which is why, when Sutton Publishing invited me to write a companion volume to the one I completed some years ago for them on the US Army, I jumped at the chance; and this is the result.

It is definitely not a detailed history of the USMC in the Second World War, although I have included a short account of the Marine divisions' individual wartime combat records in the Pacific theatre in one of the chapters. Neither is it a complete history of the USMC since its formation. Rather, it is offered as a 'nuts and bolts' pamphlet, hopefully describing in some detail what made the USMC 'tick' during the Second World War, so it includes such mundane, but important, details as organisation tables, descriptions of weapons, vehicles and equipment, etc., and of course, most importantly, the ships of all kinds that took them to war. I sincerely hope that readers will find it both interesting and of value, and above all, that I haven't made too many errors. Of course I would have been completely unable to attempt such a task without the continuing expert help I have received from the USMC Chief Historian, Maj Charles D. Melson, to whom I owe an enormous debt of gratitude. The same applies to the renowned American historian Gordon L. Rottman, whose *US Marine Corps World War II Order of Battle* must be the most comprehensive treatise on the USMC ever written. His kindness in allowing me to quote from it is very much appreciated. The breadth and depth of his knowledge of the USMC is apparent from the range of his other relevant publications, such as those in the various Osprey series – Elite, Warrior, Battle Orders and Campaigns.

Of course, there are other British writers who have also kindly assisted me, who have written excellent books on specific aspects of the US Marine Corps, for example Jim Moran, who is an undoubted expert as far as USMC uniform and equipment are concerned, and Derrick Wright, who has written countless books on the battles that the Marine Corps fought during their 'island hopping' campaigns, such as his latest, *Pacific Victory*. I must thank both of them for their kindness, help and support, and also for the loan of numerous photographs. The Bibliography lists the books I have studied, but in particular, I must mention the series of pamphlets entitled 'World War II Commemorative Series' produced by the History and Museums Division at the Marine Corps Historical Center, in Washington, DC, which covers most aspects of their wartime service. Some of the photographs in this book come from their pages and I am most grateful for their permission to use them, as I am for the other USMC, USN and National Archive photographs that I have used. Sources are listed, but include Real War Photos of Indiana, Do You Graphics, USA, and Compendium Publishing of London. I have made every effort to contact the owners of images included here, and apologise if I have overlooked anybody.

The main US Marine Corps role in the Second World War was in the Pacific theatre. True, they still maintained such peacetime tasks as providing legation guards in important places like London; they also provided (for a while anyway) part of the garrison in Iceland, and found a token landing force for D-Day in north-west Europe. However, they were mainly to be found in the Pacific theatre, which stretched from Pearl Harbor to Okinawa, from the Solomons to Iwo Jima, a vast area into which, as one historian succinctly put it, 'you could drop the entire African–

European theatre and hardly notice it'. They were in many ways isolated from the rest of the war, suffering, as did the British Fourteenth Army in Burma, from being forgotten by the general public at home for long periods of time. While Eisenhower's armies were receiving rapturous welcomes all over Europe, all that greeted the Marines were Japanese 'banzai' charges, cowed natives, jungles full of poisonous insects and the most awful tropical diseases from malaria upwards. And the fighting went on for longer too – 'All in all . . . a grim, lonely war . . . a war that seemed to have no end.'

Because their main role was in the Pacific, I have chosen to start the book with a brief description of 'Landing Operations', beginning with a short amount of pre-war history, a period that produced the 'Tentative Manual for Landing Operations' that was the basis of the tactics employed in their endless beach landings. This opening chapter also includes an example of an amphibious landing (on Iwo Jima) during which the various elements of the landing force can be seen to play their essential roles.

As an ex-professional soldier, one can only bow in admiration at the continued bravery and courage that the individual Marines from general down to 'grunt' displayed throughout the long and difficult days that must never have seemed to have any end in sight. Theirs was a hard and bloody war, fought in the most difficult conditions and against a suicidally brave and implacable enemy. Gen George S. Patton once remarked that 'in Landing Operations retreat is impossible', so there was only one direction for the Marines to go and that was forwards against the enemy, whatever the cost.

Adm Chester Nimitz probably encapsulated the feelings of all in the last sentence of the victory communiqué that he issued on 17 March 1945 when Iwo Jima had fallen, in which he said, 'Among the Americans who served on Iwo Jima, uncommon valor was a common virtue.' Undoubtedly this is what had been displayed by the USMC from the very first bullet of the very first battle of the war they fought so bravely and so well in the Pacific theatre during the Second World War.

George Forty
Bryantspuddle, Dorset
April 2006

THE MARINES' HYMN

From the Halls of Montezuma,
To the shores of Tripoli;
We fight our country's battles
In the air, on land, and sea;
First to fight for right and freedom
And to keep our honor clean;
We are proud to claim the title of
United States Marine.

Our flag's unfurled to every breeze
From dawn to setting sun;
We have fought in every clime and place
Where we could take a gun;
In the snows of far off northern lands
And in sunny tropic scenes;
You will find us always on the job –
The United States Marines.

Here's a health to you and to our Corps
Which we are proud to serve;
In many a strife we've fought for life
And never lost our nerve;
If the Army and the Navy
Ever look on Heaven's scenes;
They will find the streets are guarded by
United States Marines.

CHAPTER ONE

LANDING OPERATIONS

A SMALL BEGINNING

According to the *Encyclopaedia Britannica*, the United States Marine Corps (USMC) is a separate military service within the US Department of the Navy, and is charged with the provision of Marine troops for the seizure and defense of advanced bases and with the conducting of operations on land and in the air, coincident with naval campaigns. The Corps is also responsible for the provision of detachments for service aboard certain types of naval vessels and for the provision of security forces to protect US Navy shore installations and US diplomatic missions in foreign countries. They also specialise in amphibious operations, such as those they undertook against Japanese-held islands in the Pacific during the Second World War.

It was on 10 November 1775 that the Marine Committee of the Continental Congress held a meeting in the Tun Tavern, on King Street, Philadelphia, at which they passed a resolution that a force of Marines was to be formed for duties as landing forces for the American fleet: 'that two Battalions of Marines be raised consisting of one Colonel, two Lieutenant Colonels, two Majors & Officers as usual in other regiments, that they consist of an equal number of privates with other battalions . . .

and are good seamen, or so acquainted with maritime affairs to be able to serve to advantage by sea, when required'.

From this small beginning evolved the present-day multi-functional organisation that combines skilled ground, sea and air combat units which have fought all over the world, as their famous 'Hymn' explains. This is not the place to go into detail about the early years of Marine history, when the Corps was developing, nor the period up to and including the First World War, when the Corps was evolving into an expeditionary force and winning glory, not only against the sophisticated German army in Europe, but also in the many 'brush fire/banana republic' wars that followed the end of the 'war to end all wars'. However, we do need to look at the interwar period, between 1919 and 1941, during which the Fleet Marine Force (FMF) came into being, as did the new, innovative tactics for amphibious landing operations that were evolved at the same time and that would, during the Second World War, become the primary reason for their very existence. In doing so they moved away from the traditional functions that they had espoused in the past, such as ship guards and landing parties. As Chester G. Hearn rightly says in his *Illustrated*

Directory of the United States Marine Corps, 'Without this action, there would have been no Marine Corps in 1942 to lead the fighting in the South and Central Pacific and no amphibian vehicles to breach the enemy defenses.' Having laid the foundations during this run-up to the 'Day of Infamy', they went on to prove themselves masters of their craft in the Pacific theatre against a ferocious and implacable enemy, their other roles – and there were still quite a few of those – assuming a lesser importance as they proved their courage and ability time and time again, 'island hopping' across the Pacific ever closer to the heartland of Japan.

PLAN ORANGE

Before the First World War, American operational military plans for dealing with their potential enemies were known by a series of colours. The one involving the most likely enemy in the Pacific area was entitled 'Orange'; hence codeword 'Orange' became synonymous with Japan, as did the plan to deal with war with that country. The 'Orange Plan' had to be constantly revised in order to keep pace with the ever-changing international situation, at no time more relevant than when, after the First World War, Japan was given control of the former German possessions in the Carolines, Marshalls and Marianas under a League of Nations mandate. This made the Philippines ever more vulnerable to attack by the Japanese.

The interwar years were a period in which many new ideas about how future wars would be conducted were endlessly discussed. The Germans, for example, enthusiastically supported the revolutionary tactics of armoured warfare that were being expounded by British military 'gurus' such as J.F.C. Fuller and Basil Liddell Hart. However, they did more than just discuss them, but rather fully embraced such teachings, with their own armoured expert, Gen Heinz Guderian, using them as the basis of his new form of warfare, which he called 'Blitzkrieg'. In the USA, the Office of Naval Intelligence was studying what would happen if 'Orange' became a reality. Clearly US forces would have to fight their way across the Pacific before they could relieve the Philippines, and the USMC, among others, was directed to help in the study. MajGen John A. Lejeune, the then Marine Commandant, assigned Maj (later Lt Col) Earl H. Ellis, the brilliant former adjutant of

The thirteenth Commandant of the USMC was MajGen John A. Lejeune. He commanded the Corps in the 1920s and did much to lay the groundwork and develop the Marine Corps's expertise in amphibious operations, enshrined in the 'Tentative Landing Operations Manual' of 1934. *(USMC 308342)*

4th Brigade, which had fought so well in France, to study the problems of the current Plan Orange. The result was a paper entitled 'Advanced Base Operations in Micronesia' that he wrote in 1921, which, having been given Lejeune's blessing, became the basis of 'Operational Plan 712D' that was the USMC contribution to the Orange Plan. Ellis had concentrated upon just one segment of possible war against Orange, namely the seizure of an advanced base for use by the Navy as a coaling and repair station. The place he had in mind was in the Marshall Islands and he even outlined the tactics to be used against such islands in the group as Eniwetok (on which the Marines would land in February 1944). His proposals were of course limited by the equipment then available, but he still made a number of sensible recommend-ations – for example, the need for troops fighting on shore to have naval gunfire available 'on call'.

In his dissertation, Ellis had argued that the success of an opposed landing depended upon speedy ship-to-shore movement by waves of assault craft that would be pro-tected by overwhelming gunfire and aerial attacks: 'The landing will entirely succeed or fail practically on the beach,' wrote Ellis. Preceded by a naval version of the First World War 'box barrage', the assaulting troops would require not only infantry but also machine-gun units, artillery, engineers and light tanks to help them to penetrate beach obstacles and overcome beach defenses. These units would all require special landing craft and armoured vehicles armed with machine guns and light cannon. Unlike other contemporary planners, Ellis stressed that the landings should occur in daylight, so as to avoid confusion among landing craft and assault forces. Close-in naval gunfire would help to neutralise the defenders. Ellis also averred most strongly that, because an amphibious assault depended on detailed planning, continual peacetime training was necessary, together with careful tactical and logistical organis-ation 'along Marine lines. It is not enough that the troops be skilled infantrymen or artillerymen of high morale; they must be skilled watermen and skilled junglemen who know it can be done – Marines with Marine training.' Ellis subsequently went on a clandestine recce of the islands; with Gen Lejeune's approval, he took extended leave in May 1921 to visit the Marshall Islands and the Caroline Islands, posing as an American businessman. He died somewhere in the

The basic landing craft for vehicles/personnel, the LCVP, was modelled on the 'Higgins' Boat, as seen here with its bow door lowered and carrying a military-type truck. The initial design was by Andrew Jackson Higgins of New Orleans.
Gen Eisenhower once called the LCVP the most important war-fighting tool of the Second World War and described Higgins as the man who had won the war for the Allies. *(USN 73812)*

Palau island group in May 1923 in mysterious circumstances. To quote Millett: 'His disappearance made him a martyr in the eyes of Second World War Marines and gave his studies the heroic glow of prophecy.' Later, Operational Plan 712D was accepted in its entirety and would be used thereafter, to guide war planning, field exercises, equipment development and officer education.

Part of the Marine Corps plan was to provide two expeditionary forces – one located on the west coast and one on the east, both of some 6,000–8,000 men, ready at forty-eight hours' notice to embark, the former for a campaign in the Pacific, for example against the Marshalls and Carolines, the latter for any Atlantic or Caribbean emergencies. These forces would be independent of other commitments.

Unfortunately, although there was general interest expressed in planning and preparing for future amphibious operations, most of the 'powers that be' and even some influential officers within the Corps itself,

resisted these new proposals, while stressing that the provision of security detachments both at home and abroad, and of providing ships' guards and occupation forces as and when necessary, still took a higher priority than preparing for a war that might never come. As Alan Millett comments, 'War Plan Orange might represent a new concept for the Marine Corps, but it remained to be seen whether the Corps would respond to the amphibious assault role.'

Nevertheless, by the mid-1920s, a certain amount of instruction on amphibious operations, both theoretical and practical, was included in the curriculum at the Marine Corps Schools (MCS) and it was soon clear that there was much to learn. Initial exercises, held in 1924, proved to be a fiasco; for example, landing boats did not reach the beach at the correct time, the unloading of supplies was chaotic and naval bombardment was totally inadequate. Further exercises were held the following year and while there was considerable improvement, there was still a lot to be done; for example, the need for better boats, better communications and more training in debarking were seen as paramount. Then, before further training could take place, the Marine Corps had to deploy men, firstly to guard the US Mail, then to go on operations in China and Nicaragua, stripping the fleet of amphibious exercise units. However, some progress was made, and in 1927, the Joint Army–Navy Board gave the Marine Corps its new mission: to conduct land operations in support of the fleet for the initial seizure and defense of advanced bases, and such limited auxiliary land operations as are essential to the prosecution of the naval campaign.

'THE TENTATIVE MANUAL FOR LANDING OPERATIONS'

Between 1919 and 1933, the Joint Army–Navy Board had produced several manuals that attempted to explain how the two services would cooperate in joint overseas expeditions. However, a manual of landing instructions was still lacking. Such events as having to mobilise 7th Marine Regiment for duty in Cuba in 1933 drained away personnel. Eventually, though, it was agreed that all classes should be discontinued at the Marine Corps Schools, so that students and staff could devote all their time and effort towards producing a landing operations manual. Work began in January 1934 and a first version (deliberately called 'The Tentative Manual') came into being some six months later, and was used at MCS during the 1934–5 school year. It would be revised and reissued on numerous occasions in subsequent years; for example, it was revised, then adopted by the USN in 1938 as 'Fleet Training Publication 167' (also known as 'The Landing Operations Doctrine, US Navy 1938'). Wartime amendments followed, the first being based on

developments up to 1941 (it was the guide for the Guadalcanal landings in August 1941). A second followed on 1 August 1942, just six days before Guadalcanal. Change No. 3 was issued in August 1943, based upon further experiences in the Solomons and in North Africa. It was subsequently used during the rest of the Second World War.

Command relationships were described in the manual, dealing with the organisation of the landing force as well as the command procedures. Overall command would rest with a naval officer of flag rank, while the task force would have two main components:

- The landing force, consisting of FMF units
- The naval support groups, consisting of the Fire Support Group, the Air Group, the Covering Group and the Transport Group

The specific responsibilities of the various commanders during all phases of the operations were clearly enumerated, and the principle of parallelism of command, subject to the overall authority of the amphibious force commander, was defined, thus ensuring that the naval forces would be organised so as to be responsive to the needs of the landing forces.

The 'Tentative Manual' recognised that an assaulting landing force followed a similar pattern to conventional offensive action, but appreciated that the 'over-the-water' movement of the attacking troops complicated the problems of providing fire support. Naval gunfire missions had to take the place of conventional field artillery, with the inherent problems, such as fire direction, nature of projectiles, magazine capacity, muzzle velocities and trajectories, all having to be considered, and a sound doctrine for the effective delivery of naval gunfire, developed.

Additionally the manual explored the possibility of using aircraft to provide close air support and an initial doctrine was evolved, which included visual and photographic reconnaissance, air defense and airborne fire support, especially during the final run-in of landing craft to the beach.

ORGANISED FOR COMBAT

We shall be covering the detailed organisation of the wartime Marine division in a later chapter, including the various changes that were made during the war years as a result of operational experience. Here, however, we need to look at how a Marine amphibious force would be 'task-organised' for combat. Typical attachments to a Marine division from the Fleet Marine Force (FMF) for an assault landing would include:

• a signal intelligence platoon (radio direction finding)
• a detachment of 4.5in barrage rockets
• a war dog platoon
• a joint assault signal company (Navy, Army and Marine personnel to coordinate naval gunfire, artillery and air support)
• an amphibious truck company (equipped with DUKWs)
• amphibian tractor battalions (both LVTs and LVT(A)s to provide both transport and close fire support)

In his book *US Marine Corps 1941–45*, Gordon Rottman explains how the task-organised and reinforced regiments were initially called 'combat groups' and their battalions 'combat teams'. However, in late 1943, these were redesignated as 'regimental landing teams' and 'battalion landing teams' respectively. He quotes two examples of how such groups/teams were organised:

1st Marine Division for the August 1942 landing on Guadalcanal

Combat Group A (5th Marine Regiment) and Combat Group B (1st Marine Regiment). Each comprised an infantry regiment, an artillery battalion, a tank company, an engineer company, a pioneer company, an amphibian tractor company and a medical company, plus scout, special weapons and transport platoons. Within combat groups, the infantry battalions were designated Combat Teams A1, A2, A3, B4, B5 and B6. As well as the infantry battalion, each had a 75mm pack howitzer battery, plus an engineer platoon, a pioneer platoon and an amphibian tractor platoon, together with small service elements. Additionally a divisional support group was formed, which had four subgroups of artillery, and engineer, pioneer, amphibian tractor, headquarters, communications, medical and special weapons elements, plus 1st Parachute Battalion. The division was not only organised to land and fight under this structure but also embarked on to its transport as groups and teams.

2nd Marine Division for the November 1943 landing on Tarawa (Betio)

The first two regiments were organised as Regimental Landing Teams 2 and 8 (bearing the designation of their parent regiment), and reinforced by a 105mm artillery battalion and various combat support units. Battalion landing teams were designated Red, White and Blue for 1st, 2nd and 3rd Battalions. Each was reinforced by a 75mm pack howitzer battalion, a tank company and an engineer platoon.

Battalions and companies also task-organised their assets for greater effect. For example, for the Roi-Namur landing in 1944, 4th Marine Division formed their landing companies into assault and demolition teams. Each company formed six such teams, each led by an officer and comprising a four-man LMG group, a five-

man demolition group, a three-man bazooka group and a four-man support group (with two Browning automatic rifles). A team was carried in an LVT(2). Follow-on reserve companies also formed 'boat teams' but were lacking the LMG group. They would be carried in an LVCP.

Essential last-minute briefings were normally carried out on board the troop transports, before boarding the landing craft. Here Marines of 2nd Marine Division receive a briefing on the landing plan for the assault on Betio, largest island of the Tarawa atoll, code-named Operation 'Galvanic', 20–3 November 1943. *(USMC 10180)*

A TYPICAL ASSAULT LANDING

Perhaps the best way of illustrating how all these elements worked together is to examine a typical amphibious assault landing in which Marine Divisions were heavily involved. I have chosen the assault on 'Sulphur Island' (Iwo Jima) on 19 February 1945. First we shall consider command relationships. Adm Nimitz had given the mission to the same team that had succeeded in the earlier amphibious assaults in the Gilberts, Marshalls and Marianas, so the overall commander for Iwo

Jima was Adm Raymond A. Spruance (commanding Fifth US Fleet). Vice Adm Richmond Kelly Turner commanded the Expeditionary Forces, while Rear Adm Harry W. Hill headed the Attack Force. In addition, the highly regarded Rear Adm William H.P. Blandy was in command of the Amphibious Support Forces, who were responsible for minesweeping, underwater demolition and the preliminary naval air and gun bombardment. Gen Holland M. Smith himself was designated Commander of Expeditionary Troops. (Smith was CG of the newly created Fleet Marine Force Pacific Command). The Marine forces immediately available for the operation were 3rd, 4th and 5th Marine Divisions, which were assigned to V Amphibious Corps, commanded by Gen Harry Schmidt, Smith's immediate subordinate in the chain of command and commander of the landing forces. The actual strength of the assault force was some 70,600, augmented by Army garrison troops and naval personnel assigned to shore duty (construction and beach logistics), bringing the expeditionary force strength up to just over 111,300.

To assist with the landing, the force was allocated:

- 2nd Armored Amtrac Battalion – sixty-eight LVT(A)4s for armoured support
- Four battalions of cargo-carrying amtracs (3rd, 5th, 10th and 11th) to provide the troop-carrying amtracs for the landing and subsequent logistics support; these were LVT(2)s and LVT(4)s

They would spearhead the operation, the first five waves of the landing using 400 LVTs to carry eight battalions of 4th and 5th Marine Divisions on to the south-eastern beaches of the island. The cargo tractors would be preceded by 2nd Armored Amtrac Battalion, who in turn would be preceded by LCI gunboats firing rockets and machine guns. Heavy firepower in the first wave was the order of the day, the LVT(A)4s being in line formation so that all had maximum freedom to fire their 75mm howitzers and machine guns. They would also land and proceed a short distance inland, so as to provide continued close support to the assault troops.

Troop tractors were to land and discharge their troops on the beach, then return to sea for logistic duties. The line of departure for the landing was some 4,000yd offshore and from there a thirty-minute run-in was expected. The interval between waves of LVTs was to be 250–300yd. The combined width of the landing beaches for the two assault divisions was 3,500yd, which meant that there would be an armoured amtrac every 50yd as the first wave approached the beach.

Once the forces were ashore, the plan was simple: 4th and 5th Marine Divisions would land abreast (5th on the left), with 3rd Marine Division in reserve. The extreme

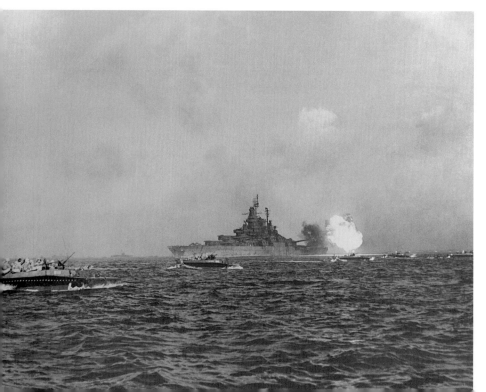

'Land the Landing Force!' Heavily loaded amtracs head for shore, under the cover of naval gunfire, the naval equivalent of a land artillery barrage and just one of the elements of the detailed fire support programme necessary to ensure a successful landing. *(USMC B-23477 via Real War Photos)*

'A Thumbs Up from the Leathernecks!' Men of 1st Marine Division give a cheerful 'thumbs up' as their LVT2s make for the beaches of Peleliu, 15 September 1944. There appear to be only some fifteen Marines in the nearest landing craft, but it was capable of carrying twenty-five. There was no ramp, so the Marines had to dismount over the sides. *(USMC B-23424 via Real War Photos)*

Marking time. Loaded landing craft circle offshore as they wait for the signal to move in towards the beaches. *(USMC B-23473 via Real War Photos)*

Above: Heading towards the beaches of Peleliu. This LVT(A)1 (nearest vehicle) and these LVT(A)4 amphibious tanks were photographed during the assault on the smoke-shrouded beaches of Peleliu. They belonged to 3rd Armored Amphibian Tractor Battalion. *(US Navy via Derrick Wright)*

Left: 2nd Marine Division storms ashore at Agune Jima, 20 miles west of Okinawa, on 9 June 1945. The island is wreathed in smoke from the pre-invasion bombardment by the US Pacific Fleet, plus the air strikes, rocket and mortar barrages. *(USMC 80-G-49886 via Compendium Publishing)*

left-hand regiment of 5th Marine Division (27th Marine Regiment under Col Harry 'The Horse' Liversedge) was to attack straight across the neck of land, then turn south-west and take Mount Suribachi. Other regiments of the division were to attack forwards, then turn right and attack north-east up the long axis of the island. On D+3, 3rd Marine Division was to land over the same beaches and move into the centre between the other two divisions.

Landing 'on call' over their parent division beaches would be 4th and 5th Tank Battalions and it was anticipated that their firepower would be needed to help get the Marines off the beach quickly. It was on the beach that the intelligence analysts expected the toughest battle as that had been the experience of past Japanese tactics. However, this would not be the case at Iwo Jima, the enemy remaining virtually silent during the early phase of the battle, then

Above: Firing salvoes of 4.5in rockets from their twenty-four multiple rocket launchers (twelve a side), two LCI (Rocket) blast away at the enemy. They could fire as many as 600 rockets in one run into the beaches. *(USMC B-23419 via Real War Photos)*

Below: Zero-hour on Peleliu. An aerial view of loaded landing craft moving on to the beaches. Some of the landing craft are on fire, having been hit by enemy counter-bombardment. *(USMC B-23427 via Real War Photos)*

Marines landing on the Marshalls. Riflemen leap ashore from their just-beached amtrac while under enemy fire during the January 1944 landing. Note the .30 and .50 heavy Browning machine guns on the amtrac to provide close fire support while the Marines 'hit the beach!'. *(USMC 72411)*

opening devastating fire after the landing had moved inland. When 3rd Marine Division came ashore, they brought their 3rd Tank Battalion. Thus there were some 150 Sherman M4A2 medium tanks on the island and their high-velocity 75mm had almost twice the hitting power of the 75mm howitzer on the LVT(A)4 – of considerable value in dealing with the numerous heavy enemy fortifications that abounded on Iwo Jima.

'LAND THE LANDING FORCE!'

At Annexe A to this chapter are, by way of example, details of the Task Organisation of 4th Marine Division for the Iwo Jima landing. Weather conditions around Iwo Jima on the morning of 19 February 1945 (D-Day) were almost ideal and at 0645 hr Adm Turner signalled: 'Land the landing force.'

Space does not permit a complete 'blow by blow' account of the entire landing and battle for Iwo Jima. However, here is an extract from 4th Marine Division's history, which graphically tells of the first moments of the assault:

Early on the morning of February 19, the Division arrived off Iwo. It was D-Day! Lying off the island was the now familiar spectacle of the vast armada of an invasion force. From every side the guns of the warships were laying down their bombardment, and overhead wave after wave of planes hit the island: torpedo bombers firing rockets, fighters strafing and dive bombers coming straight down to drop their load.

The assault BLTs (Beach Landing Teams) were boated at an early hour in their LVTs. The reserve battalions and the reserve regiment (RCT 24) were to use LCVPs. The Division landing plan provided for RCT 23 to land on the left (Yellow) beaches, while RCT 25 would use the right (Blue) beaches. From left to right, the assault BLTs were: 1/23, 2/23, 1/25, and 3/25. Because of the damage to the LCI(G)s caused by Japanese fire on D-1, close-in fire support for the assault waves was to be furnished by LCS(L)s. In addition, the leading LVTs were preceded by LVT(A)s. H hour was set for 0900.

By 0815, the first three waves of assault troops were formed and waiting behind the Line of Departure. At 0830, they were on their way in. The weather was good and the surf moderate. The naval gunfire, air strikes and rocket and mortar barrages from the gunboats were saturating the beaches now, and only moderate enemy fire fell on the leading waves. As they neared the shore, the support fire moved inland in a 'rolling barrage' [a 'navalised' form of the traditional army rolling barrage, this was aimed

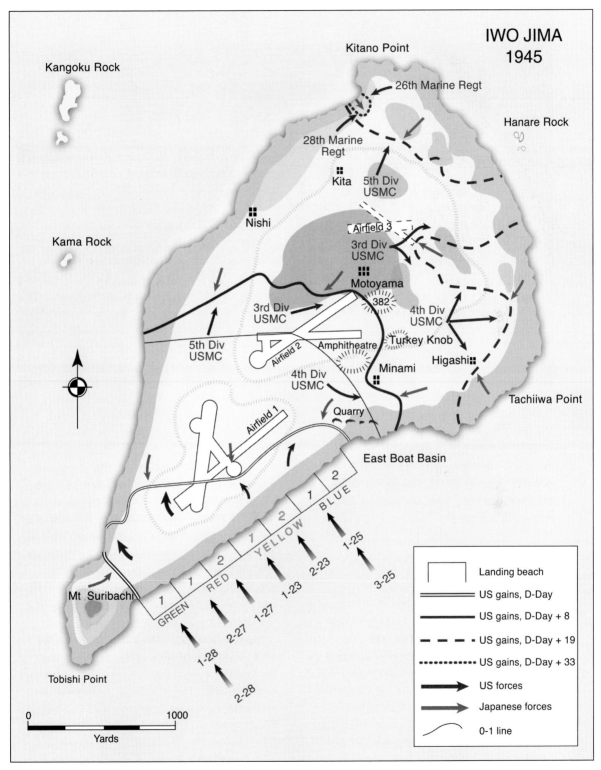

Iwo Jima – 4th Marine Division zone of action.

Iwo Jima. The 25th Marine Regiment were pinned down by accurate and heavy enemy fire on the right side of the V Amphibious Corps line. In the background can be seen landing craft bringing supplies and vehicles, which pile up in the surf behind them. *(USMC 110108)*

against beach-front targets just before H-Hour, then advanced progressively inland as the troops landed, always remaining 400yd in front of them, and controlled by air spotters]. At 0902 they hit the beach. A Japanese observer who was watching from a cave on Mount Suribachi said: 'At nine o'clock in the morning several hundred landing craft rushed ashore like an enormous tidal wave.'

And then came trouble – in large quantities. As the naval gunfire lifted, the Japanese 'opened up' with every weapon they had, and soon a solid sheet of fire was pouring down on the beaches and the incoming waves. It was (according to the Division report on Iwo) the 'heaviest enemy mortar and artillery fire yet seen in any operation'. Boats were hit; they broached and clogged the beaches. Personnel casualties mounted rapidly. Vehicles ashore found the sandy volcanic ash and the first terrace (with its 40% grade) nearly impassable. Even tanks bogged down. Every move was under direct observation of the Japanese on top of the cliff line on the right flank and on Mt Suribachi on the left.

Nevertheless, supporting arms and personnel kept coming ashore as rapidly as conditions on the beaches would permit. Tanks were on Yellow Beach by 0940. The reserve BLTs of the assault regiments were coming ashore by 1233. The Shore and Beach Parties began landing. Around 1500, two battalions of artillery were going ashore to furnish direct support for the assault troops and 1/14 was firing missions by 1740.

14

Above: Personnel of 5th Marine Division land on Red and Green Beaches at the foot of Mount Suribachi, also under heavy fire from enemy positions overlooking the black sand beaches. The 28th Marine Regiment have not yet wheeled towards Mount Suribachi. As Gen George S. Patton once remarked, 'In landing operations, retreat is impossible.' *(USMC 111691)*

Right: Moving inland. Once the beaches were secure, then the task force moved inland, as here on Okinawa, 3 April 1945. This aerial panorama shows the fleet offshore and the leading troops, supported by tanks, moving inland. *(USMC 80-G-339237 via Compendium Publishing)*

BLTs 1/24 and 2/24 of the Division Reserve were sent in at 1615 to be attached to the assault regiments. The command posts of RCT 23 and RCT 25 were set up by 1700. RCT 24 (minus detached elements) was completely ashore at 1945 and then it moved to its assembly area.

By the night of D Day, the Division had all three of its rifle regiments (less some Support Group elements), two battalions of artillery and some heavy Shore Party equipment ashore. Despite the withering enemy fire and extremely heavy casualties, the assault units had driven ahead and established a line that included the eastern edge of Airfield No. 1 and was (as reported in the Division Report on Iwo): 'of sufficient depth inland from Blue Beaches to guarantee the successful holding of the beachhead'. Full contact with the Fifth Division had been established and adequate supplies were ashore for a continuation of the attack the next day.

I hope this short, but detailed, account of a typical assault landing will help to explain how the Marines operated in their Pacific campaigns. To close this first chapter, this quotation from the Corps history, *Semper Fi*, should equally help to explain the major change that had thus occurred to the *raison d'être* of the Corps:

The Corps had made a major contribution (perhaps the major contribution) to create an essential Allied military speciality, the amphibious assault against a hostile shore. At the same time the Corps' ability to grow and adapt to the Pacific war remains impressive. When Pearl Harbor came Navy and Marine planners envisioned a Corps balanced between FMF assault divisions and base defense forces, made up of infantry, coastal and AAA, and aviation. By VJ Day the ground element of the FMF was an amphibious assault force without peer and the Marine divisions had gone through four basic organisational changes to find the right mix of men and weapons for each succeeding campaign.

The FMF also had created corps troops of heavy artillery, tanks, amtracs, recce units, and varied service units where none had existed in 1942. These changes represented rapid organisational responses not only to the tactical and logistical challenges of ship to shore movement, but also to the shifting character of the fighting ashore. Essentially the Corps fought four different ground wars against the Japanese: the jungle warfare in the South Pacific; the atoll warfare of the Gilberts & Marshalls; the mobile warfare of the Marianas; the cave warfare of Peleliu, Iwo Jima and Okinawa. Each war made its special demands and the Corps met them. It did so by adjusting its infantry training, increasing the firepower of its infantry and artillery regiments, using tanks, and armoured amphibians not only as mobile artillery but also as flamethrowers and stressing the coordination of supporting fires. By 1945, the Corps had made important conceptual and practical advances in using artillery, naval gunfire, and close air support against ground targets, but it was also aware that it needed further experience in fire support coordination.

ANNEXE A

TASK ORGANISATION OF THE FOURTH MARINE DIVISION ON IWO JIMA

Regimental Combat Team 23

23rd Marine Regiment
3rd Band Section
Company C, 4th Tank Battalion
Company C, 4th Engineer Battalion
Company C, 4th Medical Battalion
Company C, 4th Motor Transport Battalion
133rd Naval Construction Battalion (less
    Company D, plus Company A,
    4th Pioneer Battalion)
3rd Platoon, 4th Military Police Company
3rd Platoon, Service and Supply Company,
    4th Service Battalion
Detachment, 1st Joint Assault Signal
    Company
10th Amphibian Tractor Battalion
Company B, 2nd Armoured Amphibian
    Battalion
3rd Sec., 7th Marine War Dog Platoon
Detachment, 8th Field Depot Shore Party
3rd Platoon, 442nd Port Company
2nd Sec., 1st Provisional Rocket
    Detachment
Liaison and Forward Observation Parties,
    2/14

Regimental Combat Team 25

25th Marine Regiment
1st Band Section
Company A, 4th Tank Battalion
Company A, 4th Engineer Battalion
Company A, 4th Medical Battalion
Company A, 4th Motor Transport Battalion
4th Pioneer Battalion (less Company A, plus
    Company D, 133rd Naval Construction
    Battalion and Headquarters Detachment,
    8th Field Depot)
1st Platoon, 4th Military Police Company

1st Platoon, Service & Supply Company,
    4th Service Battalion
Detachment, 1st Joint Assault Signal
    Company
5th Amphibian Tractor Battalion
Company A, 2nd Armored Amphibian
    Battalion
7th War Dog Platoon (less 2nd and
    3rd Secs)
Detachment, 8th Field Depot
30th Replacement Draft (less detachment)
    (Self-Propelled)
1st Platoon, 442nd Port Company
1st Sec., 1st Provisional Rocket
    Detachment
Liaison and Forward Observation Parties,
    1/14

Regimental Combat Team 24 (Divisional Reserve)

24th Marine Regiment
2nd Band Section
Company B, 4th Tank Battalion
Company B, 4th Engineer Battalion
Company B, 4th Medical Battalion
Company B, 4th Motor Transport Battalion
2nd Platoon, 4th Military Police Company
2nd Platoon, Service & Supply Company,
    4th Service Battalion
Detachment, 1st Joint Assault Signals
    Company
2nd Sec., 7th War Dog Platoon
Detachment, 24th and 30th Replacement
    Drafts
442nd Port Company (less 1st and 3rd
    Platoons)
Liaison and Forward Observation Parties,
    3/14

Divisional Artillery

14th Marine Regiment
4th Amphibian Truck Company

476th Amphibian Truck Company
VMO-4 (Marine Observation Squadron)

Support Group
Headquarters Battalion (less detachment)
4th Tank Battalion (less Companies A, B, C; plus Tank Maintenance (Main) Platoon, Ordnance Company, 4th Service Battalion)
4th Engineer Battalion (less Companies A, B, C)
2nd Armored Amphibian Battalion (less Companies A, B, C, D, and Detachment Battalion Headquarters)
4th Service Battalion (less detachments)
Divisional Reconnaissance Company
1st Joint Assault Signal Company (less detachments)
1st Provisional Rocket Detachment (less 1st and 2nd Secs)
Detachment, 726th SAW Company
Joint Intelligence Centre Pacific Ocean Area Team
Detachment, Signal Battalion, V Amphibious Corps
Corps Liaison Group

CHAPTER TWO

MARINE CORPS STATIC ORGANISATIONS

This chapter covers the general static elements of the United States Marine Corps and explains how their organisation evolved during the war, highlighting the main important elements, such as the Headquarters Marine Corps and the training establishments. Not included here are the operational elements of the USMC, such as the Fleet Marine Force, the amphibious corps, the Marine divisions, brigades and tactical groups, and finally, the defense battalions and balloon squadrons, which are covered in the next three chapters. More specialist outfits, like the Marine aviators, the Marine paratroopers, Marine raiders and the Women's Reserve, all of whom merit chapters to themselves, follow later. Tucked in with the paratroopers is the short-lived Marine Glider Group.

Before 1941, the largest existing Marine formations were 1st and 2nd Marine Brigades, which had been formed on the east and west coasts of the USA in 1935–6. Each brigade had as its central core an under-strength Marine infantry regiment and an aircraft group. If either brigade had to deploy to meet an emergency, then numbers would, in theory, be made up from ships' guards (see later). General foreign policy at that time dictated that the Fleet Marine Force was to be more focused on possible operations in the Atlantic and the Caribbean rather than in the Pacific. This policy was vindicated when the Second World War began and German U-boats became a major threat to shipping to and from the USA through the North Atlantic. Additionally, after the fall of France in 1940, there was the distinct possibility that Germany might occupy erstwhile French possessions in the Caribbean, almost directly on America's 'doorstep'. Unfortunately that was not all. By late spring 1941, when Britain was fighting alone against Germany and Italy, the British Prime Minister asked President Roosevelt to send troops to Iceland to replace the British garrison there, the danger being that, with Norway and Denmark overrun, Iceland could be the next to fall, which strategically would have adversely affected Britain's North Atlantic 'lifeline'. This was agreed, with the proviso that the Icelandic government approved, which they did with some reluctance. The only operationally ready troops available were 1st Marine Brigade (Provisional), and so the 4,095-strong brigade left Charleston for service in Iceland on 22 June 1941. It would not return to the USA until the end of March 1942.

Thus it was that American attention would not really be directed towards the Pacific area until after Japan had become the third member of the Axis in September 1940, and they had made their unprovoked attack on Pearl Harbor on 7 December 1941. For the Marine Corps, this would lead not only to a massive expansion but also a drastic change of operational theatres, the Pacific theatre now becoming virtually their *raison d'être*.

MISSIONS

The USMC is a component of the Navy Department serving under the Secretary of the Navy. It is not a component of the US Navy. The Corps was subject to the Articles for the Government of the Navy. It is commanded by the Commandant of the Marine Corps, who was known as the Major General Commandant before January 1942. It was (and still is) tasked to support the Navy with the following specific missions:

1. Maintain a mobile force in immediate readiness as a part of the US Fleet for use in operations involving shore objectives.
2. Maintain Marine detachments as a part of the ship's crew on battleships, aircraft carriers and cruisers.
3. Provide garrisons for the safeguarding of Navy yards and naval stations at home and in outlying possessions of the United States.
4. Provide forces for the protection of American lives and property abroad.

(Source: Rottman, *US Marine Corps World War II Order of Battle*)

However, as Gordon Rottman goes on to explain, during the Second World War the USMC missions went far beyond these straightforward tasks and would soon encompass the broad spectrum of global warfare. This would include such tasks as the defense of remote island bases, fleet amphibious operations, prolonged offensive land campaigns, amphibious reconnaissance, naval base and installation security, close air support, offensive air strikes, aerial reconnaissance and patrols, ships' guards, landing forces, native militia and foreign troops training, foreign advisory missions, embassy guards, logistical support, ceremonial duties; clandestine operations, disarming and repatriating surrendered enemy forces, and occupation duties; the list was endless. Moreover, these often-complex duties had to be carried out in a joint environment operating together with the Army, Navy and Allied forces, and with those services' air arms.

THE MARINE CORPS ESTABLISHMENT

This comprised all the Marine Corps supporting activities, posts, stations, etc. that were located in the USA and its outlying territories and stations overseas. Hence there were establishments such as supply depots, procurement (recruiting) divisions and stations, recruit depots, Marine Corps Schools, administrative and security activities, bases, stations, yards, depots and air stations, etc. The list is a long one, made all the longer here by also including ships' detachments, as this is a convenient place to cover them. However, they were strictly part of a ship's crew and thus a part of the fleet, while during the war most training establishments were strictly part of the FMF.

Headquarters Marine Corps (HQMC)

In 1941, the senior Marine Corps headquarters was located in the Navy Department Building on the Mall in Washington, DC, where it had been since 1919. In 1941, it was relocated to the Arlington Annex of the Navy Department, some 1¼ miles from

HQ USMC. From 1941, the Headquarters of the Marine Corps was located in the Arlington Annex of the Naval Department some 1¼ miles from the yet to be completed Pentagon building. Here, WRs are hard at work at their desks. By the end of the war, 87 per cent of the enlisted staff jobs at HQMC were filled by women Marines. *(USMC 304979 via Do You Graphics, USA)*

the yet-to-be-completed Pentagon (opened 15 January 1943). Here it remained throughout the war. The HQ had six main responsibilities: the procurement, education, training, discipline, distribution and discharge of all Marine Corps personnel. By the end of the war, some 87 per cent of the enlisted staff posts at HQMC were filled by women Marines.

As the chart overleaf shows, in December 1941, HQMC comprised three main elements: the Office of the Major General Commandant (a small personal staff, including his deputy, the Assistant to the Major General Commandant); the planning staff in the form of the Division of Plans and Policies; and the administrative, technical, supply and operating staff. Both the latter two elements were subdivided as shown, the former into four 'M' sections, the latter into three departments and four divisions. (The Division of Plans and Policies originally had a fifth section – the War Plans M-5 Section. However, this was abolished in the autumn of 1941 and its functions were taken over by the M-3 Section.)

Inevitably organisational changes were made during the war years, as a result mainly of wartime expansion, and the second drawing shows the HQMC organisation in July 1944.

During the war years the USMC had just two Commandants: Lt Gen Thomas Holcomb from 1 December 1936 to 31 December 1943, and Gen Alexander A. Vandegrift from 1 January 1944, for the rest of the war. MajGen Holcomb was promoted to lieutenant-general in January 1942, the first Marine general officer to reach that rank, while Lt Gen Vandegrift was promoted to full general in March 1945, also the first Marine general officer to achieve that rank. He would retire on 1 January 1948.

HQ Battalion, HQMC

To provide security at the Navy Department and Marine Corps offices and facilities in the Washington, DC, area, there was an HQ Battalion, later, in 1943, split into two battalions, one of which was deactivated in late 1945. The Guard Battalion, Navy Building (1st, 2nd and

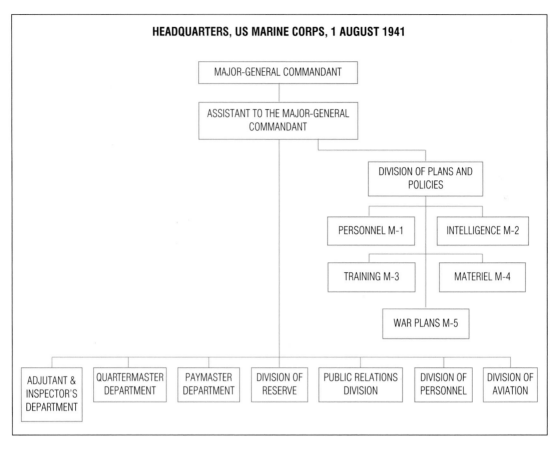

HEADQUARTERS, US MARINE CORPS, 1 AUGUST 1941

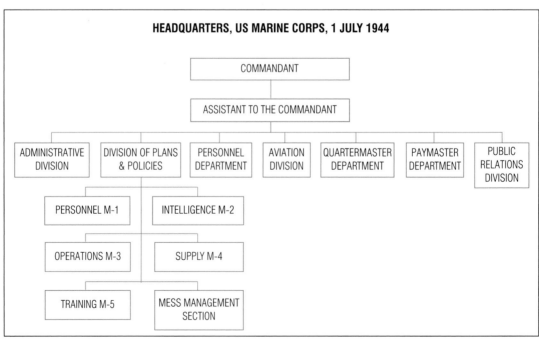

HEADQUARTERS, US MARINE CORPS, 1 JULY 1944

3rd Guard Companies) was activated on 1 March 1942, with 770 troops. It was disbanded in late 1945.

The Marine Corps Band

Established on 11 July 1798, but tracing its roots back to 1775, and designated 'The President's Own' by Thomas Jefferson (third US president), it is the oldest military band in America. It was stationed throughout the war at the Marine Barracks, Navy Yard, Washington, DC. The USMC Band Symphony Orchestra is one and the same unit. Throughout the war years it performed ceremonial duties, including occasional national tours.

One of the four USMC major posts at the start of the war was located at San Diego. The photograph shows a Friday afternoon parade in progress, with 1st Battalion, 6th Marine Regiment, marching past their CO (Lt Col Oliver P. Smith) at the Recruit Depot, before leaving for Iceland. West Coast USMC units rotated between the new Camp Elliott, 12 miles north of San Diego, and this base, every three months. *(National Archives 127-G-515852)*

In addition to the Marine Corps Band, the amphibious corps, Marine divisions, brigades, separate infantry regiments, defense and anti-aircraft artillery battalions, posts and the larger barracks all possessed their own bands or drum and bugle corps. In battle, the bands accompanied their regiments ashore and were employed as litter- (stretcher-) bearers (cf. British Army).

Posts and Stations

When the Second World War began in September 1939, the USMC had just four major posts in the USA: Quantico in Virginia, Parris Island in South Carolina, San Diego and Camp Elliott in California. Hence they were ill-prepared for the coming expansion of the Corps, and desperately needed training facilities both for recruits and for individual secondary and operational training. In addition to the more traditional training facilities such as firing ranges, obstacle courses, drill fields (i.e. parade grounds) and tactical training areas, new facilities such as amphibian tractor training areas, parachute training centres, sniper and flame-thrower ranges

and radar sites were required. The most important of those set up were:

East Coast
- Marine Barracks, Parris Island, South Carolina
- Marine Barracks, Quantico, Virginia
- Camp Lejeune Amphibious Base, NC (Camp New River before 1943, then renamed after Gen Lejeune's death)
- Marine Barracks, Navy Yard, Washington, DC

West Coast
- Marine Corps Base, Navy Operating Base, San Diego, California

- Camp Elliott, California
- Camp Joseph H. Pendleton, Marine Corps Base, California

Additionally, there were a number of posts/stations on Hawaii to house/cater for units arriving from the USA for training, preparing for operations and recovering from combat.

Training Establishments

The two main Marine recruit training establishments throughout the war were at Parris Island, South Carolina and San Diego, California. However, they did not become properly organised as recruit depots (known as 'boot camps') until August 1940; before then, only recruit training companies had existed. The depots now formed recruit battalions, each containing a varied number of lettered companies and up to twenty-five recruit training platoons (each sixty strong), which were the mainstay in making Marines out of the young recruits. The 'nitty gritty' of this task was mainly carried out under the all-seeing eye of the DI (drill instructor). To quote from a short book published soon after the war ended, entitled *Uncommon Valor* (McMillan *et al.*): 'The process of turning the recruit into a Marine began at boot camp, where he was shorn of his hair and his individuality at the same time. This was accomplished under the expert supervision of one of the most fabulous characters in the Corps, the Drill Instructor or, as he is commonly called, the "DI". The DI is a non-

Camp Lejeune, North Carolina. Originally named Camp New River but renamed in 1943, after Gen Lejeune's death, it was one of the East Coast USMC training centres. Here a column of Marine Women Reserves marches past a column of male Marines in Camp Lejeune, November 1943. *(USMC 6153 via Do You Graphics, USA)*

As sure-footed as mountain goats, these Marine Corps raiders tackle the obstacle course at Camp Pendleton, California, January 1943. Note that the man in the middle of the front trio is armed with a Browning automatic rifle (BAR), which, at 19.4lb, weighed some 10lbs more than the standard M1 Garand rifle. *(USMC 35206 via Do You Graphics, USA)*

commissioned officer who probably joined up twenty years before at the age of seventeen. Years of running errands, standing guard, polishing belt buckles, doing sea and foreign duty and marching in parades have given him a particularly bilious outlook on life. Needless to say, it is the recruit who suffers.'

Initially, training units were somewhat chaotic as the Corps endeavoured to meet the constantly changing training demands of the newly evolving tactics of amphibious warfare. To quote from Allan R. Millett's incomparable *Semper Fidelis*: 'Hard pressed to handle the patriotic, naïve, but eager hordes, the recruit depots concentrated on creating Marines, not combat-ready infantrymen. Lashed by drill instructors' tongues (physical violence seems to have been rare), the "boots" drilled, hiked, exercised and learned the rudiments of the Marine Corps traditions and customs. . . . As agencies of socialization the recruit depots were superb. Clad in loose green twill dungarees and pith helmets, the recruits labored, sweat running from their shaved

skulls, and soon learned unique behaviours and attitudes that made them Marines.'

By 1943, the situation had stabilised and more speciality training battalions had been formed, while other recruits received 'on the job' training, as is explained in *Uncommon Valor*: 'Later he (the Recruit – known as the 'Boot'!) received specialised training in the branch of the Corps to which he was assigned. Most of the recruits went to the Fleet Marine Force and out of these the combat divisions were organised. Two large camps, Lejeune in North Carolina and Pendleton, at Oceanside, California, were the principal training grounds. There men became specialists in some detail of war: riflemen, machine gunners, mortarmen, truck-drivers, clerks, scouts, artillerymen, cooks, tankmen. To this work was added training in amphibious assault. On the average it took about a year to turn a boot into a qualified Marine, ready to go into battle. No fighting men in the world ever received better training.'

In December 1944, the Marine Replacement and Training Command, San Diego

Area was formed from the HQ FMF, San Diego area, under the command of MajGen Charles F.B. Price. By early 1945, it was considered that the Marine Corps possessed all the trained personnel it needed and, despite ongoing operations and the impending invasion of Japan, some types of training were reduced/suspended. As soon as war ended, the process speeded up even more and training establishments were rapidly disbanded. The Replacement

Montford Point. 'Boot Camp' for the African-American Marines was Montfort Point, west of Camp Lejeune, New River, NC. Here Cpl Tony Ghazlo, an unarmed-combat instructor, demonstrates how to disarm his assistant, Pfc Ernest Jones. *(National Archives 127-N-5334)*

and Training Command formed the Redistribution Regiment (Provisional) at Camp Pendleton, with the Separation Battalion and 1st and 2nd Casual Battalions being responsible for separating Marines from the service (i.e. demobilising them) as they returned from overseas.

Marine Corps Schools (MCS)

The school for the formal training of officers was located at the Marine Barracks, Quantico, in 1921 and called the Marine Corps Schools (MCS). It comprised the Basic, the Company Officers' and the Field Officers' Schools. The Basic School provided basic Marine officer training to Naval Academy and Platoon Leader Course (PLC) graduates and newly commissioned officers from the enlisted ranks. In 1924, the Basic School was

Right: Cpl Jerry Cargill has his parachute straps adjusted by Cpl Glenn Riggs as he gets ready to make a controlled jump at Camp Gillespie Parachute Training Centre, near San Diego, California, December 1942. *(USMC 35096 via Do You Graphics, USA)*

Below: Paratroopers under training used jump towers for controlled jumps. The first to be used by USMC paratroopers in training were at Highstown, New Jersey, where two civilian towers belonging to the Safe Parachute Company were located. Later, training was moved en masse to Camp Gillespie, near San Diego. *(National Archives 127-YC-121 via Do You Graphics, USA)*

relocated in the Marine Barracks, Navy Yard, Philadelphia, remaining part of the MCS, yet functioning independently. The Platoon Leader Course (PLC) was established in Quantico in 1935 to train officers entering the Marine Corps from college (they attended two six-week summer camps). However, that was by no means all. To quote Rottman again: 'The MCS faculty was a repository of experience and the source of much of the Corps' forthcoming doctrine as well as future key commanders and staff officers.' The Basic School was closed in 1940 and replaced by the Reserve Officers' School at Quantico to train officers commissioned through the PLC, through Officer Candidate School (OCS), which had also been established in 1940, and via the Army Reserve Officers' Training Corps (ROTC). The MCS structure evolved during the war and by 1943 it comprised MCS Detachment, OCS Detachment, Reserve Officers' School, Field Artillery Training Battalion MCS (Batteries A–C), Infantry Training Battalion MCS (Companies A–D), Ordnance School and Aviation Ground Officers' School (redesignated Air Infantry School in 1944).

OTHER MARINE CORPS SHORE UNITS AND ESTABLISHMENTS

At the time of the attack on Pearl Harbor there were considerable numbers of Marines serving with shore establishments; for example, there were 780 at HQMC, 14,707 at major training bases (this figure includes staff, instructors, students, recruits, etc.), 10,089 at other homeland posts and stations, 3,793 ship's guard detachments on board 68 ships, 847 with the 4 recruiting divisions, and 3,367 who manned 24 Marine barracks and detachments worldwide. From 1942, many of these posts in the USA were filled by Limited Service Marine Corps personnel, and from 1943 also by wounded regular Marines and those suffering from combat fatigue. During the war there were over 120 Marine barracks, mainly in the US, although over thirty were abroad, not to mention some forty-plus smaller Marine detachments. The primary responsibility of the Marines in these barracks and detachments was one of guarding the various locations, although they also provided messengers, boat crews, work parties and special details. Most detachments were not deactivated until after the war had ended.

The London Embassy

Perhaps one of the most important of the overseas detachments was the one providing Marines for security and ceremonial duties for the American Embassy in London, and the furnishing of escorts for State Department couriers (they used Harley-Davidson motorcycles equipped with sidecars to operate the service between the embassy and the various governmental staff offices in London). Their unit was billeted close to the embassy at 20 Grosvenor Square (a prestigious address in peacetime but a tempting target in wartime). Initially the embassy

One of the most important American embassies was of course in Grosvenor Square, London; this view shows its Marine Detachment. The detachment commander, Maj Harry Edwards, is on the left of the rear row and PlSgt Floriano P. Sampieri, senior NCO, is on the right. The photograph was taken in Grosvenor Square. *(USMC courtesy of Lt Col Harry Edwards, USMC (Ret))*

Above: One of the important parts of the London detachment was its motor pool, seen here with their Harley-Davidson motorcycles, used to provide courier service for Commander Naval Forces, Europe, and also armed escorts for US State Department couriers. *(USMC courtesy of Col Roy J. Batterton, USMC (Ret.))*

Below: The Marine Detachment, Londonderry, Northern Ireland. Men of this detachment (from 1st (Provisional) Marine Battalion), helped to guard the US Naval Base in Northern Ireland. They are seen here on parade, being inspected by the Lord Mayor of Londonderry, Sir Frederick Simmons, in 1943. With the Lord Mayor is Maj John Bathum, while to his rear is the barracks commander, Col Lucian W. Burnham. *(USMC courtesy of Mrs George O. Ludcke)*

detachment consisted of sixty all ranks; however, that was doubled by December 1941. The detachment also served as the principal administrative HQ for the USMC in Europe throughout the Second World War and included on its rolls many Marines who had served with the Office of Strategic Services (OSS), and others who were sent to Europe and to Africa for staff duty or as observers.

The Marine Barracks, Londonderry, Northern Ireland

On 5 February 1941, the US Navy established its first base on the European side of the Atlantic, in Londonderry, Northern Ireland, on the banks of the River Foyle. Orders quickly followed for the Marine Corps to

The Irish influence on the battalion drum and bugle corps is apparent in this photograph. The men took bagpipe lessons and formed a pipe band. *(USMC courtesy Mrs George O. Ludcke)*

provide security for this base; hence the 400-strong 1st (Provisional) Marine Battalion was organised at Quantico, trained in a wide variety of skills (as no one could predict what their duties would be), then despatched in May 1942. It was followed a month later by a further 1 officer and 152 enlisted Marines, and then, in late October 1942, by another officer and 200 men. The Marines were needed not only to protect the naval base from possible sabotage by German units which might be landed by submarine, or infiltrate across the border (Eire remained neutral throughout the war, so the German and Japanese embassies were in full operation in Dublin), but also from militant elements of the IRA. In fact there were no sabotage attempts and the number of volunteers to enlist into the British armed forces from Eire was equal to the number from Ulster, where conscription was in effect. The Marine Barracks, Londonderry, was disbanded two years later, on 18 August 1944.

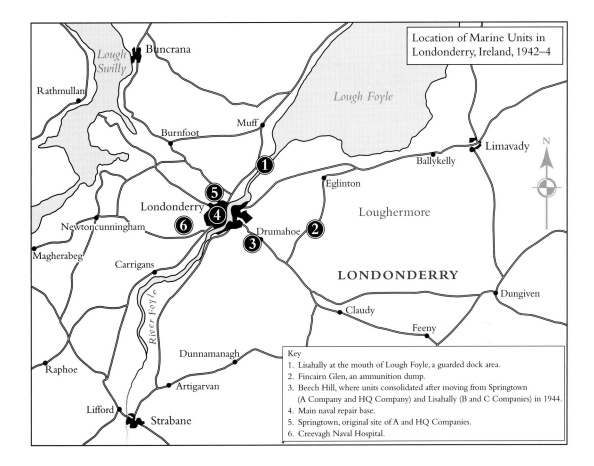

Location of Marine Units in Londonderry, Ireland, 1942–4

Key
1. Lisahally at the mouth of Lough Foyle, a guarded dock area.
2. Fincairn Glen, an ammunition dump.
3. Beech Hill, where units consolidated after moving from Springtown
   (A Company and HQ Company) and Lisahally (B and C Companies) in 1944.
4. Main naval repair base.
5. Springtown, original site of A and HQ Companies.
6. Creevagh Naval Hospital.

MARINE SHIPS' DETACHMENTS

It has been the continuing tradition within the Marine Corps that Marines serve as an integral part of the crew of the larger naval warships, and this continued to be the case during the Second World War. All the US Navy's 24 battleships, 24 fleet aircraft carriers, 9 light carriers, 2 battle cruisers, 39 heavy cruisers, 34 light cruisers, 15 amphibious command ships and scores of troop transports were all assigned a Marine ship's detachment. Smaller vessels had a Marine detachment only when they served as flagships. During the Second World War, a total of 3,744 officers and 18,722 enlisted men served aboard some 500 ships in all theatres of war. The detachment's size varied with the type of ship, for example 3 and 100+ on a modern battleship, 2 and 80 on the smaller, old battleships, fleet carriers and heavy cruisers, and so on down to just a two-man detachment on each of the transport ships. Training of these Marines for sea duty took place at sea schools that were established before the war in Portsmouth, Virginia, and San Diego, California. Marines for ships' detachments had to meet the following criteria (pre-war):

- They had to be volunteers. This was no problem, because sea duty was very popular, giving those selected both travel and adventure, including perhaps some action on foreign shores. On a more mundane level, they also got free laundry.

- They had to be over 18 years old.
- They had to be at least 5ft 8in tall.

Courses lasted for eight weeks and among the subjects taught were the operation of the ships' guns to which they would be assigned as gun crews (including gunnery practice firing), naval terminology and naval etiquette; boat drills, damage control, fire fighting, emergency drills, shipboard ceremonies, sentry duties and, of course, the duties of landing parties. The detachment was also primarily responsible for maintaining internal security on board, manning the secondary gun batteries in action and forming landing parties as needed. These duties were much the same in wartime.

Ship's detachments, like this one on board the aircraft carrier USS *Lexington*, served in all major combatant ships both before and during the Second World War. Their main duties were as gun crews for secondary gun batteries and for forming landing parties as and when needed. *(USN 51363)*

As Lt Col Harry W. Edwards explains in his booklet *A Different War: Marines in Europe and North Africa*, 'A Marine officer on board ship could anticipate assignment as the legal counsel or law officer for most courts-martial held on board and duty as a shore patrol officer. He also would have an assignment at a battle station, stand quarterdeck watches when in port and be prepared to lead his detachment when called upon to protect American lives and property.'

MARINE CORPS DEPOTS AND SUPPLY DEPARTMENTS

At the beginning of the war, the Marine Corps had just two small supply depots, at Philadelphia and San Francisco, clearly insufficient to meet the demands of the rapidly expanding Corps. More were therefore needed in order to receive, maintain, store and distribute supplies and *matériel* to units. The following is the full list of Marine supply depots:

Marine Corps Depot of Supply, Navy Yard, Philadelphia, Pennsylvania

Oldest Depot of Supplies (established 1880) and situated with the Marine Barracks (established in 1875). Two warehouse annexes were added in 1942.

Marine Corps Depot of Supply, San Francisco, California

Established in 1923 to support the West Coast FMF.

Marine Base Depot, Norfolk, Virginia

Formed as the Base Depot, FMF in 1942 and situated with the Navy Supply Depot. Redesignated as the Marine Base Depot in late 1944. It serviced all the Marine posts and stations on the east coast.

Marine Corps Depot of Supply, Barstow, California

Activated in January 1943, and located in the Mojave Desert some 150 miles from San Diego, it served as the major storage facility for the San Diego Depot of Supply. After the war ended, it remained as the main storage site for Marine equipment recovered from the Pacific theatre.

Marine Corps Depot of Supply, San Diego, California

Established at Camp Elliott in 1942 to support Marine units staging overseas. However, it proved inadequate and could not be expanded and, in late 1942, it was redesignated as the Base Depot FMF, San Diego. In January 1945, it became the Base Depot for the Marine Training and Replacement Command.

Depot of Supply, Marine Barracks, Navy Yard, Pearl Harbor, Oahu, Hawaii

The Office of the Defense Force QM, Marine Garrison Forces, 14th Naval District provided supply functions to all Marine units assigned to 14th Naval District in Hawaii and outlying islands until the office was abolished in October 1942 and the Depot of Supplies, Marine Barracks, Pearl Harbor, was established. Besides supporting Marine units in the garrison, the depot supported Pacific Fleet ships' detachments, defense battalions, forces in Johnston, Midway and Palmyra Islands, and also Marine air units and other FMF units as they arrived in the Hawaii area. In October 1943 it became the 6th Base Depot.

Other Marine Shore Establishments

Among other shore-based establishments were such important organisations as:

- Recruiting – four regional recruiting division HQs, each supervising seven USMC recruiting stations (only six in Western Recruiting Division).
- Effects Bureaus – to receive, screen and forward personal possessions of deceased and missing Marines to their next of kin.
- Paymasters' Offices – to disburse pay and allowances to Marines in units and organisations in the USA, including those on leave or convalescing in hospitals and retirees.
- Reclassification and Redistribution centres – to determine the needs of returnees from overseas and deal with excess personnel in new military specialities and oversee their reassignment to new units, training units or replacement drafts.

'Legal Eagles'. Photographed at Camp Lejeune on 7 January 1944 are the members of the camp's legal section, seen here 'in session' during a General Court Martial. Capt Lily S. Hutcheon, the first WR Judge Advocate stands to the rear, while the court reporter, Sgt Gladys R. Deeley, is seated on the left. (USMC 9195 via Do You Graphics, USA)

- Separation Centres – to expedite demobilisation at the end of the war.
- Service and Signal Battalions at Quantico and San Diego – provide service and administrative functions for the Corps's largest installations.

RECRUITING ACTIVITIES

A recruiting division was organised administratively into general service, platoon leader and special service units. In May 1943, the existing recruiting divisions were redesignated as procurement divisions. To quote Rottman: 'The redesignation was because of the elimination of voluntary recruiting the previous December. After voluntary enlistment was eliminated in December 1942, the recruiting/procurement division oversaw the procurement of 224,000 conscripts inducted into the Corps via Marine liaison NCOs at Armed Forces Induction Centres. The Marines ceased accepting conscripts in 1946. From 1943, recruiters were allowed to enlist 17-year-olds in the USMCR, enlisting almost 60,000 to enter active duty when they turned 18. Women Marines were assigned to the procurement divisions in 1944 to assist with administrative functions.' It is interesting to note that prior to Pearl Harbor a 'high' recruiting figure would be some 550 in a week; after Pearl Harbor, however, that figure soared as high as 6,000. And the quality of the volunteers was excellent.

THE USMC RESERVE

Established on 29 August 1916, some eight months before the USA entered the First World War, there were 7,000 Marines in the Reserve, representing nearly a tenth of the total Marine Corps strength at that time. After the First World War, despite the considerable part paid by the USMC on the Western Front, the Marine Corps Reserve was allowed just to disappear, as Rottman explains: 'Most Marine Reservists were inactive and there were no constituted units. An exception to this was Marine Corps Reserve companies serving as components in Naval Militias in those states and territories possessing such militias.' He goes on to explain that the naval militias were the nautical equivalent of the US Army National Guard; however, only a few fielded a single Marine company, and dual enrolment in the Marine Corps Reserve and the naval militia was no longer permitted after June 1923. Thus, by July 1925, there were under 700 Marine Reservists. Fortunately the situation was about to change, the Naval Reserve Act of 28 February 1925 establishing the US Marine Corps Reserve as a permanent component of the Marine Corps. Personnel were required to carry out sixty four-hour drill periods and attend fifteen days of field training every year. The unpaid volunteers could only be called to active duty in time of war or other national emergency. Four regiments were formed on 1 December 1925, but only 'on paper' for administrative purposes. They did not carry the lineage of the then four inactive regular 3rd, 7th, 8th and 9th Marine Reserve Regiments. However, the regiments had HQ and service companies and their three battalions each had an HQ company and four rifle companies.

USMC Reserve Area Units Home Station

Eastern	Philadelphia, Pa.
7th Regiment	New York City, NY
8th Regiment (less 3rd Battalion)	Philadelphia, Pa.
Southern	New Orleans, La.
3rd Battalion, 8th Regiment	New Orleans, La.
Central	Chicago, Ill.
9th Regiment	Chicago, Ill.
Western	San Francisco, Ca.
3rd Regiment	San Francisco, Ca.

Additionally each reserve area had a casual company and an aviation squadron. In 1926,

the Fleet Reserve regiments were only about 25 per cent of their authorised strength.

Two new Fleet Reserve units were formed in early 1929 – 401st (Washington, DC) and 402nd (Roanoke, Va.) Companies. Known as 'New Reserve' they proved highly popular, the troops attending as formed units rather than as individuals. Late in 1929, the Fleet Marine Corps Reserve was reorganised into homogeneous units, leading to the formation in 1931 of the 2,000-strong 6th Reserve Marine Brigade, with its HQ at Quantico, Va., and its units spread around in New York, Philadelphia, New Orleans, Chicago and elsewhere. Expansion of the USMCR continued; however, it was found that the brigade and regimental structures were ineffective because of their wide dispersion. Battalion level was deemed to be the most effective and so, by late 1935, the entire Fleet Reserve had converted into thirteen Marine battalions (some 2,900 all ranks), and 6th Marine Reserve Brigade was disbanded, the battalions being directly subordinate to Reserve Areas. At the same time, the Volunteer Reserve was enlarged, by encouraging newly discharged regulars to join. By November 1935, both reserve components had a combined total strength of some 9,200 all ranks. Additional Fleet Reserve battalions were also formed as more funding became available.

MARINE AVIATION RESERVE BEFORE 1938

Between 1928 and 1935, ten squadrons, including both fighter (VF-MR) and observation (VO-MR) squadrons, were formed in the Marine Aviation Reserve, which was a component part of the Fleet Reserve. Later, all were reorganised as observation units, then in 1937, all became scouting squadrons (VMS-R). In line with reserve ground units, the squadrons were considered as training and manpower augmentation pools.

'ALL MARINES'

On 1 July 1938, the USMCR was reorganised into three classes of Reserves: the Fleet (Class I), Organized (Class II) and Volunteer (Class III) Marine Corps Reserves. The first of these classes now consisted of discharged regular Marines with four or more years of active service. The separate battalions/squadrons now comprised the Organized Reserve, while the unpaid Volunteer Reserve was made up of men who had little or no previous service and were not assigned to reserve units. The Commandant, MajGen Holcomb, directed that in future all Marines, regular or reserve, were to be referred to as 'Marines' whatever their status, except when the law required them to be designated 'Reserve' or 'USMCR'.

In order to meet the demands of the limited emergency that the President declared on 8 September 1939, the USMCR was terminated on 10 November 1940 and integrated into the regulars, the Organized Reserve being ordered to active duty. All battalions reported to their mobilisation stations (see below) between 6 and 9 November, which provided 232 officers and 5,009 men to the growing USMC. (These figures do not include some 2,000 reservists who were unfit for active duty, or who were deferred or in a reserved occupation and so were not mobilised.) The mobilised battalions soon lost their identity when their personnel were absorbed into existing or newly raised regular units. By 30 June 1941, the Fleet and Volunteer Reserves had been completely mobilised, with 9,468 reservists of all categories returning to active duty.

Battalion	Home Station	Mobilisation Station
1st	New York, NY	Quantico
2nd	Boston, Mass.	Quantico
3rd	New York, NY	Quantico
4th	Newark, NJ	Quantico
5th	Washington, DC	Quantico
6th	Philadelphia, Pa.	Navy Yard, Philadelphia
7th (artillery: 75mm guns)	Philadelphia, Pa.	Quantico
8th	Toledo, Ohio	Quantico
9th	Chicago, Ill.	San Diego
10th	New Orleans, La.	San Diego
11th	Seattle, Wash.	San Diego
12th	San Francisco, Ca.	Navy Yard, Mare Island, Ca.
13th	Los Angeles, Ca.	San Diego
14th	Spokane, Wash.	San Diego
15th	Galveston, Tex.	San Diego
16th	Indianapolis, Ind.	San Diego
17th	Detroit, Mich.	Quantico
18th	St Paul, Minn.	San Diego
19th	Augusta, Ga.	Navy Yard, Norfolk, Va.
20th	Los Angeles, Ca.	Navy Yard, Puget Sound, Wash.
21st	Portland, Oreg.	Navy Yard, Norfolk, Va.
22nd (artillery: 75mm guns)	Los Angeles, Ca.	San Diego
23rd	Roanoke, Va.	Navy Yard, Norfolk, Va.

The recently formed 20th–23rd Battalions were under-strength, while some of the older battalions were depleted because of previous individual voluntary mobilisations.

(Source: Rottman, *US Marine Corps World War II Order of Battle*)

MARINE AVIATION RESERVE AFTER 1938

All the scouting and service squadrons were located at Naval Aviation Reserve Stations (NARS). All reported to their mobilisation stations on 16 December 1940 and like their ground counterparts were quickly absorbed, losing their unit identity.

Squadron	Home NARS	Mobilisation Station
VMS-1R	Squantum, Mass.	Quantico
VMS-2R	Brooklyn, NY	Quantico
VMS-3R	Anacostia, DC	Quantico
VMS-4R	Miami, Fla.	Quantico
VMS-5R	Grosse Isle, Mich.	Quantico
VMS-6R	Minneapolis, Mich.	San Diego
VMS-7R	Long Beach, Ca.	San Diego
VMS-8R	Oakland, Ca.	San Diego
VMS-9R	Seattle, Wash.	San Diego
VMS-10R	Kansas City, Kans.	San Diego
VMS-11R	Brooklyn, NY	Quantico
SMS-2R	Grosse Isle, Mich.	Quantico
SMS-3R	Seattle, Wash.	San Diego

(Source: Rottman, *US Marine Corps World War II Order of Battle*)

Counting all categories of reserves, a total of 15,138 individuals were mobilised. When this had been achieved, the Division of Reserves at HQMC had little to do, so was switched to officer procurement until 1942, when it was absorbed into the Personnel Department as the Reserve Personnel Section.

LIMITED SERVICE MARINE CORPS RESERVE (CLASS IV)

In order to ensure that all physically qualified Marines were available for FMF duty, Congress approved, on 20 January 1942, the establishment of the Limited Service Marine Corps Reserve (Class IV) as guards for Marine barracks and detachments at naval shore establishments within the continental United States. Then in March 1942 a fifth category was established; this was the Specialist Volunteer Marine Corps Reserve (Class V), which was to provide for the appointment or enlistment of the Marine Corps Reserve officers and men who possessed special qualifications that might be utilised in the Marine Corps at a time of war or national emergency, but who, because of physical defects, age or lack of training, were not qualified for general service and were to be appointed for specialist duty only.

CONSCRIPTION

From December 1942, the Marine Corps was required to accept conscripts. However, as conscripts were allowed to select their branch of service, most of those accepted had chosen the Corps already (they were known as 'handcuffed volunteers'.) They were designated USMC(SS) – Selective Service. Gordon Rottman points out that, out of over 224,000 conscripts who were inducted into the Corps from 1943, all but 70,000 volunteered to become regulars or active duty reservists. Also, from 1943, recruiters were allowed to enlist 17-year-olds in the USMCR. Almost 60,000 of these young men were ordered to active duty to complete training prior to their eighteenth birthday, when they became eligible for overseas deployment. Undoubtedly the Marine Corps recruiters did a marvellous job, helped no doubt by the rash of movies about the exploits of the USMC that appeared during the war years – films like *Wake Island, Guadalcanal Diary, Gung-Ho, Pride of the Marines* and, probably everyone's favourite, *Flying Leathernecks*; there were many more. And of course the Marines themselves were the best promoters of the Corps; an Army public relations officer once said, 'In the Army a squad consists of thirteen men. In the Marine Corps it consists of twelve men and a press agent!' (MacMillan *et al.*, *Uncommon Valor*).

1ST SAMOAN BATTALION USMCR

Undoubtedly worth a special mention in this brief section on the Marine Corps Reserve is the only USMCR unit to serve as a unit on active duty. It was a development of the 'Fita Fita' (Samoan for 'Courageous') Guard and Band that was raised in 1904 by the US Navy to guard naval installations there. It was assigned a single first sergeant – arguably the smallest Marine detachment ever. The Second World War unit, raised on 1 July 1941, comprised some 494 enlisted men up to and including the rank of sergeant, who were Samoans, and 44 officers and most of the NCOs, who were Ameri-

cans. The unit could not be deployed outside the islands, although attempts were made to detach scouts for duty in the Solomons. Organised by 7th Defense Battalion at Pago Pago, Tutuila and American Samoa, it helped the defense battalion in various ways:

- manning coast defense guns (150 Samoans plus thirty members of the Fita Fita Guard)
- beach patrols
- maintaining remote lookout posts

Fully mobilised on 9 December 1941, it was assigned firstly to 2nd Marine Brigade (Reinforced) on 20 January 1942, then to its 8th Marine Regiment on 24 February 1942, but remained tactically attached to 7th Defense Battalion (one of the original 'Rainbow Five') until it was reattached to 2nd Defense Battalion on 1 September 1942, then to the Harbor Defense Group on 1 October 1943. It was disbanded on 15 January 1944.

CHAPTER THREE

MARINE CORPS MOBILE ORGANISATIONS

THE FLEET MARINE FORCE (FMF)

This was the very core of the Marine Corps during the Second World War, consisting as it did of all the active ground and air units, together with all their necessary support units. The growth of the wartime FMF was evolutionary and to trace its development one must go back to just before the turn of the last century, when, in 1894, Congress had tasked the Corps with the mission of establishing and defending outlying naval bases as and when required by the Fleet. Four years later, during the Spanish–American War, this had been successfully achieved, Marine landings being made at Guantánamo Bay, Cuba, by 1st Battalion USMC and in the Philippines by ships' Marine guard detachments. However, although these landings were successful, the forces used had really been too small and had not had the relevant training that such

In 1940, FMF units stationed at the San Diego Recruit Depot conducted some small-unit training in the open fields of the Mission Bay area. Note that they are still in pre-war khaki uniforms and First World War-pattern steel helmets, while they are armed with the Springfield M1903 rifle and are wearing the MIV1 gasmasks that continued to be issued until 1944 when they were replaced with a lighter version. *(USMC courtesy Col James A. Donovan USMC (Ret.))*

tricky operations demanded. 'If there had been 5,000 Marines under my command at Manila Bay,' wrote Adm Dewey after the war, 'then the city would have surrendered to me . . . and could have been properly garrisoned. . . . The Filipinos would have received us with open arms, and there would have been no insurrection.' As Rottman comments, 'The concept of a Marine Corps combined arms expeditionary force has its origins with the 657-man 1st Battalion of Marines in Cuba. Formed from East Coast Marine companies, it possessed five infantry companies and a 3-inch landing gun company. Because of this battalion's success, the Colonel Commandant of the Marine Corps, Charles Heywood . . . previously a proponent of maintaining Marines only as naval base and ships' guards, proposed that a 20,000 Marine force be raised of "well drilled and equipped Marines . . . without the necessity of calling on the Army".' Had such a force been available during the Spanish–

American War, they would have proved invaluable, as Adm Dewey had said.

It was fully recognised, therefore, that there was a need for a separate Marine force of all arms, readily available and capable of seizing and defending advanced naval bases. At the same time it was appreciated that a school was necessary to teach amphibious warfare, rather than to rely on ad hoc operations using ships' longboats as had been the case in the Philippines. This school initially came into being in 1901 at Newport, Rhode Island, and comprised just five officers and forty men. It would later move to New London, Connecticut, then to Philadelphia and become known as the Advance Base School in 1910. The following year, a 300-man Advance Base Battalion was formed at the Marine Barracks, Philadelphia Navy Yard, Pennsylvania, and situated with the Advance Base School.

By 1913, a 1,600-man Marine Advance Base Force had been organised in the same location, comprising 1st Advance Base

The activation of 2nd Marine Division, 1 February 1941. Here MajGen Clayton B. Vogel, first commander of 2nd Marine Division, activates his division at a parade and review, held at the Marine Corps Base, San Diego. The parade uniform was, for officers, green breeches and polished boots, while the men (who paraded twelve abreast in battalion masses) wore cotton khaki shirts and ties, winter service green trousers, wrapped tightly into tan, blancoed leggings and polished chocolate-brown-coloured boots. (USMC)

Brigade with 1st Regiment (Fixed Defense) and 2nd Regiment (Mobile Defense). This force had the distinction of being one of the first combined arms formations in the American armed forces. However, it was soon heavily involved in missions for which it had not been intended, namely protecting American citizens and their interests worldwide, the advance base force concept being relegated to a secondary role. During the First World War, this was even more the case, with the expanded Marine Corps being used in France, where it played an important role on the Western Front, but the last thing that was needed or contemplated was amphibious warfare. Nevertheless, by late 1917, the Advance Base Force had been reconstituted, in case Germany should try its luck in the Caribbean, and also to protect oil fields at Tampico.

After the war, in 1919, the Advance Base Force was redesignated 1st Advance Base Force, with 2nd Advance Base Force also being activated at San Diego as its west coast counterpart. In 1921, 1st Advanced Base Force was replaced by the Marine Corps Expeditionary Force, a 3,300-strong all-arms force built around 5th Marine Regiment, with artillery, engineers, signal, gas and aviation units, plus a tank platoon. Landing exercises continued to be held and proved extremely valuable.

Unfortunately, however, during the 1920s and 1930s, Marine expeditionary forces had to be despatched to both Nicaragua and China, which seriously interrupted the amphibious training. Eventually, it was proposed that a suitable portion of the Marine Corps should be assigned on a permanent basis to the naval fleet, with the primary task of making amphibious landings. This conviction had long been held by the Assistant Commandant of the Marine Corps, MajGen John H. Russell, who then suggested it to the Commandant, MajGen Ben H. Fuller. Fuller approved, and a letter was sent to the Chief of Naval Operations, outlining the proposals, which also recommended that the name of this force should be the Fleet Marine Force (FMF). If approved it had the added advantage that it would immediately dedicate a body of Marines to the full-time study, development and practice of amphibious warfare.

Supplies to keep the FMF fighting. This fascinating photograph shows the crammed deck of LST 202 as it nears Cape Gloucester, New Britain, on 24 December 1943. It contained just a fraction of the myriad items that FMF units (in this case 1st Marine Division) required to function. They included trucks, Jeeps and trailers loaded with supplies, rolls of barbed wire, drinking water trailers and much more – the list is endless. *(USN N-25809A via Real War Photos)*

As Maj Alfred Bailey explains in his *Alligators, Buffaloes and Bushmasters*, 'This historic letter was fully endorsed by the Chief of Naval Operations, the Director of War Plans (Navy) and the Commander in Chief US Fleet, in four weeks, a remarkably short period of time considering the scope of the letter and the levels of endorsement required. The entire concept drew relatively little comment in view of its future impacts. With one decision to implement the concept of the letter, the Secretary of the Navy, Claude A. Swanson, created the force that would fight its way across the Pacific during the Second World War using a new form of warfare.' This approval was enshrined in Navy General Order Number 241 of 7 December 1933, which became the charter for the Fleet Marine Force of the Second World War. Certain parts of the Order are worth repeating here as they clarify the new status of the Marine Corps.

The Fleet Marine Force

1. The force of Marines maintained by the Major General Commandant in a state of readiness for operations with the Fleet is hereby designated as Fleet Marine Force (FMF) and as such shall constitute a part of the organisation of the United States Fleet and shall be included in the Operating Force Plan for each fiscal year.
2. The Fleet Marine Force shall consist of such units as may be designmated by the Major General Commandant and shall be maintained at such strength as is warranted by the general personnel situation of the Marine Corps.
3. The Fleet Marine Force shall be available to the Commander in Chief for operations with the Fleet or for exercises either afloat or ashore in connection with Fleet problems. The C in C shall make timely recommend-

ations to the Chief of Naval Operations regarding such service in order that the necessary arrangements may be made.
4. The C in C shall exercise command of the FMF when embarked on board vessels of the Fleet or when engaged in Fleet exercises either afloat or ashore. When otherwise engaged, command shall be as directed by the Major General Commandant.
5. The Major General Commandant shall detail the Commanding General of the FMF and maintain an appropriate staff for him.

This Order was thus the starting point of all serious trials and experimentation into every aspect of amphibious warfare. It also meant that the FMF was 'ring-fenced' against constant demands for troops which had in the past prevented landing exercises from taking place. As Bailey says, 'The Marine Corps now entered an era of accelerated training for amphibious war.'

When war was declared against the Axis powers on 8 December 1941, the USMC was just under 66,000 strong and, of these, over 31,000 belonged to the ground and air units of the Fleet Marine Force, while the rest were manning shore establishments in the USA and overseas, or serving on board ships of the US Navy. By the end of the war there had been a staggering sevenfold increase in the USMC to nearly half a million men and women. However, one must remember that, compared with the United States Army, the United States Marine Corps was but a fraction of the size. For example, during the Second World War, the US Army contained some twenty-four corps, of which six served in the Pacific theatre, as compared with the USMC, which had only two corps (I/III and V). At division level the Army had eighty-nine divisions, of which twenty-two served in the Pacific, while the USMC had just six.

The first wave of Marines to hit the beach on Saipan in the Marianas invasion take cover behind a sand dune while they wait for the following three waves to come in. This dramatically shows the FMF 'in action' – and what a bloody business the Marines faced on almost every island on which they landed. *(USMC 80-G-234712 via Compendium Publishing)*

FMF Initial Deployment (All located in USA apart from as shown)

Atlantic Fleet
Headquarters Amphibious Force
1st Marine Division (8,918 all ranks)
1st Marine Aircraft Wing (110 aircraft) (one scouting squadron at St Thomas, Virgin Islands)
1st and 2nd Marine Barrage Balloon Squadrons
1st Marine Brigade (Provisional) (3,972 all ranks), stationed in Iceland
1st Base Depot

Pacific Fleet
2nd Marine Division (-) (7,540 all ranks)
2nd Marine Aircraft Wing (91 aircraft) (squadrons at Wake, Ewa, Oahu and onboard carriers *Saratoga* and *Lexington*)
2nd Defense Battalion
Marine Forces 14th Naval District (Pearl Harbor) (including detachments of 1st Defense Battalion at Wake, Johnston and Palmyra Islands)

3rd Defense Battalion (Pearl Harbor)
4th Defense Battalion (Pearl Harbor)
2nd Engineer Battalion (-) detached from 2nd Marine Division (Pearl Harbor)
6th Defense Battalion (Midway)
7th Defense Battalion (-) (Samoa)
2nd Base Depot

Asiatic Fleet
4th Marine Regiment (-) (Olongapo, Philippines)
1st Separate Marine Battalion (Cavite, Philippines)
Marine Forces in northern China (Peking and Tientsin)

During the war, the FMF would grow from a force of six infantry regiments and one artillery regiment, plus seven defense battalions, to two amphibious corps, with six divisions containing eighteen infantry regiments and thirty-six artillery battalions, not to mention a mass of anti-aircraft, amphibious tractor and engineer battalions, plus all manner of special and service units.

Marines of 2nd Marine Division, who had stormed ashore at Agune Jima, 20 miles west of Okinawa on 9 June 1945, prepare to move inland. Now many of the items similar to those seen on the deck of LST 202 in an earlier picture have been moved ashore, while every Marine carries his personal weapons and equipment (his '782 gear'). *(USMC 80-G-49891 via Compendium Publishing)*

As Gordon Rottman comments, 'Such an accomplishment is a credit to the foresight and adaptability of the officers and men of the Marine Corps. No less remarkable was those Marines' ability to change from the "Old Corps" of a small group of tradition-bound professionals to one capable of employing amphibian vehicles, multiple-rocket launchers, electronic warfare, and a complex air arm. It is a testament to the professionalism, convictions and abilities of these officers and NCOs that they were able to maintain and instil the values and principles of the Old Corps on the new and adapt to new technologies and techniques while continually increasing combat efficiency.' In his history of Marine Corps Aviation, Robert Sherrod puts the change in an even more down-to-earth manner: 'In other words, the Marine Corps shifted from a simple, rough-and-ready gang, which could fight banana wars or serve the Army as infantry, to a specialised organisation with a primary mission. The Marines seized their new assignment with gusto, and if they were not the only service dealing in

amphibious warfare, they were the most sincere practitioners. The sceptics could (and did) say, after reading the gloomy details of Gallipoli's failure, that it was impossible to land and stay landed in the face of heavy enemy opposition, but the Marines had their assignment and they worked on it.'

THE AMPHIBIOUS CORPS

On operations, an amphibious corps was designed to control two or more divisions, together with a number of special and service troops in support, which were tailored to suit the operation in which the corps was involved, so the two corps were 'task organised' differently for combat. Thus a corps had no fixed organisation, although specific divisions and FMF units were regularly assigned to a specific corps. The assigned service units were there to provide their obvious service functions (see below). At the beginning of hostilities, a USMC corps was commanded by a senior major-general and it was not until 1944 that

A natural hazard for men and vehicles on many beaches was the pools left by the receding tide. Here, on Okinawa on 1 April 1945, a number of LVT(A)4s, armed with 75mm M3 howitzers in M7 mounts, wait to cross one of these pools. Note also the armoured dozer. The LVT (Armoured) provided much-needed close fire support, but were not as good as the Sherman M4 medium tanks once these were able to get ashore from the LCTs. *(USMC 80-G-48849 via Compendium Publishing)*

a Marine corps commander was granted the rank of lieutenant-general.

Assigned Corps Troops

These were for example:

Headquarters, Amphibious Corps
Corps Headquarters and Service Battalion
Corps Signal Battalion
Corps Motor Transport Battalion
Corps Medical Battalion
Headquarters Battery, Amphibious Corps Artillery
Headquarters Battery, Corps Defense Troops
    (not always assigned)
Corps Transient Centre

(Source: Rottman, *US Marine Corps World War II Order of Battle*)

I Marine Amphibious Corps (I MAC), FMF

Established on 10 October 1942 at San Diego under the command of MajGen Clayton B. Vogel, it was initially only intended to carry out administrative functions. However, as more Marine units arrived in the Pacific Ocean area, an operational HQ was clearly needed, so I Marine Amphibious Corps (I MAC) headquarters left for the South Pacific and was soon established at Pearl Harbor. Two months later it moved to New Caledonia. All USMC units in the South Pacific were assigned to IMAC, with the following exceptions: Marine aviation, ships' detachments, the Samoan Group Defense Force and those in the Ellice Islands. I MAC would soon become responsible for USA's first South Pacific offensive, which included operations on Guadalcanal, the Russell Islands and New Georgia, and would involve both 1st and 2nd Marine Divisions. On 10 July 1943, MajGen Alexander Vandegrift became the corps commander. He would hand over to MajGen Charles D. Barrett on 15 September 1943. However, Barrett died in an accident and so Vandegrift had to reassume command briefly, before MajGen Roy S. Geiger took over on 10 November 1943. Further operations would result, with the following divisions being attached:

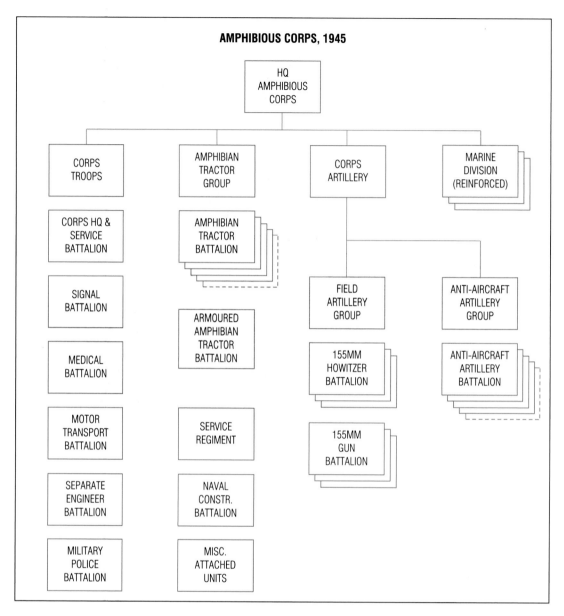

AMPHIBIOUS CORPS, 1945

HQ
AMPHIBIOUS
CORPS

CORPS
TROOPS

AMPHIBIAN
TRACTOR
GROUP

CORPS
ARTILLERY

MARINE
DIVISION
(REINFORCED)

CORPS HQ &
SERVICE
BATTALION

AMPHIBIAN
TRACTOR
BATTALION

SIGNAL
BATTALION

ARMOURED
AMPHIBIAN
TRACTOR
BATTALION

FIELD
ARTILLERY
GROUP

ANTI-AIRCRAFT
ARTILLERY
GROUP

MEDICAL
BATTALION

155MM
HOWITZER
BATTALION

ANTI-AIRCRAFT
ARTILLERY
BATTALION

MOTOR
TRANSPORT
BATTALION

SERVICE
REGIMENT

155MM
GUN
BATTALION

SEPARATE
ENGINEER
BATTALION

NAVAL
CONSTR.
BATTALION

MILITARY
POLICE
BATTALION

MISC.
ATTACHED
UNITS

Opposite, above: This photograph shows some of the elements that invariably made up the 'island-hopping' invasion armadas. In the background are the ships that brought them, and which still provide sustenance and comfort for the men ashore; nearer is the marshy beach area (this was Okinawa, Easter 1945) on which are some of the many grounded landing craft; in the foreground is part of the landing force with, most prominently, men working on an amtrac. *(USMC 80-G-48850 via Compendium Publishing)*

Opposite, below: Engaged in the bitter struggle to establish the Peleliu beachhead in September 1944, Marine infantrymen take cover on top of and behind the (well-named) beached amtrac that brought them ashore. Casualties were high, as always in such difficult beach landings; during the war, the USMC suffered nearly 87,000 casualties, of which just under 20,000 were killed or missing in action. *(USMC G 5487 via author's collection)*

1st Marine Division, 1942–4 (for Guadalcanal and North Solomons)

2nd Marine Division, 1942–3 (for Guadalcanal)

3rd Marine Division, 1943–4 (for Bougainville)

American Division (US Army), 1943 (North Solomons)

37th Infantry Division (US Army), 1943 (North Solomons)

3rd New Zealand Division 1943–4 (North Solomons)

III Amphibious Corps (III AC), FMFPac

The III Amphibious Corps (III AC) was formed on Guadalcanal on 15 April 1944, by redesignating I MAC (MajGen Geiger still in command) and it served as Third US Fleet's amphibious landing force with the mission of seizing Guam, while V AC took Saipan and Tinian. The III AC provided the Southern troops and the landing force of the Marianas Expeditionary Force. During operations between July and August 1944, 3rd Marine Division, 1st Provisional Marine Brigade (which later became 6th Marine Division) and 77th Infantry Division were all under the command of III AC.

Then, on 12 June 1944, III AC formed a planning staff for the invasion of Peleliu which was known as 'X-Ray Provisional Amphibious Corps' and put in under the command of MajGen Julian C. Smith. While 1st Marine Division prepared for the assult on Peleliu, the rest of III AC was committed to the assault on Guam. III AC reabsorbed X-Ray Provisional Corps on 15 August 1944 when MajGen Geiger and his staff returned from Guam. In September and October 1944, III AC (1st Marine Division with 321st Infantry Regiment attached from 81st Infantry Division) fought on Peleliu. The 81st Infantry Division first secured Anguar Island, then relieved 1st Marine Division on Peleliu.

The III AC then moved to Guadalcanal to prepare for the Okinawa Group assault, under the command of Tenth US Army, with 1st, 2nd and 6th Marine Divisions attached for this operation in April–July 1945, 2nd being held as a floating reserve until 11 April. On 18 June, the Army commander, Lt Gen Simon B. Buckner, Jr, was killed and his place taken by MajGen Geiger. (This was the only time that a Marine general ever commanded a field army. Lt Gen Geiger, who was promoted on 19 June 1945, was relieved on 23 June by Lt Gen Joseph W. Stillwell, US Army.) On 30 June 1945, MajGen Keller E. Rockey took command of III AC when MajGen Geiger took command of the FMFPac. The III AC then returned to Guam to prepare for the invasion of Japan.

Divisions and major units attached to III AC were:

1st Marine Division, 1944–6 (for Peleliu, Okinawa, China)

2nd Marine Division, 1945 (Okinawa)

3rd Marine Division, 1944 (Guam)

4th Marine Division, 1944–6 (Okinawa, China)

77th Infantry Division, US Army, 1944 (Guam)

81st Infantry Division, US Army, 1944 (Anguar, Peleliu)

1st Provisional Marine Brigade (became 6th Marine Division), 1944 (Guam)

V Amphibious Corps VAC, FMF/FMFPac

V Amphibious Corps (V AC) was formed on 24 August 1943 at Camp Elliott, California. The following month it moved to Pearl Harbor, its training commitments being assumed by Troop Training Unit, Amphibious Training Command, Pacific Fleet. Formed as the amphibious landing force for Fifth US Fleet, to support Central Pacific operations, V AC was commanded by MajGen Holland M. Smith and its first task was to seize the Gilbert Islands, in preparation for an assault in the Marshalls. This included two operations in November 1943:

Marines prepare for embarkation on Christmas Eve. They are bound for New Britain on 24–6 December 1943. Note the differing headgear that includes overseas/garrison caps and the earlier type of utility sage-green P1941 cap. Strewn on the ground are their personal kit and weapons, while they chat and prepare to be embarked on the troop transport to their rear. *(USMC B-23997 via Real War Photos)*

2nd Marine Division's assault on Tarawa and 27th Infantry Division's seizure of Makin.

In January–February 1944, V AC with 4th Marine Division, 7th Infantry Division and elements of 27th Infantry Division, seized Roi-Namur, Kwajalein, and Eniwetok in the Marshalls. Its next task was to take the Northern Marianas between June and August 1944, which included 2nd and 4th Marine Divisions seizing Saipan and Tinian with 27th Infantry Division and XXIV Corps's artillery attached.

In February 1945, V AC assaulted Iwo Jima with 4th and 5th Marine Divisions, with 3rd Marine Division as a floating reserve (later landed). The V AC suffered heavy casualties at Iwo Jima and so its future operations against Miyako (near Formosa)

were cancelled. It was also to have taken part in the invasion of Japan, with 2nd, 3rd and 5th Marine Divisions, but instead landed in Japan at Yokosuka and Kyushu in September 1945 and was relieved of occupation duties by Eighth US Army in September 1945.

Divisions and major units attached to V AC were:

2nd Marine Division, 1943–6 (Tarawa, Saipan, Tinian, Japan)

3rd Marine Division, 1945 (Iwo Jima)

4th Marine Division, 1944–5 (Roi-Namur, Iwo Jima)

5th Marine Division, 1945 (Iwo Jima, Japan)

7th Infantry Division, US Army, 1944 (Kwajalein)

27th Infantry Division, US Army, 1943–4 (Makin, Saipan)

A demolition crew from 6th Marine Division watch as dynamite charges explode, destroying a Japanese cave position. Note also the large man-pack radio that one man is carrying. *(USMC 127-G-122154/SI-1227 via Compendium Publishing)*

32nd Infantry Division, US Army, 1945 (Japan)

XXIV Corps's artillery, US Army, 1944 (Saipan, Tinian)

22nd Marine Regiment (Tactical Group I), 1944 (Eniwetok)

USMC DIVISIONS AND BRIGADES

The basic USMC fighting formation was the division and it was organised so as to be able to carry out major amphibious assaults with the aim of capturing island objectives. However, the six Marine divisions that were formed during the Second World War began as brigades, being formed for a specific purpose, such as a rapid deployment, and only one actually saw combat before becoming a division. As Gordon Rottman says in his *US Marine Corps 1941–45*, 'It has long been said that the Marines deploy as brigades but fight as divisions.' As explained at the start of this chapter, the organisation of the six USMC divisions is covered in the next chapter; here, we look only at the organisation of Marine brigades.

Before early 1941, there were just two permanent Marine brigades: 1st Marine Brigade, located on the east coast of the USA, and 2nd Marine Brigade on the west coast. Both were all-arms formations with, as their central core, an infantry regiment and an aircraft group, backed up with all the necessary special troops. All units were under-strength, the intention being that they would be brought up to full strength with ships' guards, barracks

A wrecked LSM(3) lies dangerously close to LST 764, with a lorry and some pressed steel planking (PSP) to its front. Also beached to its right is LST 390, with an LVT(4) parked in front. *(National Archives N25690-A via Real War Photos)*

companies and other Marine detachments. The organisation of such a brigade was as follows:

Marine Brigade FMF (1939–40)

Headquarters Company Marine Brigade
Infantry Regiment (three infantry battalions)
Artillery Battalion (three 75mm pack howitzer batteries)
Brigade Special Troops
    Engineer Battalion
    Medical Battalion
    Tank Company
    Chemical Company
    Guard Company
    Signal Company
    Service Company
    Motor Transport Company
    Anti-aircraft Machine Gun Battery
Marine Aircraft Group
    Group Headquarters Squadron (HS)
    Marine Scouting Squadron (VMS)

Marine Bombing Squadron (VMB)
Marine Fighting Squadron (VMF)
Marine Utility Squadron (VMJ)
Base Air Detachment

(Source: Rottman, *US Marine Corps World War II Order of Battle*)

During the war, various Marine brigades (or brigade-sized 'tactical groups' for special missions) were formed. Examples are:

1st Marine Brigade (Provisional) formed 1941, disbanded 1942
2nd Marine Brigade (Reinforced) formed 1941, disbanded 1943
3rd Marine Brigade, FMF, formed 1942, disbanded 1943
Tac Group I formed and disbanded 1944
Task Group A formed and disbanded 1944
1st Marine Brigade (Provisional) formed and disbanded 1944

Also, just after the war, Task Force A, Third Fleet Landing Force.

1st Marine Brigade (Provisional) (1941)

This was the brigade that went to Iceland to allow the British garrison (49th Infantry Division) to be used elsewhere. It was formed around 6th Marine Regiment, which had been originally warned and prepared to secure the Azores in May 1941. That mission was cancelled and it was next tasked for Iceland. It arrived there on 7 July 1941 and remained until relieved by an Army task force, returning to the USA in February/March 1942, to be disbanded on 25 March and its units returned to 2nd Marine Division in San Diego.

2nd Marine Brigade, Reinforced (1941)

Hurriedly formed around 8th Marine Regiment in December 1941, it left the USA on 6 January 1942 and arrived at American Samoa as a defense force on 19 January 1942. The only action took place on 11 January 1942, when Pago Pago Harbour on Tutuila Island was shelled by a Japanese submarine. It left Samoa on 25 October 1942 and was redeployed on Guadalcanal on 3 November, being replaced on Samoa by 3rd Marine Regiment (Reinforced).

3rd Marine Brigade FMF (1942)

With Samoa still liable to Japanese invasion in early 1942, it was agreed that the USA would take over the defense of Western Samoa, and 3rd Marine Brigade was formed around 7th Marine Regiment at New River in March 1942. They arrived at Upolu on 8 May. Four months later, they were redeployed to Guadalcanal and their place taken in 3rd Marine Brigade by 22nd Marine Regiment, who had arrived at the end of July. The brigade was disbanded on 8 November 1943.

Tactical Group I

This unit was formed by V Amphibious Corps in early November 1943 on Oahu, with the task of supporting the Marshall Islands campaign the following year. It was built around 22nd Marine Regiment who had been relocated from Samoa, as already explained, and augmented by the attachment of 106th Infantry Regiment (Reinforced), US Army. The 22nd Marine Regiment took Engebi, and 106th Infantry Regiment Eniwetok, the latter then reverting to Army control. The 22nd Marine Regiment moved to Kwajalein Atoll for area security and later cleared many of the islands in the Marshalls group. Tactical Group I was disbanded on 22 March 1944 and 22nd Marine Regiment moved to Guadalcanal.

Task Group A

Task Group A was formed on Guadalcanal by I AC on 22 February 1944, its core unit being the recently reactivated 4th Marine Regiment (reactivated after the demise of the four raider battalions), with the aim of assaulting Kavieng, New Britain, but this operation was later cancelled. Between 20 March and 12 April it made an unopposed landing and occupation of Emirau. Later, 4th Marine Regiment were relieved by 147th Infantry Regiment (Separate) and returned to Guadalcanal. Task Group A was disbanded on 2 May 1944.

1st Marine Brigade (Provisional) (1944)

This was the largest of all the wartime brigades, being formed on Guadalcanal under III AC, with its core being both 4th and 22nd Marine Regiments, so it was not far short of division size. It was V AC's 'floating reserve' for the Saipan assault, then landed on Guam, fighting there until mid-August 1944. Later, as will be explained in the next chapter, it would be reorganised

Once the fighting had moved inland and the beachhead was secure, then all manner of ships, landing craft, Seabee vehicles, mobile cranes, etc. were brought in. This was the scene at Iwo Jima as supplies arrived in late February/early March 1945. *(USMC 38647 via author's collection)*

and redesignated 6th Marine Division on 7 September 1944.

Before closing the discussion of brigade-sized forces, it is appropriate to mention Task Force A, Third Fleet Landing Force, which was formed just after the war by III AC using 6th Marine Division assets on Guam on 11 August 1945. The reinforced 4th Marine Regiment (5,400 men) was made up to nearly 9,000 men at sea, with the addition of two extra regimental-sized landing forces, from the ships of Third US Fleet, including a single battalion-sized British landing force (200 Royal Marines and 250 Royal Navy personnel) from three aircraft carriers attached to Third US Fleet. (The choice of 4th Marine Regiment was, as Gordon Rottman explains, both 'symbolic and natural. The original 4th Marines had defended the Philippines and was surrendered on Corregidor in 1942. The new 4th Marines would lead American occupation forces into the Home Islands [of Japan].') Task Force A's mission would be to occupy the Tokyo Bay area in advance of Third US Fleet's arriving to accept the Japanese surrender. The task force began to land at Yokosuka naval base on 29 August, four days before the formal surrender took place, and on 6 September they were returned to their ships. Task Force A was dissolved on 20 September, but 4th Marine Regiment remained at Yokosuka as a base security force.

CHAPTER FOUR

THE MARINE DIVISION

THE MAJOR UNIT OF COMBAT

During the Second World War the Marine division was the major formation of combat in the United States Marine Corps, in the same way as the division was the major formation of combat in the US Army. However, while there were several different types of division in the US Army – infantry, armoured and airborne being the main ones – there was only one type of division in the USMC, although from the outset, it was a formation composed of all arms and services. All six of the Marine divisions that were eventually activated were built around a core of numbered infantry and artillery regiments (normally three infantry and one artillery) that formed the backbone of each division, the infantry regiments being known as 'Marines' – e.g. '1st Marines', '5th Marines', etc., rather than '1st Infantry Regiment', '5th Infantry Regiment', and so on. These regiments were supported by various units of other arms (e.g. engineers and tanks) and services (such as transport), so as to produce a balanced force well capable of tackling the range of tasks involved in achieving their main mission,

When it comes to closing with the enemy, taking on his positions and killing him, then it is the individual infantryman (the 'grunt') who must perform these essential tasks. Here, members of a Marine patrol surround and cover a Japanese cave position while a demolition charge is detonated in its entrance. *(USMC B-23490 via Real War Photos)*

which was, as we have seen, conducting amphibious assaults on the Japanese-held islands in the Pacific theatre.

ORGANISATIONAL CHANGES

In addition to changes in some of their weapons, uniforms, vehicles and equipment, etc., as improvements came on stream, the basic composition of the Marine division underwent a number of alterations in organisation during the war years. These affected its overall manpower strength, and were designed to enhance such basic characteristics as firepower and mobility, while making command and control easier and more effective. However, at all times the division remained a balanced, self-sufficient formation, so that, if necessary, it could operate on its own in the most difficult and unfriendly conditions.

As already explained, the intention to form Marine divisions was first mooted in early 1940 (approved on 7 May 1940), the first two Marine divisions (1st and 2nd) being activated from the existing two permanent brigades of the FMF. In September 1940, the Secretary of the Navy directed that the first Marine Divisional Tables of Organization should be prepared. This was done, the proposed organisation including three infantry regiments, one artillery regiment, an aircraft group, engineer and medical battalions, headquarters and guard companies, and an anti-aircraft machine-gun battery. The Navy General Board, commenting on the expansion of the Marine Corps, concluded that the new proposals were satisfactory for 'the overseas landing operations to be required of the Marine Corps ground troops'.

These ambitious tables of organisation called for the elements as outlined. However, it was soon apparent that this ideal structure was impossible to achieve

immediately, bearing in mind the current levels of manpower, weapons and equipment, and the fact that, as the number of active divisions was set to increase, even newly raised units were soon required to produce cadres for additional units in other embryo formations. This shortage of men meant, for example, that initially there was only enough manpower for two infantry regiments per division instead of three, and even when the Japanese attacked Pearl Harbor, the two divisions so far activated were still at less than 60 per cent strength (with only 40 per cent of weapons and equipment) and with few special troops or service units. In addition, as Gordon Rottman explains, the Navy so jealously protected its Marine divisions, that they did not ask for any advice from the Army, who of course had far more experience in organising divisions and developing their internal command and control than the Navy. Consequently, the fleet landing exercises that were taking place at the time soon showed up numerous flaws in organisation, logistical support, tactics and so on.

As a result, for example, a pioneer battalion was added to the division in January 1942 in order to provide the necessary capability to move supplies from the landing beaches to forward combat units. This new unit, together with the divisional engineer battalion and an assigned naval construction battalion (Seabees), was put under the command of a new engineer regimental headquarters in July 1942. Additionally, a special weapons battalion was added at the same time, plus a headquarters battalion (to consolidate all the command and control elements). These additions made the Marine division (on paper anyway) larger than any other type of division in the entire US armed forces.

Two further changes took place in 1943: the parachute battalion was transferred to

One of the infantry weapons most feared by the enemy was the highly effective man-portable flame-thrower. Here, one is used while the infantrymen who make up the flame-thrower escort take cover. *(USN M 209 via Derrick Wright)*

FMF Troops in January 1943, and six months later a motor transport battalion was added by transferring the existing motor transport companies from the service battalion. More changes took place in 1944: the amphibian tractor battalion, for example, was reassigned to FMF Troops in January 1944, while the special weapons battalion was deleted, its weapons and manpower being redistributed to other divisional and FMF units. By late 1944, certain FMF units were normally attached to divisions for combat operations. These were a naval construction battalion, two replacement drafts, up to three amphibian tractor battalions (Marine or Army), an armoured amphibian tractor battalion, one or two Marine/Army amphibian truck companies, a joint assault signal company, a rocket detachment, a war dog platoon, wire platoon, radio intelligence platoon and an observation squadron. (See Rottman, page 113.)

Other changes that year included re-designating the scout company of the tank battalion as 'reconnaissance' and re-assigning it to the headquarters battalion; eliminating the special troops headquarters and reassigning its remaining units to the service troops; and deleting the engineer regiment, the Seabee battalion being returned to the Navy, while the engineer and pioneer battalions remained under divisional control. FMF Troops units were assigned that were normally attached to divisions to support their operations, i.e. the assault signal company in May 1945, the amphibian truck company in July 1945, and the rocket and war dog platoons in August 1945 after the war had ended.

These additions and subtractions had their overall effect on manpower numbers; for example, the table of organisation adopted in the spring of 1943 had a division of nearly 20,000 men that included a five-battalion artillery regiment and the engineer regiment already mentioned. This was the type of division that fought at Bougainville, Tarawa and Cape Gloucester, then with minor modifications in the Marshalls and Marianas. May 1944 saw the table of organisation drastically streamlined down to 17,465, as a result of the loss of the Seabees and the other engineer/pioneer changes, the additional men being transferred to amphibious corps along with one artillery battalion, the amphibian tractor battalion and most of the special weapons units. The infantry battalions were themselves reorganised from four companies (three rifle and one machine gun) to triangular sub-units by the elimination of the machine-gun company and the distribution of the men among the rifle companies. This was the type of division fighting on Peleliu and Iwo Jima. Finally there was a further reorganisation in the spring of 1945 that increased the strength to 19,228 as a result of the additions of more motor transport and the specialised units added to the headquarters battalion, as already listed. Furthermore, the firepower of the division was increased, by changing the 75mm pack howitzers for a battalion of 155mm, which in the past had been controlled at amphibious corps level.

UNIT STRUCTURES

Before examining the various main tables of organisation, it is worthwhile explaining how the basic unit structures were organised for all types of unit, be they infantry or other arms or services. Rottman lists the following make-up of ground units:

Ground Unit Composition

Fire team	Three men led by a team leader (adopted in 1944)
Squad	Three fire teams (none prior to 1944)
Section	One to three weapons crews (sub-element of platoon or battery)
Platoon	Three or four squads, or two or three sections
Detachment	Size varies from a platoon to a small battalion
Company	Three or four platoons
Battery	Four or six gun sections
Battalion	Three to five companies or batteries
Group (organic to a battalion)	Two or three batteries (defense and anti-aircraft artillery battalions only)
Marine regiment	Three battalions (four or five in artillery regiments)
Marine brigade	One or two regiments plus brigade troops
Marine division	Three infantry regiments, an artillery regiment, plus special and service troops
Amphibious corps	Two or three divisions, corps artillery and corps troops

UNIT COMMANDERS

T/Os specified the ranks of leaders at every level; but because of the rapid expansion of the Corps and the heavy casualty rate, units were often commanded by lower-ranking officers and NCOs. The specified ranks were:

Ground Unit	Rank of Commander
Fire team	Corporal (prior to fire teams, corporals were assistant squad leaders)
Squad	Sergeant
Section	Second lieutenant or NCO
Platoon	Second lieutenant or lieutenant
Detachment	Captain or lieutenant
Company/battery	Captain
Group (organic to a battalion)	Major
Battalion	Lieutenant-colonel
Provisional group	Colonel or lieutenant-colonel
Marine regiment	Colonel
Marine brigade	Brigadier
Tactical group	Brigadier
Amphibious corps artillery	Brigadier
Marine division	Major-general
Amphibious corps	Major-general (senior)
FMF, Pacific	Lieutenant-general
Commandant USMC	General (not until March 1945; before then, major-general until January 1942 then lieutenant-general)

DIVISIONAL TABLES OF ORGANISATION

Below are listed various Divisional Tables of Organisation, beginning with the proposed 'Full-Strength Marine Division' of 1940. This was, of course, never achieved for the reasons already mentioned; however, it does provide a useful starting point for comparison purposes. As we have already outlined what happened and mentioned the unit changes, the further four organisation charts merely show the position in July 1942, April 1943, May 1944 and September 1945, so that comparisons can be made. However, we go on to discuss each of the component parts in some detail.

Marine divisions that were organised under these four tables of organisation were:

D Series: 1st, 2nd and 3rd Marine Divisions
E Series: 1st, 2nd, 3rd and 4th Marine Divisions
F Series: 1st, 2nd, 3rd, 4th, 5th and 6th Marine Divisions
G Series: 1st, 2nd, 5th and 6th Marine Divisions (implemented in January 1945 in 1st, 2nd and 6th)

INFANTRY: A TRIANGULAR ORGANISATION

As we have seen, at the heart of the Marine division throughout the Second World War were its infantry regiments. No matter what changes were made to the organisation of the division as supporting arms and services were added and subtracted so as better to meet the ongoing situation, the fundamental principle of maintaining a triangular organisation at all levels was invariably continued, the aim being that no matter the level, a commander had to control no more than three elements, be it within a basic fire team (three men led by a team leader) right up to division level. Thus (discounting the command elements and support weapons), a Marine Infantry Regiment was composed of three battalions, each of three rifle companies, each of three platoons, each of three rifle squads, each of which contained three fire teams. However, it has to be said that at the lowest level, the fighting group that became the 'fire team' had not always been the accepted norm. Before the adoption of the fire team organisation (in 1944), the infantry platoon had comprised a platoon headquarters of a platoon leader (a junior officer, usually a second lieutenant) with a platoon sergeant as his deputy and approximately five or six radio operators/ messengers; three nine-man rifle squads of a

PROPOSED FULL-STRENGTH MARINE DIVISION, 1940

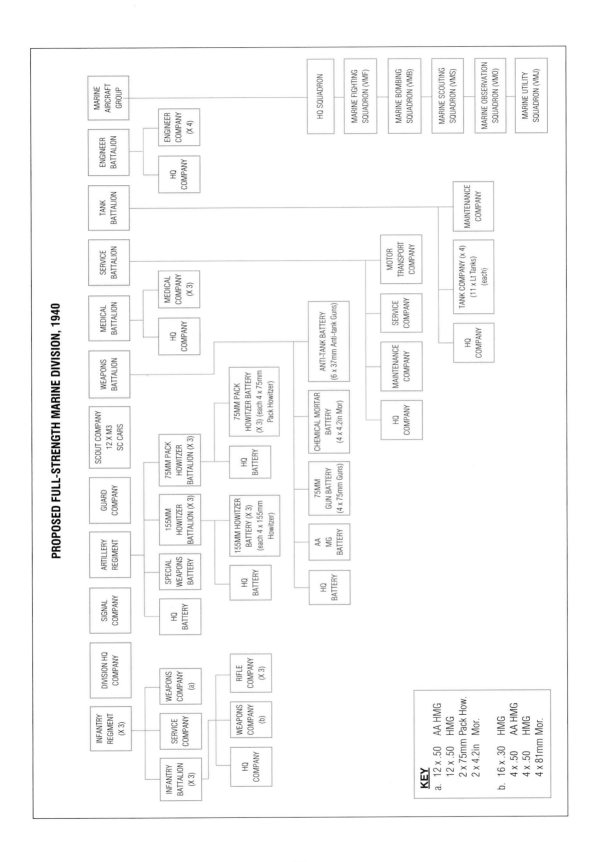

KEY

a. 12 x .50   AA HMG
   12 x .50   HMG
   2 x 75mm Pack How.
   2 x 4.2in   Mor.

b. 16 x .30   HMG
   4 x .50   AA HMG
   4 x .50   HMG
   4 x 81mm Mor.

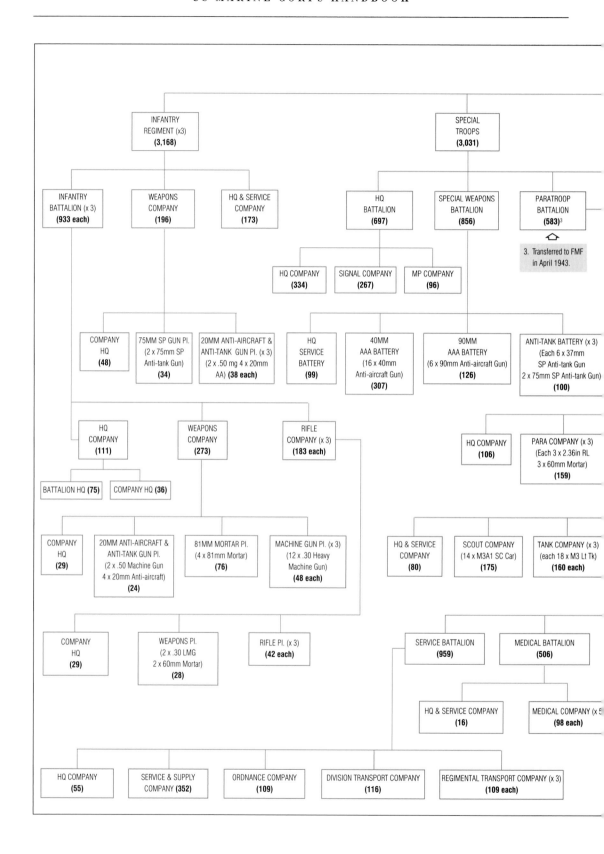

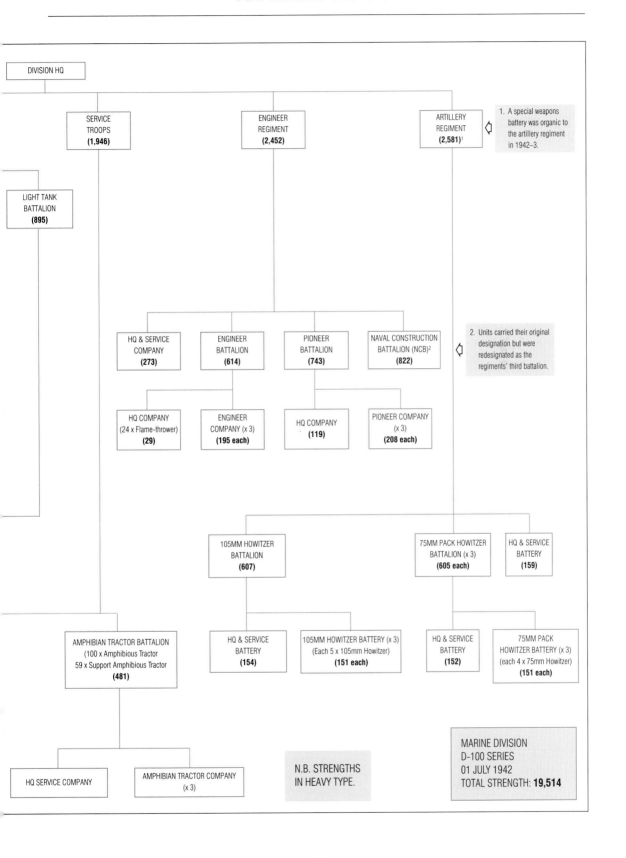

DIVISION HQ

SERVICE TROOPS **(1,946)**

ENGINEER REGIMENT **(2,452)**

ARTILLERY REGIMENT **(2,581)**[1]

◁ 1. A special weapons battery was organic to the artillery regiment in 1942–3.

LIGHT TANK BATTALION **(895)**

HQ & SERVICE COMPANY **(273)**

ENGINEER BATTALION **(614)**

PIONEER BATTALION **(743)**

NAVAL CONSTRUCTION BATTALION (NCB)[2] **(822)**

◁ 2. Units carried their original designation but were redesignated as the regiments' third battalion.

HQ COMPANY (24 x Flame-thrower) **(29)**

ENGINEER COMPANY (x 3) **(195 each)**

HQ COMPANY **(119)**

PIONEER COMPANY (x 3) **(208 each)**

105MM HOWITZER BATTALION **(607)**

75MM PACK HOWITZER BATTALION (x 3) **(605 each)**

HQ & SERVICE BATTERY **(159)**

AMPHIBIAN TRACTOR BATTALION (100 x Amphibious Tractor 59 x Support Amphibious Tractor **(481)**

HQ & SERVICE BATTERY **(154)**

105MM HOWITZER BATTERY (x 3) (Each 5 x 105mm Howitzer) **(151 each)**

HQ & SERVICE BATTERY **(152)**

75MM PACK HOWITZER BATTERY (x 3) (each 4 x 75mm Howitzer) **(151 each)**

HQ SERVICE COMPANY

AMPHIBIAN TRACTOR COMPANY (x 3)

N.B. STRENGTHS IN HEAVY TYPE.

MARINE DIVISION D-100 SERIES 01 JULY 1942 TOTAL STRENGTH: **19,514**

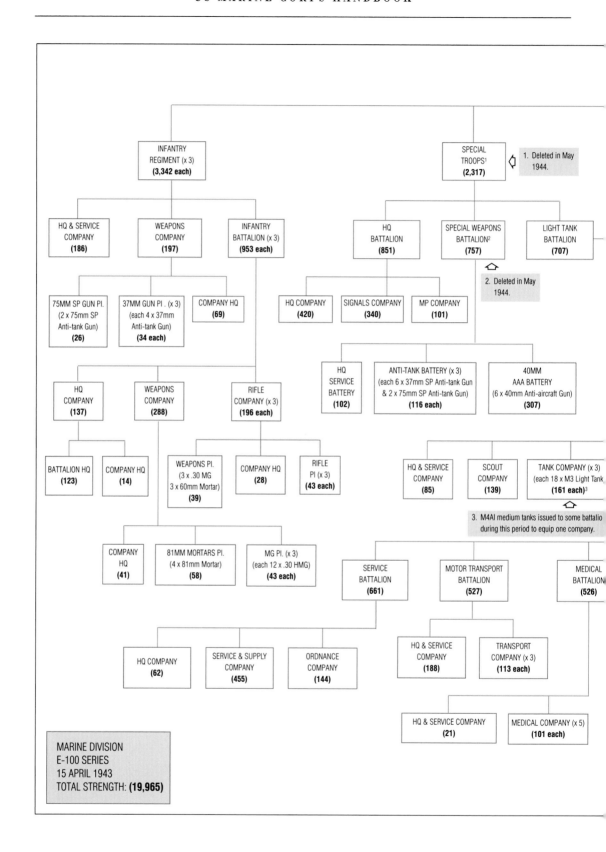

INFANTRY
REGIMENT (x 3)
(3,342 each)

SPECIAL
TROOPS[1]
(2,317)

1. Deleted in May 1944.

HQ & SERVICE
COMPANY
(186)

WEAPONS
COMPANY
(197)

INFANTRY
BATTALION (x 3)
(953 each)

HQ
BATTALION
(851)

SPECIAL WEAPONS
BATTALION[2]
(757)

LIGHT TANK
BATTALION
(707)

2. Deleted in May 1944.

75MM SP GUN PL.
(2 x 75mm SP
Anti-tank Gun)
(26)

37MM GUN PL . (x 3)
(each 4 x 37mm
Anti-tank Gun)
(34 each)

COMPANY HQ
(69)

HQ COMPANY
(420)

SIGNALS COMPANY
(340)

MP COMPANY
(101)

HQ
COMPANY
(137)

WEAPONS
COMPANY
(288)

RIFLE
COMPANY (x 3)
(196 each)

HQ
SERVICE
BATTERY
(102)

ANTI-TANK BATTERY (x 3)
(each 6 x 37mm SP Anti-tank Gun
& 2 x 75mm SP Anti-tank Gun)
(116 each)

40MM
AAA BATTERY
(6 x 40mm Anti-aircraft Gun)
(307)

BATTALION HQ
(123)

COMPANY HQ
(14)

WEAPONS PI.
(3 x .30 MG
3 x 60mm Mortar)
(39)

COMPANY HQ
(28)

RIFLE
PI (x 3)
(43 each)

HQ & SERVICE
COMPANY
(85)

SCOUT
COMPANY
(139)

TANK COMPANY (x 3)
(each 18 x M3 Light Tank
(161 each)[3]

3. M4AI medium tanks issued to some battalio during this period to equip one company.

COMPANY
HQ
(41)

81MM MORTARS PI.
(4 x 81mm Mortar)
(58)

MG PI. (x 3)
(each 12 x .30 HMG)
(43 each)

SERVICE
BATTALION
(661)

MOTOR TRANSPORT
BATTALION
(527)

MEDICAL
BATTALION
(526)

HQ COMPANY
(62)

SERVICE & SUPPLY
COMPANY
(455)

ORDNANCE
COMPANY
(144)

HQ & SERVICE
COMPANY
(188)

TRANSPORT
COMPANY (x 3)
(113 each)

HQ & SERVICE COMPANY
(21)

MEDICAL COMPANY (x 5)
(101 each)

MARINE DIVISION
E-100 SERIES
15 APRIL 1943
TOTAL STRENGTH: **(19,965)**

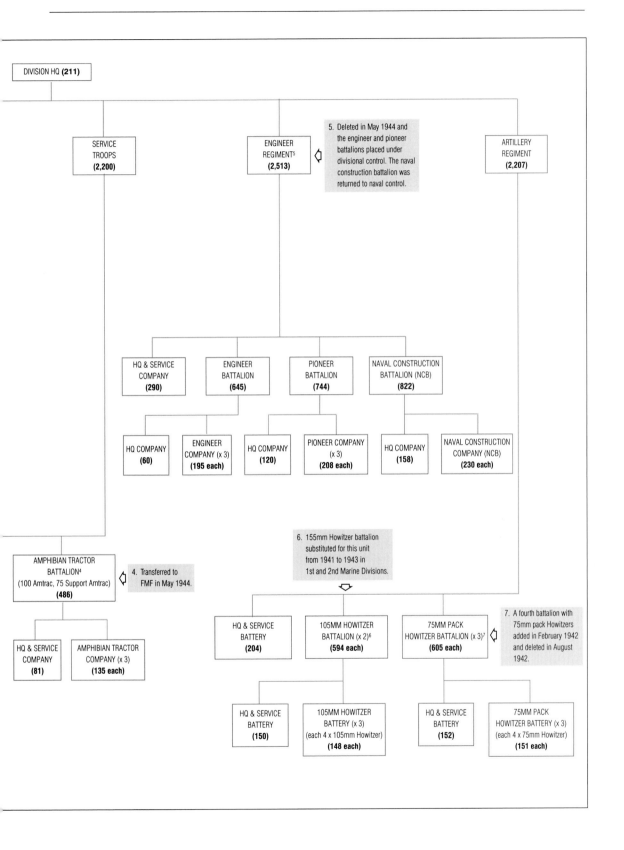

DIVISION HQ **(211)**

SERVICE TROOPS **(2,200)**

ENGINEER REGIMENT[5] **(2,513)**

5. Deleted in May 1944 and the engineer and pioneer battalions placed under divisional control. The naval construction battalion was returned to naval control.

ARTILLERY REGIMENT **(2,207)**

HQ & SERVICE COMPANY **(290)**

ENGINEER BATTALION **(645)**

PIONEER BATTALION **(744)**

NAVAL CONSTRUCTION BATTALION (NCB) **(822)**

HQ COMPANY **(60)**

ENGINEER COMPANY (x 3) **(195 each)**

HQ COMPANY **(120)**

PIONEER COMPANY (x 3) **(208 each)**

HQ COMPANY **(158)**

NAVAL CONSTRUCTION COMPANY (NCB) **(230 each)**

AMPHIBIAN TRACTOR BATTALION[4] (100 Amtrac, 75 Support Amtrac) **(486)**

4. Transferred to FMF in May 1944.

6. 155mm Howitzer battalion substituted for this unit from 1941 to 1943 in 1st and 2nd Marine Divisions.

HQ & SERVICE COMPANY **(81)**

AMPHIBIAN TRACTOR COMPANY (x 3) **(135 each)**

HQ & SERVICE BATTERY **(204)**

105MM HOWITZER BATTALION (x 2)[6] **(594 each)**

75MM PACK HOWITZER BATTALION (x 3)[7] **(605 each)**

7. A fourth battalion with 75mm pack Howitzers added in February 1942 and deleted in August 1942.

HQ & SERVICE BATTERY **(150)**

105MM HOWITZER BATTERY (x 3) (each 4 x 105mm Howitzer) **(148 each)**

HQ & SERVICE BATTERY **(152)**

75MM PACK HOWITZER BATTERY (x 3) (each 4 x 75mm Howitzer) **(151 each)**

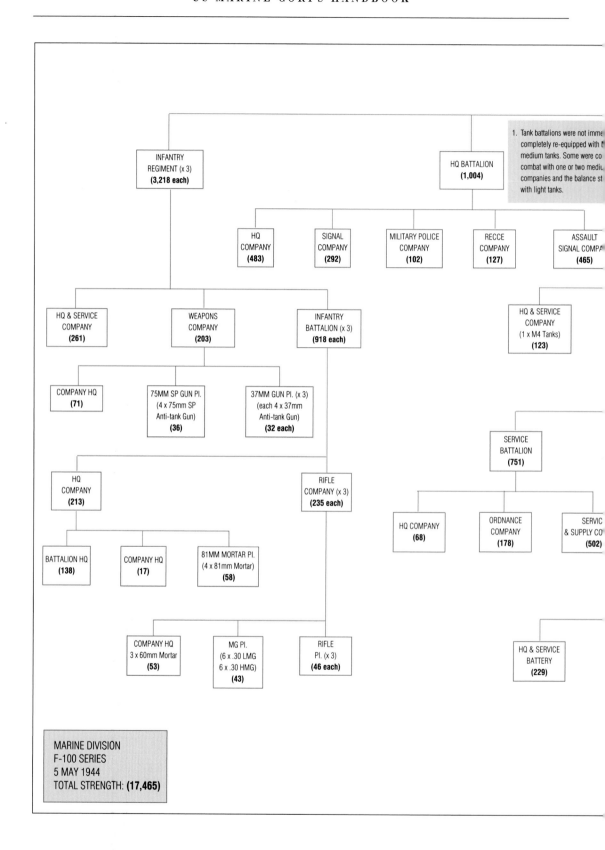

INFANTRY
REGIMENT (x 3)
(3,218 each)

HQ BATTALION
(1,004)

1. Tank battalions were not imme
completely re-equipped with r
medium tanks. Some were co
combat with one or two mediu
companies and the balance st
with light tanks.

HQ
COMPANY
(483)

SIGNAL
COMPANY
(292)

MILITARY POLICE
COMPANY
(102)

RECCE
COMPANY
(127)

ASSAULT
SIGNAL COMPA
(465)

HQ & SERVICE
COMPANY
(261)

WEAPONS
COMPANY
(203)

INFANTRY
BATTALION (x 3)
(918 each)

HQ & SERVICE
COMPANY
(1 x M4 Tanks)
(123)

COMPANY HQ
(71)

75MM SP GUN Pl.
(4 x 75mm SP
Anti-tank Gun)
(36)

37MM GUN Pl. (x 3)
(each 4 x 37mm
Anti-tank Gun)
(32 each)

SERVICE
BATTALION
(751)

HQ
COMPANY
(213)

RIFLE
COMPANY (x 3)
(235 each)

HQ COMPANY
(68)

ORDNANCE
COMPANY
(178)

SERVIC
& SUPPLY CO
(502)

BATTALION HQ
(138)

COMPANY HQ
(17)

81MM MORTAR Pl.
(4 x 81mm Mortar)
(58)

COMPANY HQ
3 x 60mm Mortar
(53)

MG Pl.
(6 x .30 LMG
6 x .30 HMG)
(43)

RIFLE
Pl. (x 3)
(46 each)

HQ & SERVICE
BATTERY
(229)

MARINE DIVISION
F-100 SERIES
5 MAY 1944
TOTAL STRENGTH: **(17,465)**

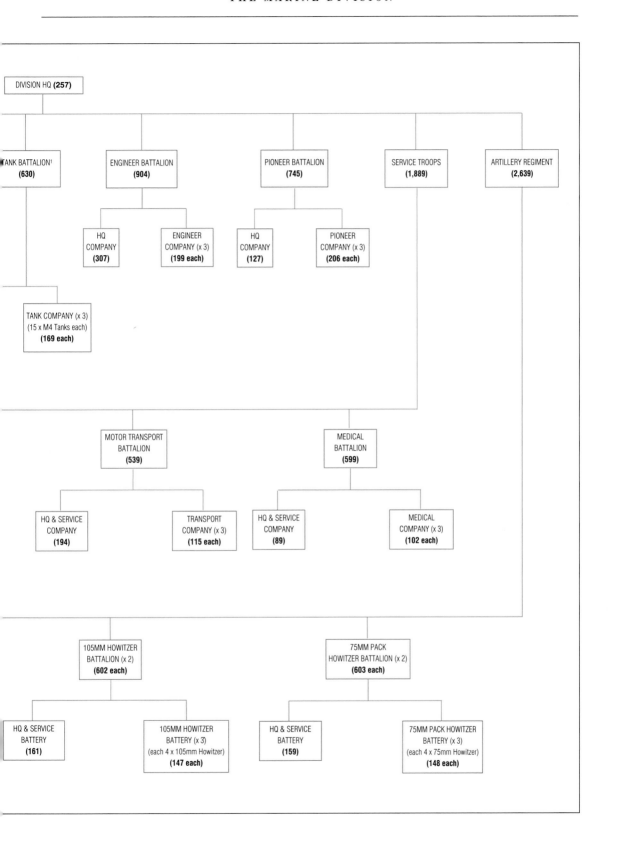

DIVISION HQ **(257)**

TANK BATTALION[1]
(630)

ENGINEER BATTALION
(904)

PIONEER BATTALION
(745)

SERVICE TROOPS
(1,889)

ARTILLERY REGIMENT
(2,639)

HQ
COMPANY
(307)

ENGINEER
COMPANY (x 3)
(199 each)

HQ
COMPANY
(127)

PIONEER
COMPANY (x 3)
(206 each)

TANK COMPANY (x 3)
(15 x M4 Tanks each)
(169 each)

MOTOR TRANSPORT
BATTALION
(539)

MEDICAL
BATTALION
(599)

HQ & SERVICE
COMPANY
(194)

TRANSPORT
COMPANY (x 3)
(115 each)

HQ & SERVICE
COMPANY
(89)

MEDICAL
COMPANY (x 3)
(102 each)

105MM HOWITZER
BATTALION (x 2)
(602 each)

75MM PACK
HOWITZER BATTALION (x 2)
(603 each)

HQ & SERVICE
BATTERY
(161)

105MM HOWITZER
BATTERY (x 3)
(each 4 x 105mm Howitzer)
(147 each)

HQ & SERVICE
BATTERY
(159)

75MM PACK HOWITZER
BATTERY (x 3)
(each 4 x 75mm Howitzer)
(148 each)

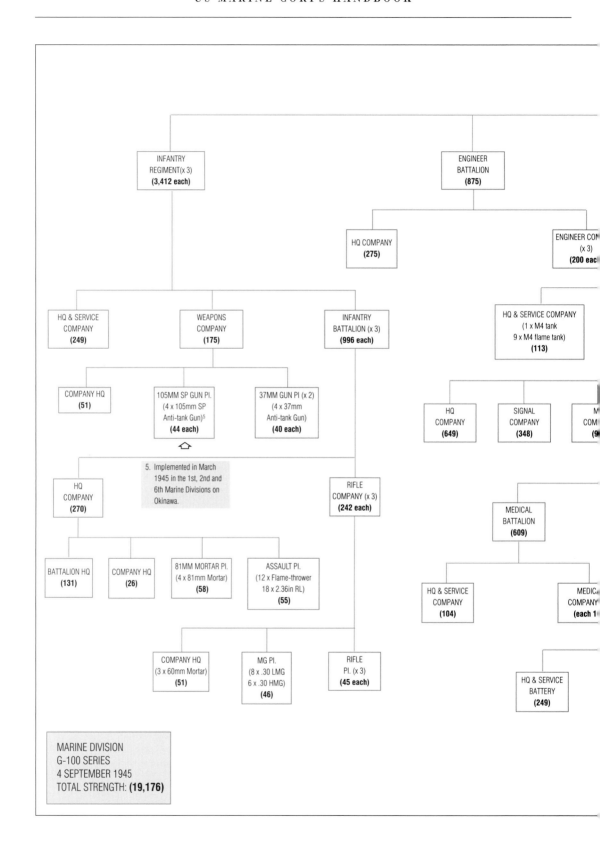

INFANTRY
REGIMENT(x 3)
(3,412 each)

ENGINEER
BATTALION
(875)

HQ COMPANY
(275)

ENGINEER CO
(x 3)
(200 eac

HQ & SERVICE
COMPANY
(249)

WEAPONS
COMPANY
(175)

INFANTRY
BATTALION (x 3)
(996 each)

HQ & SERVICE COMPANY
(1 x M4 tank
9 x M4 flame tank)
(113)

COMPANY HQ
(51)

105MM SP GUN Pl.
(4 x 105mm SP
Anti-tank Gun)[5]
(44 each)

37MM GUN Pl (x 2)
(4 x 37mm
Anti-tank Gun)
(40 each)

HQ
COMPANY
(649)

SIGNAL
COMPANY
(348)

M
COM
(9

5. Implemented in March
1945 in the 1st, 2nd and
6th Marine Divisions on
Okinawa.

HQ
COMPANY
(270)

RIFLE
COMPANY (x 3)
(242 each)

MEDICAL
BATTALION
(609)

BATTALION HQ
(131)

COMPANY HQ
(26)

81MM MORTAR Pl.
(4 x 81mm Mortar)
(58)

ASSAULT Pl.
(12 x Flame-thrower
18 x 2.36in RL)
(55)

HQ & SERVICE
COMPANY
(104)

MEDIC
COMPANY
(each 1

COMPANY HQ
(3 x 60mm Mortar)
(51)

MG Pl.
(8 x .30 LMG
6 x .30 HMG)
(46)

RIFLE
Pl. (x 3)
(45 each)

HQ & SERVICE
BATTERY
(249)

MARINE DIVISION
G-100 SERIES
4 SEPTEMBER 1945
TOTAL STRENGTH: **(19,176)**

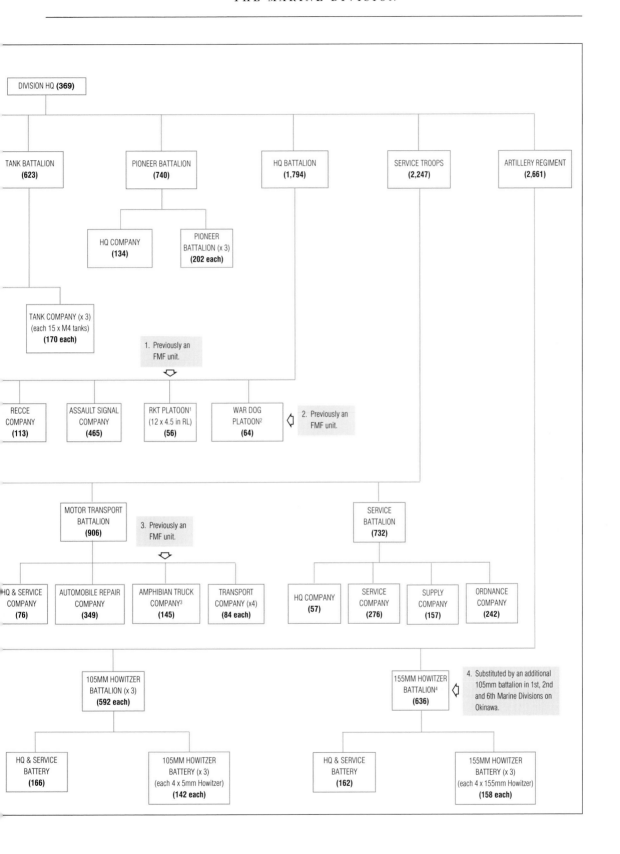

DIVISION HQ **(369)**

TANK BATTALION **(623)**

PIONEER BATTALION **(740)**

HQ BATTALION **(1,794)**

SERVICE TROOPS **(2,247)**

ARTILLERY REGIMENT **(2,661)**

HQ COMPANY **(134)**

PIONEER BATTALION (x 3) **(202 each)**

TANK COMPANY (x 3) (each 15 x M4 tanks) **(170 each)**

1. Previously an FMF unit.

RECCE COMPANY **(113)**

ASSAULT SIGNAL COMPANY **(465)**

RKT PLATOON[1] (12 x 4.5 in RL) **(56)**

WAR DOG PLATOON[2] **(64)**

2. Previously an FMF unit.

MOTOR TRANSPORT BATTALION **(906)**

3. Previously an FMF unit.

SERVICE BATTALION **(732)**

HQ & SERVICE COMPANY **(76)**

AUTOMOBILE REPAIR COMPANY **(349)**

AMPHIBIAN TRUCK COMPANY[3] **(145)**

TRANSPORT COMPANY (x4) **(84 each)**

HQ COMPANY **(57)**

SERVICE COMPANY **(276)**

SUPPLY COMPANY **(157)**

ORDNANCE COMPANY **(242)**

105MM HOWITZER BATTALION (x 3) **(592 each)**

155MM HOWITZER BATTALION[4] **(636)**

4. Substituted by an additional 105mm battalion in 1st, 2nd and 6th Marine Divisions on Okinawa.

HQ & SERVICE BATTERY **(166)**

105MM HOWITZER BATTERY (x 3) (each 4 x 5mm Howitzer) **(142 each)**

HQ & SERVICE BATTERY **(162)**

155MM HOWITZER BATTERY (x 3) (each 4 x 155mm Howitzer) **(158 each)**

squad leader (sergeant), an assistant squad leader (corporal), two scouts, three rifle-men armed with Garand M1 semi-automatic rifles (introduced in 1942) or the earlier much-loved Springfield M1903 rifle, a grenadier with his rifle fitted with a rifle grenade launcher, and one Browning automatic rifleman. Backing up these three rifle squads had been an automatic-rifle squad comprising a squad leader (with a Tommy Gun or other sub-machine gun), two Browning automatic riflemen and five riflemen as close protection/ammunition carriers/assistant BAR men.

The change to the fire team organisation came about through the combat experience gained by raiders, both before the war and during the early war years (see Chapter 9). It had been proved to work better than the normal organisation in jungle fighting, especially in difficult conditions when isolated or under heavy fire. By late March 1944, the new organisation of four-man fire team organisation had been adopted throughout the Marine Corps. Now the squad comprised a squad leader (sergeant) with three fire teams, each of four men, with a corporal (team leader), a rifleman (with grenade launcher) and two BAR men (one to fire the weapon and one to assist him).

While this was an important change in the basic grouping within the infantry squad, the actual total strength of the infantry platoon varied only minimally ('D' – 42 men, 'E' – 43 men, 'F' – 46 and 'G' – 45). The organisation of the rest of the regiment also remained much the same throughout the war years, except for the changes in support weapons (usually improvements in weapon performance or the adding/substitution of new weapons for old) and in their actual administrative location within the regiment/battalion organisation – for example, support weapons such as the smaller infantry-manned artillery pieces, anti-tank guns, mortars, rocket launchers and flame-throwers (hand-held), etc., were either grouped in weapons companies, both at regimental and battalion level, or located under HQ Company control, or a mixture of the two, as the organisational charts on pp. 59–67 demonstrate. When carrying out their supporting role, of course, they would be located where they were required operationally, so their command arrangements were naturally flexible. The actual manpower total of the infantry element in the division also varied very little – just 244 between the first and last total strengths, of which as we have seen, only a fraction were actual riflemen.

ARTILLERY

As the table in Annexe B shows, the numbered Marine artillery regiments always remained an integral part of their specific Marine division; however, the number of battalions within the regiments varied from one table of organisation to another, as did the calibre, size and type of carriage of the weapons concerned. For example, up to early 1943, there were three 75mm pack howitzer battalions and one 105mm howitzer battalion; then an additional 105mm battalion was added, which significantly increased the regiment's fire-power by adding twelve 105mm howitzers. The final increase in firepower came later, when the 75mm pack howitzers were all withdrawn and the regiment now had three battalions of 105mm howitzers (thirty-six in total) and one of twelve 155mm M1A1 guns nicknamed 'Long Toms' that became the main long-range artillery.

Anti-tank and Anti-aircraft Artillery

Be they within special weapons battalions at division level, or in weapons companies at

An indispensable support weapon in Marine division artillery regiments was initially the 75mm M1A1 pack howitzer, as seen here in the early days on Tulagi, Guadalcanal, set up in a Japanese gun position. Note the camouflage-painted sandbags. *(USMC B-23329 via Real War Photos)*

Later, the 105mm M2A1 howitzer came into service, becoming the backbone of American field artillery; over 8,500 were produced and used in almost every theatre of war. This Marine howitzer was photographed on Iwo Jima. *(National Archives M 220 via Derrick Wright)*

regimental or battalion level, there was certainly no shortage of such supporting weapons as anti-tank guns ranging from 20mm and 37mm, towed, to 75mm self-propelled guns, or anti-aircraft artillery of 20mm and 40mm, and even 90mm guns. Many had dual use and their organisation within the division varied, as the charts show. The special weapons battalion, for example, at division level, originally had two anti-aircraft artillery batteries – one of sixteen 40mm and one of six 90mm; however, the latter were removed in April 1943. It also had, at the same time, three anti-tank batteries each with six 37mm anti-tank guns and two 75mm self-propelled half-track-mounted anti-tank guns. Another example is the special weapons battery in the artillery regiment of 1942–3, which had twelve .50-cal. anti-aircraft machine guns, four 37mm self-propelled (truck-mounted) anti-tank guns and two 75mm self-propelled (half-track-mounted) anti-tank guns.

TANKS

In the 1920s there were a few light tank companies in the Marine Corps, equipped with the 6-ton American copy of the highly successful First World War French Renault light tank. However, when the 'Proposed Full-Strength Marine Division' was advocated in 1940, they had at least moved on to include a more modern armoured fighting vehicle, namely the Marmon-Herrington light tank (see Chapter 7). When the Series D organisation came in (i.e. with the formation of 1st and 2nd Marine Divisions), then the light tank battalion comprised seventy-two M3 light tanks (four companies of eighteen each) plus a scout company of fourteen M3A1 scout cars (scouting/ reconnaissance units are dealt with separately). As the tables show, tank battalions were a standard part of every Marine division, irrespective of on which Series (D, E, F or G) it was organised, the only

Another important supporting element in the Marine Division was the tank, such as these M4 medium Shermans, operating with Marine infantry near the town of Naha, on Okinawa. Note the spare track plates on the side of the hull. These were carried to replace damaged plates and also provided additional protection against hand-held anti-tank weapons. (USMC B-23502 via Real War Photos)

This Sherman has the additional advantage of being fitted with a flame-thrower (in action). This one replaces the main armament, while on some other tanks they were fitted in place of the bow machine gun. This Sherman is operating in support of Marine infantry on Okinawa on 11 May 1945. *(USMC 121929 via author's collection)*

difference being the progression from light to medium as the Sherman M4A2 or M4A3 replaced the earlier light tanks, and flame-throwers also became widely used. Of course, this did not happen all at once and tank battalions would often have a mixture of light and medium tanks at the same time. The tank battalion was never organised to operate as a complete unit, but rather each infantry regiment was normally allocated one tank company (the fourth company in the D-100 Series was allocated to Divisional Reserve). Companies were organised on either a three- or four-platoon basis, so the D and E Series had three platoons of five light tanks each and three tanks in HQ Section, while the F and G Series had four platoons

of three medium tanks, plus three in Company Headquarters (and one in Battalion Headquarters). The G Series was also supplemented with nine mediums armed with flame-throwers, while the scale of recovery vehicles went up massively (from three to fourteen). After Okinawa, it was recommended that platoons should go back to five tanks, but the war ended before this could be put into effect. Also, of course, like all organisational tables, they were always only a guide and were frequently altered to suit a particular operation.

Strengths and Types of Tanks in Tank Battalions

Type of Armoured Fighting Vehicle	D	E	F	G
Light tank M3	72	54	–	–
Medium tank M4A2 or M4A3	–	–	46	46
Flame-thrower tank	–	–	–	9
Light recovery tank	–	3	–	–
Medium recovery tank	–	–	3	14
Total	72	57	49	69

A column of vehicles, including Jeeps and Sherman M4 tanks, moving through Agana, Guam, in July 1944. They belong to C Company, 3rd Marine Tank Battalion.
(Sgt Robert Riebe via Derrick Wright)

SCOUT/RECONNAISSANCE COMPANY

The first scout companies in the initial two Marine divisions were trained to reconnoitre on foot, or using motorcycles and/or motorised in M3A1 scout cars. In the D and E Series Marine divisions they became part of the tank battalion with a motorised reconnaissance mission and an all-ranks strength of 175 (D Series) and 139 (E Series). However, once they arrived in the Pacific theatre, their scout cars were replaced with Jeeps and they were also issued with rubber inflatables and taught dismounted patrol techniques, 'by old-timers with "Banana War" experience in jungle terrain' (Melson, *Marine Recon 1940–90*). In May 1944, the scout companies were renamed as reconnaissance com-panies, extracted from the tank battalions and assigned to the divisional headquarters battalion. Their strength was now 5 officers and 122 men in 3 platoons (reduced to 113 all ranks in G Series organisation). This was a measure of their usefulness and they became, in part, the division commander's 'eyes' with their ability to travel on land and over water. Additionally, they were also used as independent rifle companies to protect divisional headquarters; Charles Melson aptly describes them as being at times, both the division command post's 'palace guard' and as a 'private army' on a roving commission.

With the wealth of experience in the Marine Corps in the arts of raiding and patrolling from both the raider and parachute battalions that had done so much in the early days, the techniques were widened and developed, particularly via the Amphibious Scout and Raider School formed at Fort Pierce, Florida, to train individual soldiers, sailors and Marines in raiding and patrolling techniques. While the Reconnaissance Company filled the needs of the divisional commander, those senior Marine commands lacked any equivalent organisation. This led to the formation of the Amphibious Reconnaissance Company in January 1943, then in April 1944 of the 2-company-strong Amphibious Reconnaissance Battalion (23 officers and 291 men). Known as the 'Recon Boys', the battalion operated in support of both III AC and V AC. It was deactivated on 24 September 1945.

ENGINEERS

Although 1st to 6th Engineer Battalions and 1st to 6th Pioneer Battalions were an integral part of their respective Marine divisions, initially they were only two-thirds of a three-battalion Engineer Regiment, the third battalion being a naval construction battalion (the Seabees – see below for details of USN personnel/units that were assigned to, or provided direct support to, the Marine Corps). Both the engineer and pioneer battalions had the usual three-engineer/pioneer company organisation, plus a headquarters company.

SERVICE TROOPS

Service troops within the divisions had various organisations, as the earlier organisational charts show. However, the basic elements were always present: headquarters, service and supply, ordnance, transport and medical. Additionally, another vital component of the service troops was the amphibious tractor battalion with its

100 standard amtracs and 59 support amtracs (raised to 73 in 1943). The battalion was taken away from divisional control in 1944, but there still were a large number of amtracs within the division as numerous units (for example, some motor transport, engineer and pioneer battalions) were equipped with their own specialised support amtracs.

NAVAL PERSONNEL ASSIGNED TO THE MARINE CORPS

Medical

Various USN personnel were assigned to the Marine Corps to provide organic medical (including dental and hospital) personnel for the Corps, which included physicians and surgeons, medical administrative officers, pharmacists and technologists, hospital warrant officers and enlisted medical corpsmen, etc. Thus, Marine medical units (including malaria control units) were almost fully manned by naval personnel, down to platoon level. They even wore Marine uniforms but with USN insignia. Wounded, sick or ill Marines were also admitted to USN hospitals everywhere. Additionally the USN Chaplain Corps provided all chaplains (since 1914), while the Judge Advocate's Office supported the Corps's judicial services.

Naval Construction Battalions

One of the most important naval contributions to the USMC – indeed to the war effort as a whole – was the work of the naval construction battalions, popularly known by the acronym 'Seabees' (derived from the initial letters of 'construction battalions'). Before the war, 'civilian-type' construction work, both at home and abroad, had been carried out by contracted civilians, but clearly this was impossible in wartime, especially in the combat zone. So there was a need to form construction battalions that

Another vital direct support element in the Marine Division was the engineers, including of course the Seabees. This small dozer belonged to 4th Marine Division, as can be seen from the half-circle logo on the back of the driver's shirt. Unit markings like these were often stencilled on to unit equipment, clothing, etc., sometimes with a number inside (see p. 98). *(USMC via author's collection)*

would be able to protect themselves as well as build – hence their motto: *Construimus Batuimus* (We build, we fight). A typical Naval Construction Battalion consisted of some 1,105 all ranks, and was a well-equipped, self-contained unit, capable of tackling virtually any construction task, such as building roads, airfields, docks, railways and so on, and frequently having to defend their worksites from the enemy into the

bargain. NCBs were briefly assigned to Marine divisions, as the organisational charts show, while the majority were under naval control; a staggering 8,000 officers and 238,000 enlisted men were Seabees and were deployed all over the world.

Underwater Demolition Teams

Finally, mention must be made of the USN Underwater Demolition Teams, first formed in September 1942 and first employed during Operation 'Torch' (the invasion of French North West Africa in November 1942). Initial training for these 'Frogmen', who were responsible for the reconnaissance of proposed landing beaches and their approaches, was held at the Joint Navy–Army Amphibious Scout and Raider School in Florida. Underwater Demolition Teams were 100-man units of four platoons,

And the signals. As well as radio sets, field telephones were used whenever possible as they were more secure, despite the fact that it meant linemen laying landlines by hand. Here, two Marines of 5th Marine Division Signals race across country under fire to establish telephone contact with the front lines. *(USMC M-208 via Real War Photos)*

commanded by a commander or lieutenant commander. Their only equipment was a face mask, fins, measuring lines, plexiglas boards, grease pencils and demolition gear. They did not use scuba gear. By the end of the war, there were some 3,500 men assigned to Underwater Demolition Teams.

UNIT MISSIONS

The following provides a useful summary of the specific missions as assigned to units organic to the Marine division:

Divisional headquarters – Command and staff.

Headquarters battalion – Command and control, signals and military police support.

Infantry regiments – Locate, close with and destroy the enemy by fire and manoeuvre, or repel the assault by fire and close combat.

Artillery regiment – Provide direct and general artillery fire support.

Tank battalion – Close with, and destroy, the enemy with armour-protected firepower, shock and manoeuvre, and provide anti-tank fire support.

Parachute battalion – Provide a parachute-deployable raiding and reconnaissance force.

Support weapons battalion – Provide anti-aircraft and anti-tank fire support.

Amphibian tractor battalion – Transport supplies ashore (originally), transport assault force from ship to shore and support mechanised operations ashore.

Engineer battalion – Enhance mobility, countermobility and survivability.

Pioneer battalion – Support ship-to-shore movement of supplies and *matériel* and supplement engineer support.

Naval construction battalion – Provide construction and general engineer support.

Service battalion – Provide supply, ordnance maintenance and (originally) motor transport support.

Motor transport battalion – Divisional and regimental truck transportation support.

Medical battalion – Provide direct and general medical support.

Scout/reconnaissance company – Collect battlefield intelligence information by dismounted and mounted patrolling.

(Source: Rottman, *US Marine Corps World War II Order of Battle*, p. 114)

ANNEXE A

MARINE CORPS DIVISIONAL BATTLE CASUALTIES AS AT THE END OF THE SECOND WORLD WAR

Division	Numbers	Remarks
1st	19,284	
2nd	11,482	
3rd	8,676	
4th	17,722	
5th	8,563	Iwo Jima only
6th	8,226	Okinawa only (does not include losses of component units at Eniwetok, Saipan, Guam, and in other actions)
TOTAL	73,953	

(Source: McMillan *et al.*, *Uncommon Valor*)

ANNEXE B

MARINE DIVISIONS TABLE SHOWING MAJOR UNITS 1941–5

Division	1st	2nd	3rd	4th	5th	6th
Infantry Regiments	1	2	3	23	26	4
	5	6	9	24	27	22
	7	8	21	25	28	29
		9*				
Artillery Regiment	11	10	12	14	13	15
Engineer Regiment	17	18	19	20	16	6
Tank Battalion	1	2	3	4	5	6

N.B. From 1944 onwards there were numerous changes made to the division's Special and Service Troops, as already explained. These units invariably took the divisional number in their unit title, i.e., 1 to 6 as appropriate.

* The newly formed 9th Marines was attached to the 2nd Marine Division in February 1942, until reassigned to 3rd Marine Division in May 1944.

CHAPTER FIVE

MARINE DEFENSE BATTALIONS, ANTI-AIRCRAFT/ARTILLERY UNITS AND BARRAGE BALLOON SQUADRONS

DEFENSE BATTALIONS

Traditionally, the Marine Corps had been responsible for the capture, and subsequent defense, of naval bases in time of war. As we have seen, when, on 8 December 1933, the Fleet Marine Force was established as an integral part of the fleet organisation, one of its primary responsibilities was the seizure and temporary defense of advance bases, in concert with fleet operations. The requirement to have troops ready and able to carry out this task would become one of the main reasons why defense battalions were formed. Even during the continual round of disarmament conferences of the 1920s and 1930s, which inevitably led to savage cuts in the US defense budget, the need for such units to maintain security within the long string of American possessions that stretched out across the Pacific all the way to Manila was never in doubt and, as Charles Updegraph comments in his treatise on *USMC Special Units of the Second*

World War, it was 'perceived as a legitimate Marine Corps responsibility'. Additionally there was the school of thought, much favoured by those who constantly tried to ensure no duplication of effort between the Services, that averred that the Army should be primarily responsible for homeland defense, while the Navy (including the Marine Corps) looked after overseas defenses – and never the twain should meet.

IMPLEMENTATION

All this came together in the late 1930s when the implementation of the early phases of Plan Orange (the basic plan for operations against Japan) led to the need for the establishment of battalion-sized forces (to be known as 'Defense Detachments') on Midway, Wake and Johnston Islands. They were to be of sufficient size to be able to repel raids by small-scale enemy landing parties. The proposed Midway

Marines of 4th Defense Battalion man a 5in sea-coast gun at Guantánamo Bay, Cuba. They were deployed there to defend the naval base. Later they were moved to the Pacific theatre, in time to become one of the 'Rainbow Five' battalions, and were divided between Pearl Harbor and Midway. (USMC 185054)

proposed units had become known as defense battalions, and the tentative armament was proposed as being:

six naval 5in guns
twelve 3in anti-aircraft guns
forty-eight .50-cal. anti-aircraft machine guns
forty-eight .30-cal. anti-aircraft machine guns
six searchlights
six sound locators

As we shall see, both the numbers of personnel and the weapons/equipment allocated depended very much upon the assignment/location of the defense battalion. For example, during the war some defense battalions included both infantry and tank platoons, together with a variety of anti-aircraft weapons and/or coast artillery. To quote Updegraph again:

detachment, for example, would consist of 5in coastal defense guns, 3in anti-aircraft guns, a machine-gun battery and a search-light battery, with an estimated detachment strength of some twenty-eight officers and 482 enlisted men. The Wake and Johnston detachments would be a similar mix of armament and manpower, but on a smaller scale. The Commandant authorised an inspection/survey trip of the three islands in the autumn of 1938, with special attention being paid to locating possible gun positions, determining fields of fire and working out what personnel support would be required. By the summer of 1939, the

The enlisted complement of each battalion would total 711 and each man would be assigned a battle station as on shipboard. Under this arrangement, the battalions would be essentially immobile after they had landed, but a mobile anti-aircraft battalion could be organised if the heavy guns and searchlights were left behind. A total of four such battalions were planned initially, and their relative importance in relation to the total Marine Corps is noteworthy. A request to increase the personnel ceiling from 19,000 to 27,000 had been submitted with indications that, of the new total, 9,000 would be in the FMF, and 2,844 of these would be in the four defense battalions.

Above: On 4 June 1942, during a Japanese air raid on Midway, a number of Marines belonging to the garrison, including some from 6th Defense Battalion, were killed. The 6th had relieved the 3rd on Midway in September 1941. The battalion earned a Naval Unit Commendation for its bravery and remained on Midway for the rest of the war. Here survivors bury their dead with full military honours. *(USN 12703)*

Below: The first defense battalion to operate in a potentially hostile location was 5th Defense Battalion, who went to Iceland with 1st Marine Brigade (Provisional). Here, Marines pause during field training, wearing fur hats and 'polar bear' flashes on their shoulders. This was the shoulder flash of the British 43rd Infantry Division, from whom they took over in Iceland. *(USMC 185021)*

The actual formation of defense battalions started in late 1939 and, by the time of the attack on Pearl Harbor, seven were in existence. The 1st, 2nd, 6th and 7th were formed at the Marine Base, San Diego while the 3rd, 4th and 5th were organised at the Marine Base, Parris Island.

SERVICE IN ICELAND

In fact the first defense battalion to operate in a potentially hostile location was not in the Pacific, but rather in the North Atlantic, when 5th Defense Battalion, under the command of Col Lloyd L. Leech went to Iceland with 1st Marine Brigade (Provisional), sent there to relieve the British garrison. The defense battalion's anti-aircraft weapons (3in guns and .30 and .50-cal. machine guns) were integrated into the British air defense system that was deployed to protect the airfield and harbour at the capital, Reykjavik. This gave them much

useful experience and saved them from irksome labour and construction duties. As time passed and it became clear that a German invasion of Iceland was becoming less and less likely – mainly because they were now heavily committed in Russia – it was decided to withdraw the Marine brigade and replace it with a US Army force. Col Leech brought his battalion back to the USA in March 1942, and four months later, in July, they sailed to the South Pacific, the bulk going to the Ellice Islands, while detachments went to Noumea, New Caledonia and Tulagi in the Solomons (after 1st Marine Division had landed there in August 1942).

Manoeuvring in the half-light of an Icelandic winter was not too cold for those Marines with winter clothing, but the chap in his 'forest greens' must have been freezing. Note that all are armed with the Springfield M1903 rifle. *(USMC 524213)*

A 6th Marines staff NCO demonstrates bayonet
fighting with his Springfield rifle and sword bayonet in
the squashy Icelandic mud. Note the heavy wool
socks and galoshes worn by all, plus the First World
War steel helmets, greatcoats and webbing. *(USMC,
Lt Col Robert J. Vrogindewey collection)*

Of the other six defense battalions that
were in existence at the time of Pearl
Harbor, all but one (2nd Defense Battalion)
were already deployed in the Pacific, 2nd
joining them in January 1942. By early
December 1941, Midway, Johnston, Palmyra,
Samoa and Wake were all defended by
Marine defense units, known as the
'Rainbow Five' after the war plan in effect
when the Japanese attacked Pearl Harbor
(i.e. 1st divided among Pearl Harbor,
Johnston, Palmyra and Wake, 3rd and 4th at
Pearl Harbor, 6th at Midway, 7th in Samoa).
At that time 2nd was still training in
California but was deployed soon afterwards.
As Maj Melson comments in his *Condition
Red*: 'Few of the battalions received group
recognition for their contributions to
victory, although the 1st, 6th and 9th were
awarded unit citations. Each defense
battalion created its own distinctive record
as it moved from one island to another. . . .'
Col Robert D. Heinl, Jr, a Marine historian
who had helped shape the concept of the
defense battalion and served in one of the
wartime units, described the members as a
'hard-worked and frustrated species'. He felt
that the defense battalions represented the
culmination of Marine Corps thinking that
could trace its evolutionary course back to
the turn of the century. The weapons, radars
and communications equipment in the
battalions at times represented the cutting
edge of wartime technology and the skill
with which they were used paid tribute to
the training and discipline of the members
of these units.

Charles A. Holmes, a veteran of the
defense battalions that fought so gallantly at
Wake Island, said that, in his opinion,
anyone could serve somewhere in a division
or aircraft wing, but:

it was an honor to have served in a special unit of
the US Marines. . . . Defense battalions deployed
early and often throughout the Pacific

campaigns, serving in a succession of distant places, some dangerous, others boring. They did not benefit from post-battle rest – though few rest areas lived up to their name – nor were their accommodations comparable to those of an aircraft wing sharing the same location. The Marines of the defense battalions endured isolation, sickness, monotonous food and primitive living conditions for long periods, as they engaged in the onerous task of protecting advance bases in areas that by no stretch of the imagination resembled tropical paradises. After putting up with these conditions for months, many of these same Marines went on to serve as replacements in the six Marine divisions in action before the war ended. . . . Throughout their existence, the defense battalions demonstrated a fundamental lesson of the Pacific War – the need

for teamwork. As one Marine Corps officer has pointed out, the Marine Corps portion of the victorious American team was 'itself the embodiment of unification'. The Corps had 'moulded itself into the team concept without the slightest difficulty. . . . Marine tank men, artillerymen, and anti-aircraft gunners of the defense battalions, interested only in doing a good job, gave equal support to . . . [the] Army and Navy.'

THE FIRST MEDAL OF HONOR

It is also worth recording here that the first Medal of Honor to be awarded to a Marine officer would be awarded to a member of a defense battalion – Lt George H. Cannon of 6th Defense Battalion on Midway on 7 December 1941. As Maj Charles D. Melson also recounts in his treatise on Marine defense battalions in the Second World War, 'As the Japanese aircraft carriers withdrew after the raid on Pearl Harbor, a pair of enemy destroyers began shelling Midway Island shortly before midnight on 7 December to neutralise the aircraft there. A salvo

Marines of 13th Defense Battalion on parade at Guantánamo Bay, Cuba, in 1943. Note that all wear the 'helmet fibre tropical', unofficially known as a 'dishpan'. The 13th were stationed in Cuba throughout the war, defending the naval base. *(US Marine Corps Historical Collection)*

Another crowded LST deck, this time crowded with weaponry rather than supplies; some of the 40mm LAA guns are ready to fire at any incoming Japanese aircraft as the LST approaches Cape Gloucester. The guns belong to 12th Defense Battalion.
(USMC 71623)

directed against Midway's Sand Island struck the power plant, which served as a command post of the 6th Defense Battalion, grievously wounding First Lieutenant George H. Cannon. He remained at his post until the other Marines wounded by the same shell could be cared for and his communications specialist, Corporal Harold Hazelwood, had put the battalion switchboard back into action. Cannon, who died

of his wounds, earned the first Medal of Honor awarded a Marine officer during the Second World War. Hazelwood received a Navy Cross.'

AN AVERAGE DEFENSE BATTALION

By October 1941, the tables of organisation for the new defense battalions had certain features in common, namely each had a headquarters battery, a sound locator and searchlight battery, a 5in sea-coast artillery group, a 3in anti-aircraft group and a machine-gun group. However, the specific allocation of personnel and equipment depended upon where the battalion was deployed and what changes the Commandant had prescribed, that is, the variations

There were two African-American defense battalions, both of which served in the Pacific theatre. Both received their basic training at Camp Montford Point and, to paraphrase the original caption to this photograph, 'cleared any obstacle on the way to earning the right to serve in the US Marine Corps'. *(USMC)*

Cpl Edgar R. Huff drills a platoon of recruits at Montford Point Camp. Huff, who enlisted in the Marine Corps in June 1942, became a legend and retired in 1972 as a sergeant-major. *(National Archives 127-N-5337)*

necessary due to time and circumstance. The average defense battalion strength during the war was 1,372 all ranks, including naval medical personnel. Like manpower, the equipment also varied, although a typical average wartime defense battalion consisted of: 8 155mm guns, 12 90mm guns, 19 40mm guns, 28 20mm guns, 35 .50-cal. heavy machine guns and, in some cases, 8 M3 light tanks.

AFRICAN-AMERICAN MARINES

Regrettably it is true to say the Marine Corps strongly resisted the introduction of black troops until they were ordered to do so, with the rest of the Navy and Coast Guard, by President Roosevelt (via Secretary of the Navy Frank Knox) on 7 April 1942. Some six weeks later it was announced publicly that the Navy, Marine Corps and Coast Guard would enlist about 1,000 African-Americans each month, starting on 1 June. These would include at least one racially segregated 900-man defense battalion (eventually two would be formed). The black recruits for the battalion would begin training at a special, segregated 'boot camp' (Camp Montford Point, west of Camp Lejeune, New River, North Carolina). In addition to defense battalions, there would be a Messman Branch formed and various base support units (over fifty depot companies and twelve ammunition companies). All would, like the women Marines, be granted only Reserve status, being considered to be just a wartime necessity. Of the 19,168 African-Americans who served in the Marine Corps during the Second World War, 12,738 went overseas in defense battalions or in combat support companies or as stewards. Their duties were, to quote one historian, 'exhausting, dangerous, and at times, boring'. Nevertheless, one of these 'Ration Box Commandos' as they

sarcastically called themselves, commented, 'If I had to do it all over again, I'd still be a black Marine . . . I think they made a man of me.'

ANTI-AIRCRAFT ARTILLERY UNITS

Reorienting the Defense Battalions

With so many tasks to perform and manpower always in short supply the Commandant (now Gen Vandegrift) faced the onerous task of using what manpower there was available to the greatest possible effect. Top priority was given to the maintenance of the six divisions, four aircraft wings and the corps troops and service establishments, all without a substantial increase in aggregate strength. Gen Vandegrift's director of the Division of Plans and Policies at HQMC at the time, was Brig Gen Gerald C. Thomas, and it was he who suggested that eliminating special units, including the defense battalions, would produce the required additional manpower. Although Vandegrift agreed, it was not easy persuading the US Navy in the shape of the then Chief of Naval Operations, Adm Ernest J. King, to accept not only that no new defense battalions should be formed, but that two should be disbanded and the remaining seventeen reorientated, so as to meet the current threat.

The process of change began in April 1944 and, five months later, the defense battalions had been converted into anti-aircraft artillery units, although some retained their old designation and, in a few instances, the 155mm artillery group remained with a battalion as an attachment rather than an integral component. The emphasis now was on 40mm and 90mm anti-aircraft weapons, although the manpower level remained unchanged, with 57 officers and 1,198 enlisted men organised into an HQ and Service Battery, a heavy anti-aircraft

This Bofors 40mm anti-aircraft gun has shot down a
fair number of Japanese planes; note the 'Rising Sun'
flags painted on the barrel, each representing a 'kill'.
The gun was part of 3rd Defense Battalion that was
deployed to Hawaii in May 1940, thus becoming one
of the 'Rainbow Five'. They helped defend Pearl
Harbor during the Japanese attack of 7 December.
(USMC 7401)

group, a light anti-aircraft group and a
searchlight battery. Only three units
retained the designation 'Defense Battalion'
until they disbanded – 6th, 51st and 52nd –
the last two being recruited from African-
Americans, commanded by white officers.
Most of the defense battalions became anti-
aircraft artillery outfits and functioned
under FMF, Pacific.

Writing in the *Leatherneck* magazine in
1944, one combat correspondent explained
how, since the beginning of the war, many

of the Marines had seen action in units far
smaller than divisions, such as defense and
raider battalions and other special commands. These Marines had already been
fighting for a long time and it would not be
until the war was won that their complete
story could be told: 'because of the vital part
they played, much information about them
. . . must be withheld, but there are no
American troops with longer combat
records in this war.'

Balloon Squadrons
The roots of USMC balloon units go back to
June 1918 when a balloon detachment was
formed for spotting duties in support of the
10th Marines heavy artillery, which was
being got ready to be sent to Europe for
service with the American Expeditionary
Force. However, the unit never went overseas and was disbanded in April 1919.
Experimentation followed intermittently

after the war, then, in 1924, the Corps formed a balloon observation squadron, ZK-1M, disbanding it five years later.

In 1940, interest was reawakened among military planners, faced with the task of defending bases against air attack. Eventually it was agreed that the Army would be responsible for barrage balloon defenses of permanent naval bases while the Navy was responsible for both advanced bases and shipboard. The Secretary of the Navy then sent out further guidance in which the responsibility for balloon and kite elements of anti-aircraft defenses not manned by the Army should be assigned to the FMF; in other words, it should become the responsibility of the Marine Corps. Opinion, however, remained divided, especially because many (the Director of War Plans Division HQMC in particular) considered that balloons were not a reliable means of anti-aircraft defense, apart from perhaps

Above: This 155mm gun, sited looking seawards, was part of the defenses on the island of Eniwetok, and belonged to 10th Defense Battalion. It was camouflaged against being spotted by enemy aircraft. *(USN photograph)*

Right: A balloon being brought on board LST 447 at Tulagi Island, Solomons, in February 1944. This must have been one of the 3rd Barrage Balloon Squadron balloons. Unfortunately they were not allowed to fly their balloons in case they drew attention to Tulagi, so the personnel were used for other tasks in the island defenses. *(USN N-25705 via Real War Photos)*

against dive-bombers, especially due to the small size of some potential island targets. Such locations would probably require movable barge bases, which could lead to difficult anchorage problems. The other view was held by the Director of the Fleet Training Division, who was full of confidence in their effectiveness, citing British experience in the Battle of Britain, especially over London.

To give adequate cover, some 50–100 balloons were estimated as being necessary to provide adequate area defense. Thus the Marine Corps would need between two and four squadrons of 24–30 balloons each, with some 200 men per squadron. All existing industrial balloon manufacturing capacity would soon be devoted to supplying the Army, so the USMC had to act quickly before any extended runs began. Agreement was given and the Chief of Naval Operations approved the formation of two squadrons, each of 10 officers and 200 enlisted personnel, by the Marine Corps. Action was also taken to procure the requisite number of balloons needed ahead of production for the Army, while a Maj Bernard L. Smith, USMCR, who was an authority in the field of ballooning, was recalled to active duty. Next a training school was established at the Marine Base, Quantico, Virginia, in late April 1941; however, classes could not begin until the balloons and equipment began to arrive in the late summer. The Commandant authorised the formation of 1st and 2nd Barrage Balloon Squadrons, with effect from 1 October 1941. Concurrently the Commandant, to quote Updegraph again, 'emphasised his desire that "every opportunity be taken to train barrage balloon units with defense battalions in base defense operations, and that a report be made covering . . . the lessons learned"'.

Barrage Balloon Squadron (10 April 1942)
Squadron Headquarters (8 officers and 32 enlisted men, including 2 men of the USN)
one communication and aerology section (21 enlisted men)
one gas section (11 enlisted men)
one maintenance section (28 enlisted men)
four balloon sections (each 6 balloons, 1 officer and 31 enlisted men)
Total: 12 officers and 216 enlisted men

By early December the school was able to advise HQMC that 1st Barrage Balloon Squadron (ZMQ-1), under Lt Charles W. May, would be ready for overseas duty on or about 15 January 1942. However, by compressing the training, the squadron was ready earlier and arrived at Fort Randolph in the Canal Zone (Panama) on 30 December 1941. It was eventually relieved by an Army balloon squadron and returned to the USA (to the school that was now at New River) in September 1942. Meanwhile, 2nd Barrage Balloon Squadron (ZMQ-2) had gone on training until late March 1942, when it was shipped to Samoa to join 2nd Marine Brigade there.

Once war had been declared, interest in barrage balloons grew rapidly, and for 1942, funding for a total of eight squadrons was approved, while the school and its supporting activities were enlarged. The 3rd Barrage Balloon Squadron (ZMQ-3), with a strength of 12 officers and 214 enlisted men, went first to New Zealand, then on to Tulagi, via Noumea and Espiritu Santo. Unfortunately, they had extreme difficulty in unloading as a result of enemy air attacks, but eventually managed to get some of their machine guns into defensive positions on the island. It was decided by the senior command in the Guadalcanal–Tulagi area not to fly 3rd Barrage Balloon Squadron's balloons, as they did not want to draw enemy attention to Tulagi, so the personnel were used either as infantry or anti-aircraft gunners.

Eventually they went to Noumea to join ZMQ-1, which had been ordered to the South Pacific after their extended stay in the Canal Zone. Also at Noumea were 5th and 6th Barrage Balloon Squadrons, making four squadrons in all there. In July 1942, 4th Barrage Balloon Squadron was the next to embark for the Pacific area, reaching Samoa, where it stayed until disbanded in February 1943.

Problems now occurred for the balloons on Noumea, some of which were flying in defense of the inner anchorage: a shortage of helium (used to inflate the balloons before hydrogen generators were operational) precluded full operations except when attack was imminent. By late December the hydrogen generator was functioning and the unit was on full operations when 1st and 6th Barrage Balloon Squadrons arrived.

By the end of 1942 there were four squadrons (1st, 3rd, 5th and 6th) in static defensive positions at Noumea and two more (2nd and 4th) similarly employed at American Samoa. Plans for 1943 provided for eight squadrons, with proposals for a further seven. However, the Bureau of Aeronautics was having a hard time keeping them supplied, the most critical shortage being the high-pressure hydrogen cylinders, of which each squadron needed some 4,000. A total of 120,355 were contracted for in June 1942, but peak deliveries of 14,500 per month could not be realised until January 1942. Partly in an attempt to remedy some of the problems, the Marine Barrage Balloon Group was activated at Noumea on 10 January 1943. Its CO was Maj Charles W. May.

Gradually it became clear that anti-aircraft guns offered a far better defense against air attack than did barrage balloons. Additionally by the spring of 1943, four squadrons at Noumea were under Army control, so really surplus to the Marine Corps mission. Fortunately the Army agreed and, on 26 June 1943, assumed full responsibility, thus freeing about 60 officers and 1,200 enlisted men who were involved in barrage balloon duties.

Commencing in March 1943, some 90mm anti-aircraft guns had been assigned to selected barrage balloon squadrons on Noumea, squadrons being reorganised into composite defense units with a balloon section and a gun battery. To release more men for gun duty, balloon flying had to be further limited and by 6 August, 6th Barrage Balloon Squadron had been ordered to secure all its balloons and devote themselves full-time to the guns. By the autumn of that year all the balloon squadrons were doing the same.

In August 1943 2nd Barrage Balloon Squadron was disbanded on Samoa, the personnel being transferred to 2nd Defense Battalion. This became the pattern for the remainder in late 1943, most of the personnel being transferred to defense battalions. The barrage balloon squadrons were no more.

ANNEXE A

DEFENSE BATTALIONS

Unit Designation	Activation	Location	New Designation (date)
1st Defense Battalion	1 Nov. 1939	San Diego	1st Anti-Aircraft Artillery Battalion (+) from 7 May 1944

One of the 'Rainbow Five'. Elements arrived in Hawaii in March 1941. Provided defense detachments for Johnston, Palmyra and Wake Islands. Wake detachment would receive a Presidential Unit Citation for the defense of the outpost, earning them the nickname 'Wake Island Defenders', while the others dealt with hit-and-run raids. In March 1942, the scattered detachments became garrison forces and a reconstituted battalion was formed on Hawaii. Unit then moved to Kwajalein and Eniwetok in the Marshalls in February 1944. It became 1st Anti-Aircraft Artillery Battalion on 7 May 1944 and then served on Guam until 1947.

Unit Designation	Activation	Location	New Designation (date)
2nd Defense Battalion	1 Mar. 1940	San Diego	2nd Anti-Aircraft Artillery Battalion from 16 April 1944

Deployed to Hawaii, December 1941. Deployed to Tutuila, Samoa, in January 1942. In November 1943, deployed to Tarawa in the Gilberts. It became 2nd Anti-Aircraft Artillery Battalion on 16 April 1944 and subsequently served in Hawaii and Guam before landing on Okinawa in April 1945. Returned to USA in 1946 and was deactivated.

Unit Designation	Activation	Location	New Designation (date)
3rd Defense Battalion	10 Oct. 1939	Parris Island	3rd Anti-Aircraft Artillery Battalion from 15 June 1944

Deployed to Hawaii in May 1940 and became one of the 'Rainbow Five'. A third of the battalion went to Midway in September 1940, followed by the rest in 1941, but returned to Hawaii in October 1941 and was there to help defend Pearl Harbor. A detachment of 37mm guns and a 3in anti-aircraft group joined 6th Defense Battalion on Midway and shared the Navy Unit Commendation with that unit for the defense of the atoll. In August 1942, took part in the landings at Guadalcanal and Tulagi. After a stay in New Zealand, they returned to Guadalcanal in September 1943, then landed at Bougainville in September 1943, remaining in the northern Solomons until June 1944. Redesignated as 3rd Anti-Aircraft Artillery Battalion on 15 June 1944. Disbanded at Guadalcanal on 31 December 1944.

Unit Designation	Activation	Location	New Designation (date)
4th Defense Battalion	1 Feb. 1940	Parris Island	4th Anti-Aircraft Artillery Battalion from 15 May 1944

Deployed in February 1941 to defend Guantánamo Bay, Cuba, then to Pacific to become one of the 'Rainbow Five', divided between Pearl Harbor and Midway. Deployed in March 1942 to Efate and Espiritu Santo in the New Hebrides. Moved to New Zealand in July 1943, then to Guadalcanal before landing in August 1943 at Vella Lavella in support of I MAC. On 15 May 1944, became 4th Anti-Aircraft Artillery Battalion. Returned to Guadalcanal in June but ended war in Okinawa, arriving there in April 1945.

Unit Designation	Activation	Location	New Designation (date)

5th Defense Battalion 1 Dec. 1940 Parris Island 5th Anti-Aircraft Artillery Battalion from 16 April 1944

Became 14th Defense Battalion with unofficial title of 'Five: Fourteenth'. Went to Iceland with Marine Brigade, then back to USA in March 1942 and in July to the Pacific. Detachments at Noumea and another at Tulagi, while rest of the battalion was on the Ellice Islands. On 16 January 1943, the detachment on Tulagi was redesignated 14th Defense Battalion. The rest of the unit was designated as 'Marine Defense Force Funafuti'. Sailed to Hawaii in March 1944, where, on 16 April, became 5th Anti-Aircraft Artillery Battalion, later seeing action during the latter stages of the Okinawa campaign.

6th Defense Battalion 1 Mar. 1941 San Diego Marine Barracks, Naval Base, Midway, from 1 February 1946

One of the 'Rainbow Five'. Moved to Hawaii in July 1941, then relieved 3rd Defense Battalion on Midway in September and helped fight off Japanese air attacks and repair bomb damage, thus earning Navy Unit Commendation. Remained at Midway until redesignated Marine Barracks, Naval Base, Midway, in February 1946. Deactivated on 31 October 1949.

7th Defense Battalion 16 Dec. 1940 San Diego 7th Anti-Aircraft Artillery Battalion from 16 April 1944

Deployed to Samoa in March 1941 as one of the 'Rainbow Five', and later to Upolu, with a detachment at Savaii. In August 1943, moved to Nanoumea in the Ellice Islands, then to Hawaii, where in April 1944 it became 7th Anti-Aircraft Artillery Battalion. As such it moved to Anguar, Palau Islands and remained there for the rest of the war.

8th Defense Battalion 1 Apr. 1942 Samoa 8th Anti-Aircraft Artillery Battalion from 16 April 1944

Raised from Marine units on Tutuila, Samoa, then in May 1942 deployed to Wallis Islands and redesignated Island Defense Force. In November 1943 the battalion was deployed to Apamama in the Gilberts. Moved to Hawaii and became 8th Anti-Aircraft Artillery Battalion and as such took part in the Okinawa campaign, remaining there until November 1945, then back to the USA.

9th Defense Battalion 1 Feb. 1942 Parris Island 9th Anti-Aircraft Artillery Battalion from 15 May 1944

Known as the 'Fighting Ninth', first in Cuba defending Guantánamo naval base. It then went to Guadalcanal in November 1942. Emphasised mobility and artillery support of ground operations at expense of coast defense. During fighting in central Solomons set up anti-aircraft guns and heavy artillery on Rendova to support fighting on nearby New Georgia, before moving there and deploying its light tanks and other weapons. Its tanks also supported Army troops on the Arundel Islands. Awarded a Navy Unit Commendation for its active service at Guadalcanal, Rendova, New Georgia and Guam. Redesignated 9th Anti-Aircraft Artillery Battalion, returned to USA in 1946.

Unit Designation	Activation	Location	New Designation (date)
10th Defense Battalion	1 Jun. 1942	San Diego	10th Anti-Aircraft Artillery Battalion from 7 May 1944

Arrived in the Solomon Islands in February 1943 and prepared for the defense of Tulagi and Banika (the latter in the Russell Islands). Its light tanks saw action on New Georgia and the nearby Arundel Islands. Landed at Eniwetok, Marshall Islands, in February 1944. Redesignated 10th Anti-Aircraft Artillery Battalion.

Unit Designation	Activation	Location	New Designation (date)
11th Defense Battalion	15 Jun. 1942	Parris Island	11th Anti-Aircraft Artillery Battalion from 16 May 1944

Deployed to Etate, New Hebrides, December 1942. From January 1943 helped defend Tulagi, in the Solomon Islands, and Banika, in the Russells. Fought on Rendova, New Georgia and in the Arundel Islands during the central Solomons campaign. Came together on New Georgia, then in March 1944 moved to the Arundel Islands. Redesignated 11th Anti-Aircraft Artillery Battalion in May 1944, moved to Guadalcanal and was deactivated by the end of the year.

Unit Designation	Activation	Location	New Designation (date)
12th Defense Battalion	1 Aug. 1942	San Diego	12th Anti-Aircraft Artillery Battalion from 15 June 1944

Deployed to Hawaii in January 1943, then on to Woodlark Islands off New Guinea (via Australia). Took part in the assault on Cape Gloucester, New Britain, in December 1943. On 15 June 1944 redesignated 12th Anti-Aircraft Artillery Battalion, moved to Russell Islands in June and to Peleliu in September, remaining there through 1945.

Unit Designation	Activation	Location	New Designation (date)
13th Defense Battalion	25 Sept. 1942	Guantánamo Bay	13th Anti-Aircraft Artillery Battalion from 15 April 1944

Formed at Guantánamo Bay, Cuba, where it remained throughout the war. Became 13th Anti-Aircraft Artillery Battalion and was disbanded after the war.

Unit Designation	Activation	Location	New Designation (date)
14th Defense Battalion	15 Jan. 1943	Tulagi, Solomon Islands	14th Anti-Aircraft Artillery Battalion from 1 September 1944

Organised from elements of 5th Defense Battalion on Tulagi, so given the nickname 'Five: Fourteenth'. Operated there and sent a detachment to Emirau, St Mathias Islands, to support landing in March 1944. Moved to Guadalcanal to prepare for future operations. Landed at Guam, then in September 1944 became 14th Anti-Aircraft Artillery Battalion and remained on the island after the war ended.

Unit Designation	Activation	Location	New Designation (date)
15th Defense Battalion	1 Oct. 1943	Pearl Harbor	15th Anti-Aircraft Artillery Battalion from 7 May 1944

Organised in Hawaii from 1st Airdrome Battalion at Pearl Harbor. Nicknamed 'First: Fifteenth'. From January 1944 served at Kwajalein and Majuro Atolls in the Marshalls. Became 15th Anti-Aircraft Artillery Battalion in May 1944.

Unit Designation	Activation	Location	New Designation (date)
16th Defense Battalion	10 Nov. 1942	Johnston Island	16th Anti-Aircraft Artillery Battalion from 19 April 1944

Formed from elements of 1st Defense Battalion on Johnston Island. Went to Hawaii after redesignation as 16th Anti-Aircraft Artillery Battalion, then on to Tinian until April 1945, when moved to Okinawa.

Unit Designation	Activation	Location	New Designation (date)
17th Defense Battalion	22 Mar. 1944	Kuai, Territory of Hawaii	17th Anti-Aircraft Artillery Battalion from 19 April 1944

Organised from 2nd Airdrome Battalion, giving rise to nickname 'Two: Seventeen' and the motto 'One of a Kind'. Move to Saipan in July 1944 after redesignation as 17th Anti-Aircraft Artillery Battalion in April, then on to Tinian in August. There it provided anti-aircraft defense of Tinian town and North Field, whence B-29s took off with the atomic bombs to drop on Hiroshima and Nagasaki.

Unit Designation	Activation	Location	New Designation (date)
18th Defense Battalion	1 Oct. 1943	New River, NC	18th Anti-Aircraft Artillery Battalion from 19 April 1944

By August 1944, echelons of the battalion were located at Saipan and Tinian, but came together on Tinian the following month and remained there until war ended.

Unit Designation	Activation	Location	New Designation (date)
51st Defense Battalion	18 Aug. 1942	New River, NC	Disbanded 31 January 1946

Composed of African-Americans with white officers. The plan was for it to be a composite battalion with infantry and pack howitzer elements, but in June 1943 it became a conventional defense battalion. Served in Nanoumea and Funafuti in the Ellice Islands, then in September deployed to Eniwetok in the Marshalls. In June 1945 sent a composite group to Kwajalein Atoll, then back to the US in November 1945 and disbanded in January 1946.

Unit Designation	Activation	Location	New Designation (date)
52nd Defense Battalion	15 Dec. 1943	New River, NC	3rd Anti-Aircraft Artillery Battalion from 15 May 1946

Composed of African-Americans with white officers and began as a composite battalion but took shape as a conventional defense battalion. Deployed to the Marshalls in October 1944 to man the anti-aircraft defenses of Majuro Atoll and Roi-Namur in Kwajalein Atoll. Between March and May 1945 deployed to Guam, remaining there for the rest of the war. Returned to the US in May 1946 to become 3rd Anti-Aircraft Battalion (Composite).

CHAPTER SIX

THE MARINE: INSIGNIA, CLOTHING AND PERSONAL EQUIPMENT

BADGES AND INSIGNIA

Emblem and Motto

The current emblem of the USMC was adopted in 1868, while the motto has been the same since 1885, when the then Commandant, Charles G. McCauley, changed the existing motto, 'By Sea and By Land', to 'Semper Fidelis' ('Always Faithful'). The new motto was inscribed on a scroll and held in the beak of the American eagle on the USMC emblem, where it remains today, perching on top of a globe (showing the American continents), with a 'foul' anchor behind it (that is, an anchor with a turn of cable round it). The initial letters 'USMC' and the emblem are to be found on nearly all field uniforms, usually on the left breast pocket.

The Marine Corps Flag and Colours

Very little information is available regarding the flags carried by early American Marines, but the standard carried by the Marines during the 1830s and 1840s consisted of a white field with a gold fringe, and bore an elaborate design of an anchor and eagle at its centre. Prior to the Mexican War, this flag bore the legend 'To the Shores of Tripoli' across the top. Shortly after the war, the legend was revised to read 'From Tripoli to the Halls of Montezuma'. During the Mexican and Civil Wars, Marines in the field apparently carried a flag similar to the national flag, comprised of red and white stripes and a union. The union, however, contained an eagle perched on a shield of the United States and a half-wreath below, with twenty-nine stars encircling the entire design. Beginning in 1876, Marines carried the national colours (the Stars and Stripes) with 'US Marine Corps' embroidered in yellow on the middle red stripe. At the time of the Vera Cruz landing in 1914, a more distinctive standard was carried by the Marines, the design consisted of a blue field with a laurel wreath encircling the Marine Corps emblem in the centre. A scarlet ribbon above the emblem carried the motto 'Semper Fidelis'. Orders were issued on 2 April 1921 which directed that all national colours be manufactured without the yellow fringe and without the words 'US Marine

Corps' embroidered on the red stripe. This was followed by an order dated 14 March 1922, retiring from use all national colours still in use with the yellow fringe or wording on the flag. Following the First World War, the Army practice of attaching silver bands carrying inscriptions enumerating specific decorations and battles was adopted; this was discontinued on 23 January 1961.

Marine Corps Order No. 4 of 18 April 1925 designated gold and scarlet the official colours of the USMC. These colours,

however, were not reflected in the official standard until 18 January 1939, when a new design was essentially that of the current Marine Corps standard. For a brief time after the First World War, the inscribing of battle honours directly on to the colours of a unit was in practice, but the realisation that a multiplicity of honours and the limited space on the colours made the system impractical and the procedure was discontinued. On 29 July 1936, a Marine Corps Board recommended that the Army

What is my Rank? This poster shows examples of Marine Corps rank insignia as used during the Second World War. (USMC 127-N-529542 via Do You Graphics, USA)

system of attaching streamers to the staff of the organisational colours be adopted. Such a system was finally authorised by Marine Corps Order No. 157, dated 3 November, and is currently in practice.
(Source: USMC History and Museums Division website)

Headdress and Collar Badges

The cap badge and collar badges of all ranks bear the eagle, globe and anchor (known irreverently as the 'bird on a ball') but without the scroll and motto. The cap badges are in gilt and silver for wear with dress blues, and dark bronze with all other forms of service uniform; there are large badges for the peaked cap and smaller ones for the garrison cap and collars. The officers' large badge had a separate rope twisted around the anchor, while the rope on the enlisted men's badges was struck as part of the badge, so the spaces between the anchor and the rope were not cut out.

Authorised shoulder insignia. The authorised Marine patches as at the end of the war (August 1945) are shown on this poster facsimile. The 2nd Marine Division's insignia is the final design. It also shows examples of defense battalion insignia, those of the FMFPac, Marine Amphibious Corps and Ship Detachments, etc. *(USMC 127-NA-707152 via Do You Graphics, USA)*

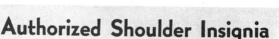

This Marine NCO was a technical sergeant, serving in III Amphibious Corps (note the distinctive Corps shoulder patch) when he was photographed in China in 1945. *(USMC 127-N-227069 via Do You Graphics, USA)*

Buttons

The device reproduced below is the oldest military insignia in continuous use in the USA. It first appeared, as shown here, on Marine Corps buttons adopted in 1804, with the stars changed to five points. The device has continued on USMC buttons to the present day.

Rank Badges – Officers and NCOs

Badges of rank for officers and NCOs were simplified at the beginning of the Second World War; for example, the number of different NCO ranks was considerably reduced. From before the war, NCO stripes have been in gold on a scarlet background for dress uniforms, forest green on scarlet for winter service uniforms and green on tan/khaki for summer service uniforms and shirts. Officers' rank badges were all in silver except for second lieutenants and majors, which are in gold.

Shoulder Insignia

The shoulder patches of the six Marine divisions, the Fleet Marine Force, the amphibious corps and the various defense battalions are shown in the photograph on p. 96. The following points were stressed in the instructions published about wearing these shoulder patches:

- They were primarily identifying marks and not heraldic designs or service decorations.

- They were not to be worn in advance areas where the enemy might observe them.
- They could be worn on overcoats, field jackets and coats, and on the field shirt when the jacket was not worn.
- They were to be worn on the left shoulder only.
- Only one patch could be worn at any time.
- Former members of disbanded units (such as the paramarines) were entitled to wear the patch of that organisation until they joined a new unit that had its own, at which time they had to change.

Unit Markings

A series of six geometrical symbols were used to differentiate between the six divisions. In addition, within the symbol, a three-/four-digit number was stencilled, which normally stood for the following:

1st digit: regiment within the division
2nd digit: battalion
3rd digit: company

UNIFORMS

The USMC Quartermaster Depot of Supplies

The USMC had its own Quartermaster Depot of Supplies in Philadelphia, set up in 1880 and, while a fair proportion of the individual items of personal equipment and weapons used by Marines in wartime was the same as that used by the Army in the Pacific theatre, this did not include the majority of the items of wartime uniform worn by Marines, which was of unique design and manufacture. Details of these wartime uniforms were as laid down in USMC Uniform Regulations dated 21 May 1937 (amended during the war years). Much of this gear was actually made at the QM Depot. Alec S. Tulkoff in his very comprehensive book *Grunt Gear: USMC Combat Infantry Equipment*

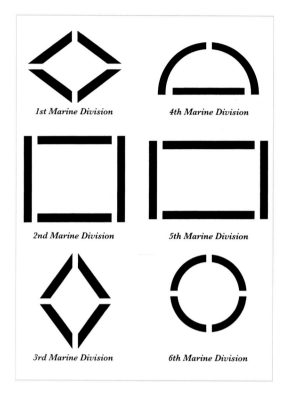

1st Marine Division   4th Marine Division

2nd Marine Division   5th Marine Division

3rd Marine Division   6th Marine Division

of World War 2 (see Bibliography), explains how this manufacturing facility at the Philadelphia Navy Yard had three divisions: Depot, Administration and Manufacturing, where, 'Between the World Wars the Marine Corps manufactured the vast majority of all equipment it used. . . . The facility consisted of seven buildings that housed clothing and equipment factories as well as other buildings for storage and other operations. The facility itself fell under military supervision, but the employees were civilian.' He then goes on to explain that written evidence of the period showed that the depot at that time employed some 1,800 civilians.

As well as manufacturing it also played a major role in the development and distribution of Marine equipment; Tulkoff quotes from the same written evidence: 'It furnishes the technical knowledge necessary

Dress uniforms. Photographed at San Diego in 1940 are examples of 'dress blues' (worn with white belt and gilt belt plate) and 'enlisted undress'. The trousers in both cases were light blue in colour, officers and NCOs having a scarlet stripe down the outside seam. Both are wearing medals awarded for shooting.
(USMC 127-N-402602 via Do You Graphics, USA)

to maintain and improve the specifications for the purchase and distribution of all standard articles used by the Marine Corps; develops and maintains the standard samples, patents, dies, drawings and blueprints necessary in the procurement of Marine Corps equipment; and provides the technical knowledge and the mechanical equipment necessary to test a large proportion of its purchases under practical operating conditions. It also does a great proportion of all the experimental work in developing suggestions for the improvement of equipment used by the Marine Corps.' Sadly, after the war and before the Marine Corps depot in Philadelphia closed and moved to the USMC Logistic Centre in Albany, Georgia, most of the records and materials were thrown away, so little remains.

When war began the USMC was wearing very much the same uniforms as their predecessors had worn in the First World War while fighting in a temperate climate or on garrison/operational duties in the Pacific/Americas area and will be considered under the four categories of 'Dress Uniforms', 'Winter Service Dress', 'Summer Service Dress' and 'Miscellaneous Items'.

Dress Uniforms

The most easily recognisable of all the USMC uniforms were the dress blues, the dark-blue coat and light-blue trousers that have been worn since the early 1900s, with few modifications being made during the intervening years. Both officers' and enlisted men's coats are edged with scarlet piping and have high-standing collars at the neck, epaulettes and cuff flaps; however, while those worn by officers have breast and skirt patch-pockets, the coat worn by enlisted men has no visible pockets at all. The coat is fastened by seven gilt buttons down its front, while the epaulettes and officers' pocket flaps are fastened with similar, smaller gilt buttons. The light-blue trousers have scarlet stripes down both outside seams which vary in thickness according to rank, except for a private's trousers, which have no stripes, and a corporal's, which have one only on the left leg. A 2in-wide white cloth belt was normally worn with the blues. From early 1942, the issue of dress blues ceased except for special organisations, such as the Marine Corps

Band, the Marine Recruiting Staff and those on guard duty at important embassies, such as the one in Grosvenor Square, London. There was also a white dress uniform for officers only, which, apart from its colour, was very similar in all other respects to dress blues.

Winter Service Dress

As the USMC expanded with the mobilisation of its reserves, so the dress blues became, as one historian put it, 'relegated to closets'. Newly returning Reservists were not required to have dress uniforms, although many still did possess them and, as already mentioned, they went on being issued to special units. The most formal

uniform remaining, therefore, was the winter service 'greens', introduced in 1912 and worn as the standard field uniform in the First World War, but with a standing collar for enlisted men, until 1926, when that was replaced by an open roll collar. This uniform was forest green in colour and included the peaked barracks cap; the peak (visor in US parlance) was made of dark cordovan leather (tanned and dressed Spanish leather, originally coming from Córdoba). It was worn with a khaki, long-sleeved woollen shirt (or a cotton shirt in warmer weather) and matching tie ('field scarf'), most Marines using a brass 'battle pin' to hold the pointed shirt collars in place. Many enlisted Marines, like other professional soldiers the world over, washed, starched and even ironed their own khaki clothing, except no doubt in the Pacific theatre, where such services were, before hostilities began, cheap and easy to obtain from the local washerwomen. The trousers were in the same green wool kersey material as the jacket, while for the officer's uniform the standard material was a fine quality 20oz wool elastique cloth. Officers were also allowed to wear tailored riding breeches with leather puttees or riding boots. Their 1935-pattern 'Sam Browne' belts were of cordovan leather with a strap over the right shoulder and brass buckles. Enlisted men wore an almost-black cow-skin

Service and field uniforms. Again photographed at San Diego in 1940 are examples of winter service and field uniforms. Note the extremely smart four-pocket, forest-green coat and trousers, worn with a cordovan leather belt and polished boots (cordovan service shoes in American vernacular). Cap and collar badges are in dull bronze. Note also the leggings and fibre tropical helmet worn with the cap emblem, again in bronze. (USMC 127-N-420600 via Do You Graphics, USA)

A far more formal group of officers photographed at the Marine Barracks, Londonderry, Northern Ireland, in June 1942, wear immaculate webbing over their greatcoats, plus the newly issued steel helmets. *(USMC via Mrs George O. Ludcke)*

'Anything goes' in Iceland, even fur-collared cold-weather gear, as seen here in the Nissen-hutted 'Main Street' of the Marine encampment. They were the lucky ones – some were in tents. *(USMC 185054)*

belt called a 'fair leather belt'. Enlisted men's trousers had no rear pockets. Enlisted men's badges of rank were in forest green on a scarlet background, while buttons were of dark bronze (changed to brown plastic during the later years of the war to save metal).

The regulation six-button overcoat was in heavy green wool, similar to the issue uniform, double-breasted and fitted, and looked extremely smart. Officers' overcoats were tailored, fitted and usually made of a heavy beaver or similar material. Also worn in such extremely cold locations as Iceland was a fur-collared cold-weather coat, sometimes accompanied by a fur hat. However, it has to be said that none of this clothing was designed for, nor proved

particularly suitable for, wear in the wet and cold climate of Iceland. On the other side of the world, when 1st Marine Division was in Australia in 1943, they were issued with British battledress (made in Australia); the blouses became popular to wear and were known, after their divisional commander, as 'Vandegrift jackets'. A US-made version of this jacket in forest green was authorised in late 1944.

Summer Service Dress

This was all made of khaki cotton, the shirts being worn with or without a khaki tie, along with khaki trousers or breeches (for mounted troops). There was also a summer service coat made of the same material. Field leggings were worn with boots (see below for 'boondockers'). The trouser belt was of narrow webbing.

Headgear

In addition to the steel helmet M117A1 pattern and the garrison cap (see below), there was a fibre helmet; known officially as 'helmet, fibre, tropical' and unofficially as the 'dishpan', it resembled the British colonial-style pith helmet. Both helmets would be replaced by the standard M1 steel helmet and inner (see later), although, as some photos show, the 'dishpan' continued to be worn by some on occasions. On both

Standard utility and summer service uniforms. The last of this trio of uniform photographs taken at San Diego in 1940 shows examples of the one-piece standard HBT suit (what the British called 'denims'), with the USMC logo stencilled in black on the left breast pocket. This uniform would soon be replaced by a two-piece. Summer service uniform was an extremely smart khaki shirt, tie and trousers. Note that both Marines wear the fibre tropical helmet. *(USMC 127-N-402599 via Do You Graphics, USA)*

the steel and fibre helmets, the USMC emblem in bronze was worn (unofficially), on the front.

Miscellaneous Items (Worn with Winter and Summer Dress)

Boondockers

Enlisted men were issued with high-top lace-up leather boots ('field shoes' in American parlance) again made of cordovan leather, rough side out. Known as 'boondockers' – the American slang term for wild, desolate, uninhabited countryside is 'the boondocks' – many thousands of pairs were manufactured by the Hermann Shoe Company of Boston, Massachusetts. Before the war, all Marines were issued with two pairs of

At the outbreak of war, a modernised version of the M1917A1 helmet was being worn in the USMC, which had a padded leather liner and two-piece canvas chinstrap. This model of the 'tin hat' was far more comfortable to wear than its predecessor. Later, it would be replaced by the Hadfield manganese-steel helmet, which had a separate fibre liner (its suspension system, as suggested by Gen George Patton, was designed by the makers of contemporary American football helmets). The new helmet was issued to the Marine Corps in the spring/early summer of 1942. *(USMC courtesy Col James A. Donovan, USMC (Ret.))*

boondockers each – one to take a parade 'spit-shine', the other for wearing in the field. However, their soles were really too thin for continual rough work, so many Marines had them double-soled.

Underwear
Known colloquially as 'skivvys', white vests and pants were issued and often dyed green in the field. Issue socks were also white.

Overseas/Garrison Cap
An ideal, easy-to-wear and easy-to-stow item of headgear was the overseas or garrison cap, which looked not unlike the British Army forage cap. It was made either in forest green wool or khaki tan cotton and worn with a Marine bronze collar-badge-size emblem on its left-hand side; officers wore rank badges, again in miniature, on the right-hand side. Other forms of headgear were the First World War M1917A1 steel helmet and, in Iceland, a locally approved fur hat.

The Campaign Hat
One of the most popular, colourful and instantly recognisable items of clothing was the olive drab, felt field hat, also called the 'campaign' hat, which was not unlike the Royal Canadian Mounted Police hat of similar design. 'It was the pride of all real "salty" Marines of the period,' wrote Col James A. Donovan in his Commemorative Series booklet on Iceland, entitled *Outpost in the North Atlantic* (see Bibliography). 'Its ancestry went back to the frontier US cavalry of the late 19th century. Marines in the Fleet Marine Force battalions wore this hat with a special jaunty flair, and the Corps' emblem on the front was often greenish from the salt water sprayed on during landing exercises.'

Dark Blue Denim Coveralls
To save the more expensive winter service greens and summer service khakis, a one-piece dark blue denim coverall was issued and was worn by working parties, for fatigue

This group of 1st Marine Division officers, photographed in New Britain in 1944, shows a wide variation in items of clothing (Marine and Army), headgear and, above all, webbing, as worn on operations. Although, at first glance, all appear to be wearing 'boondockers' and leggings, at least two pairs of paratrooper boots are on show (one of the wearers being right of the line next to Lt Col Lewis B. 'Chesty' Puller, the other third from the left). *(USMC via Compendium Publishing)*

duties, dirty field training (e.g. range firing details) and by prisoners in the guardhouse. These coveralls were perhaps the ancestors of the wartime dusty-green cotton herringbone twill utilities that became the Marines' first proper Second World War combat uniform. Those serving in Iceland took both their old blue coveralls and the new one-piece green coveralls for dirty/fatigue duties while there.

INITIAL FIELD EQUIPMENT

In the British Army, all the details of a soldier's personal clothing and equipment as issued to him on joining were (and still are) recorded on a military form known as the AFG 1157; in the USMC the same happened, and the equivalent field equipment was always known as the '782 gear', after the form on which a Marine signed for all his clothing and equipment, which was:

pack, including a haversack, worn at the top, a knapsack, worn below, and a set of adjustable webbing shoulder straps to help the wearer distribute the weight evenly (American parlance – 'belt suspenders'). Pre-war packs (M1928) remained in service until the issue of the replacement – the Model 1941. (There had been another new type of pack system tested in 1940, but dropped, as the 1941 model was far superior.)

ammunition belt with pouches for clips of cartridges, or a pistol holster and ammunition pouch. There was also a brown leather shoulder holster for those issued with the Colt .45 pistol.

eating utensils, consisting of knife, fork and spoon, and mess tin (known as a 'meat can', complete with cover).

canteen, complete with cup and cover; most Marines carried two canteens in action. Canteen covers were unlined and fitted with 'lift the dot' pressure studs.

A newish Marine Corps recruit at the recruit depot adjusts his 1941 pack system (in transport-pack mode). Note the USMC stencilled marking on some items, also the .30-cal. M1 Garand self-loading rifle and its 'sword' bayonet fixed to the side of the pack. *(USMC 127-N-041745 via Do You Graphics, USA)*

first-aid packet, usually including at least one hermetically sealed first-aid field dressing in a webbing pouch, although later in the war a more comprehensive jungle first-aid kit was issued which needed a larger pouch.

poncho, designed to replace both the raincoat and rain hat. Initially made of a resin-coated, waterproof, light khaki material, but in 1943 a newly designed rubberised, camouflaged poncho began to be issued. It normally fastened around the neck with press-studs. It also had the added advantage of being able to be turned into a makeshift one-man shelter or used as a sleeping bag cover.

shelter half with a pole, a guy line and five tent pins (a mosquito net was added for the Pacific theatre).

steel helmet, including a fibre inner liner that was sometimes camouflage-painted in the factory. There is some evidence that these liners were on occasions worn on their own in the jungle with disastrous consequences. Indeed in 1944, the QM Corps discontinued

Opposite, above: Arriving at their railway station in Australia, March 1943. These Marines have presumably arrived by train from the docks and are now loading their full field transport packs on to lorries for the last leg of their journey to the camp where they will prepare for the coming offensive. Note that they carry blankets and shelter halves. Once again there is a wide variety of headgear being worn – even a service hat (worn by the Marine on the lorry). *(USMC 127-N-054921 via Do You Graphics, USA)*

Opposite, below: A group of WRs try on the new lightweight gas mask that was issued to Marines in 1944. It was carried in an OD (olive drab) haversack. *(USMC RG-127-GC-6277 via Do You Graphics, USA)*

Below: San Diego, April 1944. Recruits under training check over their newly issued '782 gear'. The centre Marine holds his canteen and drinking cup, made of aluminium or plastic (the latter when there was a need to save aluminium). His personal washing and shaving gear is also included on show. *(USMC 127-n-042144 via Do You Graphics, USA)*

the issue of camouflage-painted liners and
ordered them repainted in olive drab.

gasmask and container. The standard issue
gasmask was the M1VA1, but was replaced in
1944, by a lightweight version.

digging aids, including an entrenching tool
(there were two varieties of this shovel – one
folding, the other rigid; the former was
superior), pick/mattock. Also various types of
machete (bolo knife).

flotation devices. The Marine Corps soon
realised that they needed flotation devices for
crossing swollen jungle rivers. They looked at
and tested the Army 'Swimaster' lifebelt and
the Navy kapok vest, but found them
unsuitable (the former did not prove very
effective when the wearer was laden with
heavy equipment, while the latter was a full-
body vest, greatly restricting the wearer's
movements). Then they tried various types of
flotation bladders and finally chose one made
by the Firestone Company.

This equipment was all in addition to the
Marine's personal weapon, for example a
rifle, complete with a canvas webbing rifle

sling (better suited to jungle conditions
than leather), bayonet and scabbard and
rifle-cleaning gear (oil bottle, 4 × 2 cloth).
Last, but by no means least, was his utility
KA-BAR Bowie knife, known universally as
the 'K-Bar' and the indispensable companion of all leathernecks.

The 1941 pack system also incorporated
other items as well as the three already mentioned: a light marching pack (normally for
such items as toiletries, change of socks and
underwear, towel and rations); a marching
pack (haversack, its contents being as per
laid-down orders, belt straps, cartridge/
pistol belt, entrenching tool); a field
marching pack (as for the marching pack,
plus shelter half and two blankets for

This photograph of Marines transferring between
Higgins boats and LCMs at Tarawa in 1943 gives a
good opportunity to see a mixture of lifebelts – some
inflated. There were two types, one being the
Swimaster life preserver belt, the other a complete life
jacket, which was far more cumbersome. *(USMC
127-NA-637581 via Do You Graphics, USA)*

Buck Delaney, a former Marine raider, explains this Second World War edged-weapons collection, on show in the Raider Room of the command museum, during a raider reunion held there in 2003. Note in particular the wide-bladed 'gung-ho' knife and the Camillus raider stiletto (at bottom of case). *(USMC via Do You Graphics, USA)*

Another kit layout of '782 gear', in Guadalcanal in April 1944. This time it is laid out on top of a camouflage-pattern shelter half. Note also the pegs and guy rope alongside the spade (known as the 'rigid entrenching tool'). Alongside the M1 carbine is a K-Bar fighting knife. *(USMC 127-N-079986 via Do You Graphics, USA)*

bivouacking); a transport pack (as for the marching pack, but with the knapsack for additional clothing instead of the bivouac gear – thus for use on a train or ship journey where accommodation was provided); a field transport pack (transport pack plus shelter half and blankets); a canvas field bag also known as the 'musette bag', pre-war M1936 model designed to be used by those who had heavy weapons to heft, so could not carry normal packs. It was also issued to officers and WRs.

FIRST MARINE UTILITY UNIFORM

'The USMC entered World War II wearing essentially the same field uniforms that it had worn during the "Banana Wars".' That is how Kenneth L. Smith-Christmas, Curator of Material History at the USMC Air and Ground Museum, began a short brief about early combat uniforms in Henry I. Shaw's pamphlet in the Commemorative Series,

First Offensive – The Marine Campaign for Guadalcanal. He goes on to explain how those Marines who were defending their country's outposts on Guam, Wake Island and the Philippines in late 1941 were still wearing khaki cotton shirts and trousers, leggings and First World War steel helmets, although plans to change this uniform had been under way for at least a year. As already explained, for work details and field exercises right up to the beginning of the Second World War, the Corps was still using the loose-fitting blue denim fatigue uniform that had been in service since the 1920s. In June 1940 it was replaced by a green cotton coverall, then a year later – on 10 November 1941, the USMC's 166th birthday – both these uniforms were replaced by a new utility uniform made of sage-green (although 'olive drab' had been the ordered colour in the specification) herringbone twill cotton, which was at the time a popular material for civilian work clothing. The

A good example of two different types of Marine footwear. The Marine with his sleeves rolled up has a pair of the new canvas and rubber jungle boots, while the other has a pair of the old 'boondockers' and leggings. The newer jungle boots were superior, being more comfortable and quicker to put on. *(USMC 127-N-066895 via Do You Graphics, USA)*

two-piece uniform comprised a loose-fitting jacket fastened in front with four steel buttons, finished in bronze, each bearing the words 'US MARINE CORPS' in relief, and similar buttons on the cuffs. The jacket had three pockets – two large patch pockets on the front skirts and a single patch pocket on the left breast. The breast pocket bore the eagle, globe and anchor emblem, together with the letters 'USMC', all stencilled on it in black ink (lettering above emblem). The trousers had two slashed front pockets and two rear patch pockets.

Issues were first made to new arrivals at the recruit depots in early 1942, while the uniform first saw combat use during the landing on Guadalcanal in August 1942. It continued to be worn for the rest of the war, in addition of course to the camouflaged uniforms (as described in Chapter 9). Sometimes the new uniform would be worn with canvas leggings, sometimes without, the choice being left normally to individual circumstance. All buttons on both jackets

This group of Marines are being interviewed by a radio reporter on Iwo Jima in February 1945. Note the camouflaged poncho and helmet covers. The reporter in the centre wears a sniper's helmet cover and is holding a small microphone. (USMC 127-N-112637 via Do You Graphics, USA)

In training at Camp Allard, New Caledonia, in March 1943, these Marines of 1st Marine Raider Battalion are wearing the newly issued camouflage uniforms. Note that they are mainly armed with the Reising M55 SMG, except for two who have M1 Garand rifles. *(USMC 127-N-055234 via Do You Graphics, USA)*

and trousers were going to be copper-plated, but a range of other finishes was then allowed in order to save copper. Towards the end of the war, a 'modified' utility uniform was also issued.

A sage-green utility cap was also issued for wear with the new uniform. There were two versions – the original P1941 and the modified P1944, which had a longer peak and was fuller, with stiffeners in the front of the crown so that the Marine Corps emblem (stencilled in black ink) was more visible.

IDENTITY DISCS

The requirement to wear identity discs was promulgated in 1916 (Marine Corps Order No. 32 of 6 October 1916), when it was stated that, 'Hereafter identification tags will be issued to all officers and enlisted men of the Marine Corps. They will always be worn when engaged in field service, and at all other times they will either be worn or kept in the possession of the owner.' By 1942, all Marines were wearing two plain

Machete
Pick-mattock
Jungle pack
M1942 first-aid pouch
Water bottles with 1st pattern covers
Early first-aid pouch

These three 'sharp-shooting' Marines go after a Japanese sniper in Engebi. They also provide good close-ups of webbing, etc. For example, the left-hand man wears two water bottles with, in between, an M1942 first-aid pouch; the middle man has a machete and a pick-mattock on his jungle pack, and also a 'gung-ho' knife behind the right-hand of his two water bottles. *(USMC B-24150 via Real War Photos)*

metal identity discs, known universally as 'dog tags', on a cord/chain around the neck. Both were engraved with the same information: name, religion, blood type, service number and status of the individual concerned. Where a Marine was killed, one disc was left on the body for identification purposes by the graves registration unit, while the other was taken so that the individual's death could be properly reported by his unit. There were a number of variations in the type of metal used, the shape (varying between round and oval), and the information shown; indeed one variety had a fingerprint etched on to its reverse side.

DECORATIONS AND MEDALS

Marine Unit Awards: Presidential Unit Citations (PUC)

Instituted by Executive Orders of 6 February 1942 and 26 February 1942 respectively, they were awarded to units that had particularly distinguished themselves in action. The unit personnel could wear the relevant emblem: the Navy PUC was a 38 × 10mm ribbon strip with three horizontal stripes of blue, yellow and red, without a gilt frame; the Army PUC was a 35 × 10mm royal blue ribbon set in a narrow gilt frame. The numbers awarded to the USMC were:

eighteen Presidential Unit Citations (Navy) (the equivalent in individual valour was the Navy Cross).
three Presidential Unit Citations (Army) (the equivalent in individual valour was the Distinguished Service Cross)
thirty-five Navy Unit Commendations (the equivalent in demonstrated unit service was the Legion of Merit)

EXAMPLES OF CAMPAIGN AND WAR MEDALS

1.

2.

3.

4.

5.

KEY
1. The American Defense Service Medal
2. World War II Victory Medal
3. American Campaign Medal
4. European–African–Middle Eastern Campaign Medal
5. Asiatic–Pacific Campaign Medal

EXAMPLES OF BRAVERY AND MERITORIOUS ACHIEVEMENT MEDALS AND DECORATIONS

6.

7.

10.

8.

9.

KEY
6. Bronze Star Medal
7. Legion of Merit (Commander's Badge)
8. Air Medal
9. Commendation Medal
10. Purple Heart

Individual Awards

The Medal of Honor

This is the highest award for bravery that can be given to any individual in the United States of America. The medal is awarded 'in the name of the Congress of the United States', which is why it is often called the 'Congressional Medal of Honor'. In judging potential recipients, the deed must be proved by the incontestable evidence of at least two witnesses and it must be so outstanding that it clearly distinguishes the recipient's gallantry beyond the call of duty. It must involve the risk of his life and it must be the type of deed for which no criticism could have been directed at him, if he had not carried it out. Since 1862, 294 Marines have been awarded the Medal of Honor, 82 being given during the Second World War (11 to aviators); 51 were awarded posthumously.

The Navy Medal of Honor

On 7 August 1942, Congress abolished the 'new' Medal of Honor that had been instituted in 1919 as a cross pattée and worn on the left breast, and reverted to a style very similar to the original medal instituted in 1861. The revised medal is 53mm in diameter, made of bronze, suspended by an anchor from a bright blue ribbon and is worn about the neck. The ribbon is spangled with a cluster of thirteen white stars representing the original states. The service dress ribbon shows only five stars. Each ray of the five-pointed star contains sprays of laurel and oak and is tipped with a trefoil. Standing in bas relief, circled by thirty-four stars, representing the thirty-four states in 1861, is Minerva, who personifies the Union. She holds in her left hand the

Sgt Clyde Thomson, seen here, was the first enlisted Marine to be awarded the Medal of Honor (inset) in the Second World War. He was posthumously decorated for his leadership in turning back a Japanese counter-attack during the raiders' Makin Raid in August 1942. *(USMC via Do You Graphics, USA)*

fasces, an axe bound in staves of wood, which is the ancient Roman symbol of authority. With the shield in her right hand, she repulses the serpents held by the crouching figure of Discord. The reverse of the medal is left blank, allowing for the

Divine Service in progress on the crowded deck of an LST, en route for Cape Gloucester on 24 December 1943. *(USMC B-23992 via Real War Photos)*

engraving of the recipient's name, and the date and place of his deed. It is worn round the neck; in the centre the ribbon is made up into a rectangular pad with turned-in corners (making it virtually octagonal).

Other individual awards were:

Navy Cross: instituted 1919; dark-blue ribbon with white centre stripe; 1,026 awarded.

Distinguished Service Medal (Army): instituted 1918; ribbon was white and navy-blue stripes, with red edging); 30 awarded.

Silver Star Medal: instituted 1932; ribbon was blue/white/red/white/blue, all equal; 3,952 awarded.

Legion of Merit: instituted 20 July 1942 and established in four degrees – Chief Commander, Commander, Officer and Legionnaire; 606 awarded.

Navy and Marine Corps Medal: instituted 7 August 1942; ribbon was 3 equal stripes of navy blue, golden yellow and scarlet, subsequent awards indicated by gilt stars; 354 awarded.

Soldier's Medal (Army): instituted 1926; ribbon was 7 narrow white, 6 narrow red centre, wide dark-blue edge; 29 awarded.

In addition, of course, there was the Purple Heart (instituted in 1932; the ribbon was purple with narrow white edges, awarded to all wounded in action against the enemy) and campaign medals, eligibility depending upon having the correct length of service in the correct area.

RATIONS

Of the five basic types of field rations issued to the US armed forces, the two which the Marines found themselves mainly living on were 'K' and 'C' rations. The former soon became the staple diet of the front-line Marines. One meal was packed into a cardboard box some 6⅓in long and waterproofed by means of a waxed paper covering. Boxes were marked 'Breakfast', 'Dinner' or 'Supper'. Each contained some type of meat course and supplementary items, such as packets of biscuits (crackers), small tins of cheese and/or jam, coffee, sugar, chewing gum, lavatory paper, even cigarettes, matches, sweets/chocolate. Other drinks were bouillon or lemonade

powder. The 'C' rations were considerably more appetising, with varied meat and vegetable contents that were certainly more sustaining than the endless 'K' rations. Additionally, they contained all the 'goodies', as for the 'K' rations, and, most importantly, a tin opener.

Although there were small stoves for heating up the 'K' and 'C' rations that worked on solid fuel tablets, most of the time combat conditions did not allow many opportunities for cooking, so food was eaten cold, which did not help to sustain fitness levels. Units did have cooking stoves and, when conditions allowed, 'chow' would be prepared centrally. Of the other rations: 'A' was very similar to garrison rations, with at least 70 per cent fresh foods, 'B' was similar but with the perishable items replaced by non-perishable (e.g. dehydrated potatoes and eggs), while 'D' rations were just highly concentrated chocolate bars, containing cocoa, oat flour and skimmed milk powder, in a pack of twelve 4oz bars – a last resort that took the place of First World War iron rations.

'Food, glorious food!' 'K' rations being issued on Iwo Jima in February 1945. Boxes were marked with different menu numbers, so that, although they were often the staple diet in the front line, at least some variation of diet was possible. *(USMC 127-N-109761 via Do You Graphics, USA)*

Left: More palatable than the monotonous 'K' rations were the tinned 'C' rations, seen here being heated over an ad hoc stove. *(USMC 127-N-082381 via Do You Graphics, USA)*

Opposite, above: Stretcher-bearers carry a wounded comrade along the beach at Saipan on 24 June 1944, to load him on to a landing craft for transfer to a hospital ship. *(USMC M-119 via Real War Photos)*

Opposite, below: Sadly, this stretcher contains a dead Marine. The body has been covered with a camouflaged poncho as it is removed for burial. *(USMC 127-n-70172 via Do You Graphics, USA)*

Below: Wounded Marines lie on stretchers and are given blood by medical corpsmen on the beach at Eniwetok. The man nearest the camera wears a first-aid dressing around his head. *(USMC B-24135 via Real War Photos)*

CASUALTIES

Out of the total casualty figures for the USA in the Second World War, of 291,557 killed and 670,846 wounded, the Marine Corps suffered 19,733 who were killed in action or died of their wounds, and 67,207 wounded in action; their total casualty figure from all causes is 90,709. It is also worth noting that the USMC sent most of its men overseas; by VJ Day for example, 98 per cent of USMC officers and 89 per cent of enlisted men had served in the Pacific, while the average for the entire armed forces was only 73 per cent. By VJ Day there were 485,053 all ranks (officers, men and women) in the Corps. Eighteen different Army divisions made a total of twenty-six opposed amphibious landings, while the six USMC divisions made fifteen.

Marines visit the graves of fallen comrades to say their final farewells. This graveyard was on Guadalcanal. *(USMC B-23336 via Real War Photos)*

USMC STRENGTHS

Year	Officers	Enlisted	Total
1936	1,199	16,040	17,239
1940	1,556	26,369	27,925
1943	21,938	287,621	309,559
1945	37,664	447,389	485,053
1948	6,765	76,844	83,609

WAR DOGS

Just a word on 'Man's Best Friend', who served the Marine Corps so faithfully and so well in the Pacific theatre. It was in the late summer of 1942 that the Marine Corps first decided to experiment with the use of dogs, and in due course there were hundreds of dogs and dog handlers being employed, some 465 serving on combat operations at one time. In addition to the dogs and their handlers, medics and kennelmen were needed, but it was the handlers who had to be the 'hands-on' experts, both as dog handlers and as skilled scouts. 'Man and dog searched out the enemy, awaited his coming and caught him by surprise around the Marine perimeter or while on patrol. In

Man's best friend. This war dog and his handler were leading a scout patrol on Bougainville. Such teams were invaluable for a wide variety of tasks. Over 500 war dogs were still in service with the USMC at the end of the war. *(USMC B-24934 via Real War Photos)*

addition they found snipers, routed stragglers, searched out caves and pillboxes, ran messages, and protected the Marines' foxholes as they would private homes. The dogs ate, slept, walked and otherwise lived with their masters' (O'Brien, *Liberation: Marines in the Capture of Guam*). At the end of the Pacific war there were 510 war dogs in USMC service, 491 of which were 'de-programmed' and returned home, or otherwise given to their handlers. Just four dogs would prove 'incorrigible' and considered to be unsafe for civilian life.

ESPRIT DE CORPS

To close this chapter it is necessary to mention that most difficult to quantify ingredient of soldiering, namely *esprit de corps*, the element that made the USMC so special. To quote first from *Uncommon Valor: Marine Divisions in Action*, which briefly tells

the story of the six fighting divisions during the Second World War, 'One more distinctive – if somewhat impalpable – feature of a Marine division is its well-known esprit de corps. Corps spirit is built upon two things – teamwork and a Marine's pride in his outfit, which he believes to be the best fighting organisation in the world. Believing that, he wants to keep it so. Furthermore, he derives a certain amount of personal glory through membership of the Marine Corps. He inherits an equity in the reputation of the Corps earned by those

Navajo code talkers. The Japanese were never able to decipher these Navajos, who needed no complicated codes; they simply used their own language. They would read a message in English, absorb it mentally, then deliver the words in their own native tongue, directly and quickly, and without the need for coding. *(USMC via author's collection)*

Left: Another kit layout of a Marine with his '782 gear' and uniform ready for inspection, at San Diego in May 1943. *(USMC 127-NA-035681 via Do You Graphics, USA)*

Below, left: This lethal array of demolition charges is being examined by three Marine raiders. They were widely used to blow up all manner of enemy bunkers, trench positions and caves. *(USMC 127-N-055268 via Do You Graphics, USA)*

who went before, and he strives to make himself worthy of this inheritance. A sign over the door of the Marine Sergeants Club in Pearl Harbor reads: "Through these portals pass the best damn fighting men in the world". Such immodest self-appraisal can easily pass for boorish conceit. Actually, the men who pass through the portals laugh at the sign – but in the back of their minds they like to think it is true. The man who <u>thinks</u> he is a better fighter usually is. The Marine Corps has what might be called a healthy superiority complex.'

Here is another quotation, this time from Allan R. Millett's *Semper Fidelis*, which aptly captures in just a few words, a marvellous 'pen-picture' of the individual 'leatherneck', the rifleman who was the linchpin of the Corps's fighting ability. He writes, 'On his head rests a helmet covered with camouflaged cloth; his light green cotton dungarees with the black USMC globe and anchor on the left pocket are stained and often bloody; his M-1 is scratched but clean; his leggings (if he still has them) cover soft brown work shoes; around his waist hangs a cartridge belt carrying two canteens, a first aid packet and a K-Bar knife. Burned by the tropic sun, numbed by the loss of comrades, sure of his loyalty to the Corps and his platoon, scornful of the Japanese but wary of their suicidal tactics, he squints into the western sun and wonders what island awaits him.'

ANNEXE A

COMPARISON OF RANKS OF THE USMC WITH US ARMY AND US NAVY

USMC	USA	USN
No equivalent	General of the Army	Fleet Admiral
General (introduced December 1943)	General	Admiral
Lieutenant-General (introduced January 1942)	Lieutenant-General	Vice-Admiral
Major-General (introduced 1902)	Major-General	Rear Admiral
Brigadier-General	Brigadier-General	Commodore
Colonel	Colonel	Captain
Lieutenant-Colonel	Lieutenant-Colonel	Commander
Major	Major	Lieutenant-Commander
Captain	Captain	Lieutenant
1st Lieutenant	1st Lieutenant	Lieutenant (Junior Grade)
2nd Lieutenant	2nd Lieutenant	Ensign
Chief Warrant Officer	Chief Warrant Officer	Chief Warrant Officer
Warrant Officer	Warrant Officer Junior Grade	Warrant Officer
Master Gunnery Sergeant, First Sergeant or Sergeant Major	Master Sergeant or First Sergeant	Chief Petty Officer
Master Technical Sergeant or Quartermaster Sergeant or Paymaster Sergeant	Technician 1st Grade	No equivalent
Gunnery Sergeant	Technical Sergeant	Petty Officer 1st Class
Technical Sergeant or Supply Sergeant	Technician 2nd Grade	No equivalent
Platoon Sergeant	Staff Sergeant	Petty Officer 2nd Class
Staff Sergeant	Technician 3rd Grade	No equivalent
Sergeant	Sergeant	Petty Officer 3rd Class
Corporal	Corporal	Seaman 1st Class
Private First Class	Private First Class	Seaman 2nd Class
Private	Private	Apprentice Seaman

For simplicity's sake I have only shown the 'line NCOs', but there were also 'staff NCOs' in the bands or messes, who outranked the line NCOs. In the chief warrant officer rank, there were CWO pay clerk, CWO quartermaster clerk and chief marine gunner. In December 1943, the CWO rank was redesignated as 'commissioned warrant officer'.

CHAPTER SEVEN

WEAPONS, VEHICLES AND EQUIPMENT

While the weapon requirements of the USMC, once they had reached the battle-field, were generally similar to those of the US Army, it must be remembered that they were continually faced with difficult problems that Army units did not normally have to worry about. These were, for example, restrictions on the size and weight of everything, due to constant shortages of shipping space and the need to be able to on- and offload the larger supporting weapons and other bulky items, from both large and small landing craft. Such restrictions meant adaptation, fortunately a trait in which Americans excel, for example replacing the tyres/wheels on the standard 105mm howitzer with those normally found on the 2½-ton truck, because the latter were narrower. When modified, this most important close support field artillery piece

A vital job that had to be done before going into action. Two Marines of 2nd Marine Division load magazines and clean their weapons, en route to Betio in their attack transport. *(USMC via Lt Gen Julian C. Smith collection)*

would then fit on to the DUKW amphibian for transportation from ship to shore.

In addition, all the weapons, vehicles and equipment that the Marines used had to be able to function in the difficult jungle terrain and tropical climate, with all their built-in problems. However, this was also the case for Army units fighting in the Pacific theatre, so it was not unique, but merely continual. As we shall see, in certain aspects of the conflict, such as armoured warfare, the Japanese did not show much interest until far too late, so the Marine armour, despite suffering casualties from the fanatical defenders, had things much their own way and there were few tank-versus-tank battles, even on a small scale. However, as one American armoured expert, Gen Donn A. Starry, later commented in *Mounted Combat in Vietnam*, 'In the war in the Pacific there was slow, difficult fighting in island rain forests. No armored division moved towards Japan across the Pacific islands. Neither blitzkrieg tactics nor dashing armored leaders achieved literary fame in jungle fighting. It was an infantry war, armored units were employed, but what they learned was neither widely publicised nor often studied.'

It was a 'swings and roundabouts' situation, however. For example, the enemy made up for his lack of interest in tanks by making the building of fighter and light bomber aircraft one of his pre-war priorities (together with naval vessels), so USMC detachments often found themselves having to face a superior enemy air threat, something that hardly ever occurred in the north-west European theatre. Although the Marines were able, at times, to rely upon massive naval gunfire support, the role of artillery in providing close fire support was still vital, especially further inland, once the seaborne supporting fire was no longer available.

In this chapter we look at the Marines' wide range of weapons (from personal arms to tanks), vehicles and equipment, most of which was also in service with the US Army. Some were clearly unique to the USMC and these have been highlighted, despite the fact that the quantities in service of these weapons was never very large. I have deliberately left out amtracs, which are covered with other landing craft and amphibians in Chapter 8, while wheeled unarmoured vehicles (known in British nomenclature as 'B' vehicles to distinguish them from armoured 'A' vehicles) have not been covered in any great detail, because this was already done in my *US Army Handbook 1941–1945*. However, two of the most important 'B' vehicles have been included here – the ¼-ton Jeep and the 2½-ton GMC 6 × 6 truck. While both were used (among their myriad other uses) for towing differing types and sizes of artillery, the larger guns and howitzers needed a vehicle that combined speed with great pulling power. As will be seen from the artillery section, these were the high-speed dozer/tractors D9 and D18, the latter being well able to deal with the heaviest artillery weapons in USMC service, as it was designed for towing artillery loads of up to 13.4 tons, together with their personnel, ammunition and accessories.

AN INFANTRY FORCE

Despite this significant show of supporting weapons and back-up equipment, the Marines were, as Gordon Rottman points out, 'first and foremost an infantry force. The rifle was, and is, considered a Marine's "best friend" and great care was given to marksmanship.' He goes on to emphasise how close combat in jungle terrain, especially at night and against 'banzai' attacks, required a high density of automatic

Holding their personal arms high above the surf, these Marines wade ashore from a landing craft. Those on the left have rifles, while the three in front on the right all have M1928 Thompson SMGs. *(USMC B-24002 via Real War Photos)*

weapons, while such weapons as flame-throwers, bazookas, satchel charges and grenades were needed constantly for use against enemy strongpoints in pillboxes, caves and bunkers, from which the determined Japanese had to be prised, usually preferring to be killed rather than captured alive.

The Infantryman's Creed: 'My Rifle'

Undoubtedly, at the heart of training for newly joined Marines was marksmanship. To quote from Allan Millett's *Semper Fidelis*, 'To have been a Marine and not be a rifleman was unthinkable to veteran Marines, from the Commandant (himself a crack shot) down to the DIs. In addition to the careful marksmanship training at boot camp, the young Marines memorised a new creed, "My Rifle".'

It was William H. Rupertus, later CG 1st Marine Division (8 July 1943 to 2 November 1944), who was prompted by the 'Day of Infamy' that brought America into the war, to compose his 'Infantryman's Creed', which he entitled 'My Rifle'. It epitomises the inseparable bond that was formed between every individual Marine and his rifle, a bond that paid dividends in combat.

THIS IS MY RIFLE

There are many like it but this one is mine.
My rifle is my best friend
It is my life.
I must master it as I master my life.
My rifle, without me, is useless.
Without my rifle, I am useless.
I must fire my rifle true.
I must shoot straighter than any enemy who is trying to kill me.
I must shoot him before he shoots me.
I will . . .
My rifle and myself know that what counts in war is not the rounds we
    fire, the noise of our burst, nor the smoke we make.
We know that it is the hits that count.
We will hit . . .
My rifle is human, even as I, because it is my life.
Thus, I will learn it as a brother.
I will learn its weakness, its strength, its parts, its accessories, its sights,
    its barrel.
I will keep my rifle clean and ready, even as I am clean and ready.
We will become part of each other.
We will . . .
Before God I swear this creed.
My rifle and myself are defenders of my country.
We are masters of our enemy.
We are saviors of my life.
So be it until victory is America's and there is no enemy, but Peace.

PERSONAL ARMS

This section covers those small arms carried by individual Marines. In the main, as already mentioned, they are the same as those found in the US Army.

Pistols

The Colt .45-cal. M1911A1 pistol. Standard issue from 1912 to many Marine officers, NCOs and specialists not armed with the rifle or M1 carbine. Shortages during the First World War had led to more than half a million being manufactured during the early 1920s. The revised pistol was now known as the M1911A1. Its modifications included a shorter, serrated trigger, wider sights, a contoured handgrip and a longer safety grip. Some 1.8 million A1s were produced, while all M1911 models were upgraded to the same standard. The advent of the Second World War led to the 'Parkerisation' of all pistols to give them a non-reflective matte surface. Colt could not keep up with wartime demand and six other firms had to be brought in, one of them (Remington-Rand) actually out-producing Colt by some half a million pistols. The Colt .45 was a recoil-operated, magazine-fed, self-loading weapon. The magazine held seven

MajGen Robert Pepper, Commanding General of 3rd Marine Division, is seen here with two of his senior commanders. Note that two of them wear a .45 Colt M1911A pistol in a shoulder holster. Other significant items of dress include utility caps bearing badges of rank, Pepper's new utility trousers and the officer's raincoat worn by the brigadier in the middle. *(USMC 127-NA-a17849 via Do You Graphics, USA)*

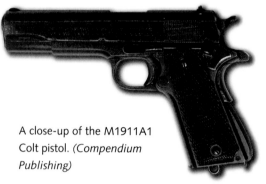

A close-up of the M1911A1 Colt pistol. *(Compendium Publishing)*

rounds and the pistol weighed just under 2⅟₄lb. It was normally carried in a leather holster together with a web pouch that held two spare magazines. A very powerful pistol with a maximum effective range of some 50yd, it was difficult to fire accurately without continual practice.

Other pistols issued included the .38-cal. Smith & Wesson double-action revolver (six-shot cylinder), with a similar maximum effective range of 50yd. It was lighter than the Colt, weighing just over 1lb, and was issued within the USMC mainly to aircrew.

Rifles and Carbines

The Springfield '03 rifle was first issued to the USMC in 1908 and was first used in combat during the campaign in Nicaragua in 1912. Service in Vera Cruz, Mexico, Haiti and Dominica was followed by its exclusive use by Marines serving in France with the American Expeditionary Force during the First World War. After that war, an improved version was issued, its accuracy now being of the highest order. The Corps designed an improved set of sights (both front and rear) for the rifle. Models still in service during the Second World War were the M1903, the M1903A1 and the M1903A3, the last of these being a redesign (to speed up production), which at 8lb was over ⅟₂lb lighter than the initial '03 model. Bolt-action, with a five-round box magazine, it was some 3ft 7in long and had a maximum effective range of 600yd. It could also be fitted with the long M1905 bayonet. Two other special models of the rifle were produced, one pre-war in the 1920s – the M1903 sniper rifle – and one during the war in 1943 – the M1903A1 sniper rifle – both of which weighed 10.4lb, being modified so as to take telescopic sights; the former used the ×5 Lyman 5A sight, the latter the ×8 Unertl. Both had an effective range of over 800yd.

As the 'Infantryman's Creed' has already demonstrated, individual Marines were extremely proud of their prowess with the Springfield '03 rifle and some still preferred

The Springfield M1903 rifle, standard issue to Marines from the early part of the twentieth century and first used in combat in Nicaragua in 1908. Its accuracy was legendary and it remained in use for snipers even after the general issue of the Garand M1 rifle and the M1 Carbine. *(USMC)*

A close-up of the Springfield M1903 rifle complete with telescopic sight. *(Compendium Publishing)*

Two Marines of 1st Marine Division search badly damaged houses, armed with Garand M1 rifles with fixed bayonets. The Corps did not start receiving these rifles in sufficient quantities to replace the Springfields until early 1943. *(USMC 24674 via Real War Photos)*

A close-up of the Garand M1 rifle. *(Compendium Publishing)*

it to its successor, the .30-cal. M1 Garand rifle, and retained it even when the more modern, semi-automatic Garand was issued during the rehabilitation period following the Guadalcanal campaign. The FMF did not become fully equipped with Garands until late 1943 and the rest of the Corps not until 1944. The major advantage of the Garand was the fact that, being a semi-automatic fed by an eight-round magazine, it could deliver far more rapid suppressive fire than the bolt-action Springfield with its five-round magazine, giving Marines a vital edge in the short-range fire-fights that were the norm in jungle warfare. Designed by

John C. Garand, a civilian working in the Springfield Armoury, Massachusetts, it was a .30-cal. (7.62mm) semi-automatic, gas-operated rifle, and entered mass production in 1939. It was not as accurate as the Springfield and had an effective range of only 500yd, although its maximum range was over 3,000yd. It could also be fitted with the M1905 long bayonet.

There was one other semi-automatic rifle in contention with the Garand: the .30-cal. M1941 Johnson, designed by a Marine (Capt Melvin Johnson). However, there were several design problems and the Johnson proved to be too delicate a weapon

This photo of a signal unit hitting the beach gives a good close-up of an M1 carbine. The first relatively large consignment (250) arrived at the depot in August 1942; thereafter, much larger numbers were issued – over 170,000. *(USMC B-23385, via Real War Photos)*

A close-up of the M1 carbine. *(Compendium Publishing)*

for the rigours of jungle combat. It also took a long time to get into the hands of those 'at the sharp end'. Nevertheless, it did see limited service with some Marine raiders and Marine paratroops and some were also sold to the Dutch. After the fall of the Dutch East Indies, shipments of the Johnson rifle were held back in case they should end up in Japanese hands. The USMC then procured a quantity of both Johnson rifles and Johnson LMGs from the Netherlands Purchasing Commission.

For those not armed with a pistol or a rifle, the Winchester .30-cal. M1 and M1A1 carbine were introduced. These were extremely popular weapons, being much lighter (5.2lb) than the rifle, shorter (overall length just under 3ft), and having a magazine capacity of fifteen rounds and a high rate of fire (30rpm). Eventual production ran into millions. The M1A1 carbine was virtually the same weapon, except that it had a metal folding stock and was used by paratroopers.

Sub-machine Guns

Thompson sub-machine gun .45-cal. M1928A1, M1 and M1A1. The original 'Tommy Gun', beloved of Chicago gangsters, was the 1928 model, with the vertical foregrip and fifty-round drum magazine, some of which were still in service. However, the new model (M1928A1) issued in the early 1930s had a horizontal foregrip and a compensator on the end of the barrel. It could take either the drum magazine or the twenty-round box magazine. When war began, the need for simplified production led to the M1 version, which had various alterations; for example, the bolt cocking handle was moved from the top to the side, a permanent butt stock was fitted, it had simpler sighting and it was unable to accept the drum magazine (twenty- and thirty-round box magazines only). Finally came the M1A1, which had a simpler mechanism, including a fixed firing pin and protective 'ears' on either side of the rear sight. Despite its weight (just under 10¼lb) it was

The WR Rifle Team at Camp Mathews, San Diego, Ca., January 1944. They are armed with the M2 Standard US Rifle Cal .22. It was designed for indoor or short-range target practice and was a highly accurate small-bore weapon. *(USMC L/01612 via Do You Graphics, USA)*

Left: While one Marine aims his Thompson SMG, the other (armed with a Browning automatic rifle) ducks for cover among the stunted trees. Both these weapons did much to enhance the firepower of the Marine infantry. The photograph was taken near Shuri, on Okinawa. *(USMC 127-n-123170 via Compendium Publishing)*

Below: This Paramarine (2/Lt Gass) is heavily armed with both a K-Bar knife on his right hip and a .45 automatic pistol on his left, in addition to the Reising M55 SMG. Note also the two-piece utility suit underneath a similar-camouflage-pattern jump smock. The M55 had many problems. *(USMC 35435 via Do You Graphics, USA)*

a very popular weapon, because its heavy bullet could penetrate even the densest jungle and kill the enemy.

Reising .45-cal. M50 and M55 submachine gun. Designed and developed by noted gun inventor Eugene Reising, the M50 was patented in 1940 and manufactured by Harrington & Richardson of Worcester, Massachusetts. Tested by the US Army, but not adopted by them, the M50 (nicknamed the 'Buck Rogers Gun') was tried out by Marine paratroops and accepted by the USMC, who, at the time, desperately needed more SMGs. There were two versions: the M50 had a fourteen-finned barrel (for cooling), a Cutts compensator on the end of the barrel (to prevent upward muzzle jump when the gun was fired), and a wooden stock, while the M55 had a folding wire stock, a shorter barrel and no compensator. At 6lb, it was handier than the Thompson, more accurate and pleasanter to shoot. However, both models had reliability problems, such as rusting and jamming in the difficult, dirty and damp jungle conditions, plus the danger that the safety mechanism did not always work, so the weapon could go off if the butt was

Close-ups of shotguns. *(Compendium Publishing)*

slammed down hard on the ground. These problems resulted in the Reising being declared unreliable, and consequently it was withdrawn from front-line service in 1943, to be replaced by the M1 carbine.

Shotguns

The Marines have used combat shotguns since before the First World War, both in their 'riot' and 'trench gun' configurations, as manufactured by Winchester (two models), Ithaca (one model), Stevens (two models) and other firms. For example, the 12-gauge M97 and M12 Winchester shotguns were used in combat. They weighed about 6½lb, were just over 3ft 3in long and had a pump slide-action. The feed was six rounds from a tubular magazine and the effective range was 40–50yd.

Automatic Rifles

The .30-cal. M1918A1 Browning automatic rifle was a tried and tested weapon that had been developed prior to American involvement in the First World War. Updated between the wars, it was now a useful infantry squad support weapon, the M1918A1 version incorporating a spiked

Grenade launchers were tubular devices that could be attached to the muzzles of both rifles and carbines to fire various standard rifle grenades. Here a Marine uses one from the edge of a clearing in northern Peleliu. Such launchers could propel rifle grenades some 175–250yd, depending on the model of launcher/rifle. *(USMC 96106)*

Left: Here, one member of a Marine patrol fires a rifle grenade at a Japanese machine-gun nest on Saipan, as the leathernecks push forward towards Garapan. *(USMC M-146 via Real War Photos)*

This Marine is about to throw a hand grenade into one of the caves that honeycombed the hillsides on Saipan. The grenade is a 'grenade, hand offensive, Mk IIIA1'. When loaded and fused, it weighed some 14oz. This was primarily a blast grenade, as there was no marked fragmentation, so it could be used in the open more safely than the standard fragmentation grenade. *(USMC M-138 via Real War Photos)*

bipod, while the A2 eliminated the A1 bipod and replaced it with a more effective skid-footed one, although in combat it was often removed to save weight. Weighing some 18½lb (the A2 was a pound heavier), with an overall length of just under 4ft, it had a maximum effective range of 600yd, was fed by a twenty-round box magazine and had a rate of fire of 550rpm.

Hand and Rifle Grenades and Launchers

The most widely employed hand and rifle grenades of the Second World War were fragmentation, chemical and smoke. They were either thrown by hand or used in conjunction with rifle grenade launchers – the M1 (1941) for the Springfield M1903 rifle, the M7 (1943) for the M1 rifle and the M8 (1943) for the M1 carbine.

The rifle grenades were fired from the launcher using a special blank cartridge, which propelled the grenade some 175–250yd, depending upon which type of weapon was being used. Rifle grenades were generally lighter (21–6oz) than hand-thrown (21–32oz) grenades, apart from the Mk 3A1 (blast only), which weighed just over 15½oz.

In addition to coloured smoke and other pyrotechnics, lethal hand grenades in use included the Mk 2 (fragmentation and blast), the Mk 3A1 (blast only); the AN-M14 (incendiary) and the W15 white phosphorus (burns and smoke). Lethal rifle grenades included the M9A1 (anti-tank, shaped charge, with up to 4in penetration), the M19A1 white phosphorus (burns and smoke) and the M17 fragmentation (fragmentation and blast), which could be fitted with a delay mechanism.

CREW-SERVED WEAPONS

Light Machine Guns

The Lewis gun (.30-cal. Mk 6). Oldest of the LMGs in service with the USMC was the American version of what had been a truly

Above: Close-up photograph of the elderly Lewis gun .30-cal. Mk 6 Mod 1 LMG (Lewis), standardised in 1917. Used by raiders and on landing craft prior to 1944, then replaced by the Browning LMG. *(Compendium Publishing)*

Below: One of the best light machine guns of the war was the Browning M1919A4 .30-cal. MG (air-cooled version), seen here in action. It was the infantry squad weapon and was also used on many vehicles, including tanks. It is still in service worldwide. *(USMC 24677 via Real War Photos)*

Above: Partly hidden by one of the ammunition numbers is a .30-cal. M1917A1 Browning MG – the heavy support version, with a water-cooled jacket. *(USMC M222 via Derrick Wright)*

Centre: Somewhat dwarfed by the 37mm anti-tank gun to its rear is the .50-cal. Browning HB M2 heavy machine gun, a superlative weapon which is still in service around the world. *(USMC B-23373B via Real War Photos)*

Below: This .30 heavy support Browning MG is being carried to a new position up a steep hill. The leading Marine has the tripod (plus all his personal gear), the next one carries the water-jacketed barrel, while other members bring up the boxes of ammunition. *(USMC B-24761 via Real War Photos)*

international LMG during and after the First World War, being produced, for example, by the USA, the UK, Japan, Belgium and France during the interwar period. Many of the .30-cal. version were still in service in the USA, being used by the Marines on Guam, Wake and Corregidor. Feed was from the forty-seven-round circular drum magazine that fitted on top of the body, while the end of the barrel was supported by a bipod. The 27lb Lewis gun had a maximum effective range of some 700yd and a rate of fire of 450rpm.

The .30-cal. M1919A4 Browning was the infantry squad/company/vehicle version of the M1917A1 heavy machine gun (see below), with an air-cooled barrel instead of the heavy water jacket and tripod, thus saving over 50lb so that the weight of this widely used LMG was only 31lb, despite having a bipod, butt and carrying handle. With a rate of fire of 450–500rpm and feed via a 250-round fabric or metal-link belt, this excellent weapon, standardised in 1940, was fitted on tanks (both in flexible and coaxial mounts), landing craft and so on, as well as

The anti-aircraft version of the water-cooled M2 .50-cal. HMG in action on Guadalcanal. *(USMC B-23324 via Real War Photos)*

being used in its infantry ground-mounted role, and is still in use worldwide.

The Johnson light machine gun (M1941) was acquired in small numbers and used by Marine paratroops for a while; there was also a later version, the M1944, but it was never adopted. With a twenty-round magazine of .30-cal. ammunition, the Johnson weighed less that the BAR, but they were troublesome and were never ordered in large numbers. It was withdrawn in 1943.

Heavy Machine Guns

The .30-cal. M1917A1 Browning was the company and battalion heavy support machine gun, being the heavier (85.75lb) water-cooled version of the company .30-cal. Browning, complete with water jacket and tripod, the latter alone weighing over 50lb. However, it was possible to transport the complete weapon system on the M4A1 two-wheeled handcart.

The other heavy machine gun, the .50-cal. Browning HB M2 heavy machine gun, was basically just an enlarged version of the .30-cal. M1917 and was manufactured in greater quantity than any other US machine gun, having many uses on the ground, mounted on armoured fighting vehicles, in an anti-aircraft role and in infantry use, the last of these being on a tripod (weighing 44lb). It was also used on numerous aircraft. The Marines used it on tops of tanks and mounted it on LVTs and other types of landing craft, while there was a water-cooled version used as an anti-aircraft weapon, until it was replaced by the 20mm Oerlikon cannon in 1944. Weighing some 84lb, it was fed by a 110-round web or disintegrating metal belt and had an effective range of 1,800yd.

Battalions were well equipped with heavy MGs (of both calibres), which were often used by special weapons groups to help defend artillery and anti-aircraft artillery positions.

Mortars

The standard light mortar was the 60mm M2 mortar, with a barrel length of just

Above, left: In action on a firing range in Guadalcanal, gun crews fire their 60mm mortars. This tiny mortar had a range of some 2,000yd. Two other versions were the M19 (hand-held) and the T20 (shoulder-fired from the prone position). *(USMC RG-127-GW-76781c via Do You Graphics, USA)*

Above, right: A close-up of the 60mm mortar. *(Compendium Publishing)*

The larger 81mm mortar was the battalion-level mortar, having replaced the vintage 'Stokes'. It had an effective range out to 3,290yd. This photo was taken during the Okinawa campaign. *(USMC 80-G-329037 via Compendium Publishing)*

28.6in and a weight in action of 42lb, complete with M2 bipod and baseplate. It fired either a 3lb high-explosive or an M83 illuminating round, and was muzzle-loaded and drop-fired, the rate of fire being 18rpm. It had an effective range of just under 2,000yd. There were two other versions of this successful small mortar: one was the M19 that had a hand-held mount (cf. the Japanese 'knee mortar') as well as the conventional bipod; the other was the T20 mortar, which was shoulder-fired prone, and designed for use against pillboxes and other strongpoints. It was never standardised, as the bazooka was more effective.

The 81mm M1 mortar was the normal battalion mortar, having replaced the earlier issue First World War vintage 3in Stokes mortar. It could be hand-carried into action or transported on the M4A1 two-wheeled handcart. Weighing 136lb, its barrel length was just over 4ft and its maximum effective range 100–3,290yd (light high-explosive). Muzzle-loaded and drop-fired, its rate of fire was 18rpm. Bomb types were light high-explosive (6.87lb), heavy high-explosive (10.62lb), white phosphorus and illuminating (10.75lb).

Flame-throwers (Man-portable)

There were three types of man-portable flame-throwers: the M1, M1A1 and M2-2, standardised in 1942, 1943 and 1944 respectively. The weight (filled with 4gal of fuel) was 70lb (M1 and M1A1) and 72lb (M2-2). They were operated by projecting a stream of fuel – this varied from petrol (with or without napalm powder), naval fuel oil and diesel, to straight bunker fuel oil – ignited by an electronic spark mechanism fuelled by compressed hydrogen (M1 and M1A1) or nitrogen (M2-2). Ranges were: M1 – 15–20yd; M1A1 – 50yd, M2-2 – 60yd. A second man was needed to carry a refill (fuel can and spare gas bottle).

An excellent close-up of a man-pack flame-thrower, which weighed around 70+lb. The operator gets ready to fire as the other Marine points out the target. The flame fuel was electrically ignited and propelled by compressed hydrogen. *(USMC B-23494 via Real War Photos)*

A flame-thrower team in action. Two flame-throwers make short work of a target on Iwo Jima. They could carry some 4gal of fuel, but a second crew member was needed to carry a refill. *(USMC M223 via Derrick Wright)*

Hand-held Anti-tank Weapons

The rocket launcher M1 and M9/M9A1 bazooka were two examples of one of the most original weapons ever produced, the main difference between the two types of bazooka being the fact that the M9 could be broken down into two pieces for ease of carrying. The 3.4lb rocket could penetrate some 4.7in of armour; however, they were equally effective against enemy pillboxes. Range was some 250–300yd.

The Boys .55-cal. anti-tank rifle Mk 1. This British-designed and Canadian-made weapon had a maximum effective range of 500yd and its ammunition (fed from a five-round box magazine) could penetrate a half-inch of steel plate at 500yd. Nicknamed the 'Elephant Gun' (probably because of its considerable recoil) it was used by Marine

A bazooka team in action north of Nada, Okinawa, just behind a small patrol. This useful anti-tank weapon was also used against blockhouses and other fortifications. *(USMC 80-G-427846 via Compendium Publishing)*

A close-up of the bazooka.
(Compendium Publishing)

raiders as an anti-pillbox weapon, although it was once used successfully to down two Japanese seaplanes at Makin Atoll in August 1942.

TANKS AND OTHER ARMOURED FIGHTING VEHICLES

'If any one supporting arm can be singled out as having contributed more than any others during the progress of the campaign, the tank would certainly be selected.' (MajGen Lemuel C. Shepherd, Jr, CG 6th Marine Division, 7 September 1944– 24 December 1945).

Light Tanks

Before the Second World War the only tanks in service with the USMC were the Marmon-Herrington CTL 3 and 3A light

tanks. Early Marmon-Herringtons had been turretless, but in 1940 they produced the CTL version with a turret, specifically for the USMC. It was nicknamed 'Betty' after Adm Harold 'Betty' Stark, who had ordered the lightly armed vehicles, and armed with just three .30-cal. MGs, all in the front of the open-topped turret. They weighed some 8.4 tons, were 11.5ft long, and had a road speed of 30mph and a range of 60 miles. The majority were used for training, although some were sent to Alaska

This M2A3 light tank has stopped just clear of some enemy dead at the side of the track. This model had some improvements on the M2A2, such as thicker frontal armour. It, and the M2A4, saw limited combat service in the Pacific theatre with the USMC. *(USMC via author's collection)*

This M3A1 light tank of 1st Tank Battalion fought on Guadalcanal and saw much heavy fighting there. Although the Japanese had few anti-tank guns they often attacked US tanks using masses of 'kamikaze-type' infantrymen, armed with satchel charges and Molotov cocktails. *(USMC via author's collection)*

and to Western Samoa for local defense. None saw combat.

The M2A4 light tank was standardised in 1939 and went into mass production in 1940, the first American tank to do so. It mounted a 37mm in its turret and four MGs (one coaxial, one anti-aircraft and one in a sponson on each side of the driver). It weighed 10.26 tons, had a crew of four men and was 14ft 7in long, 8ft 4in wide and 8ft 3in in height. Its road speed was 25mph and range 130 miles. Some were used in combat on Guadalcanal, but had started to be replaced by the M3 series light tanks by late 1942.

The M3, M3A1 and M3A3 light tanks were known as the 'Honey' by the British crews who first used them in combat in North Africa – a tribute to their all-round reliability and ease of handling over the M2A4, which they replaced. Basic details were: armour plate increased in thickness from 25mm to 37mm, length 14ft 11in, width 7ft 4in, height 8ft 3in, weight 12.23 tons, speed 36mph and range 70 miles. Their armament was initially a 37mm main gun and five machine guns, but later the two sponson-mounted MGs were taken out to increase space for more ammunition. With better vision devices, radio and intercom equipment and a gyrostabiliser for the gun (M3A1 onwards), the M3s were the first American tanks to see action against the Japanese. They were used by 192nd and

'Hothead' was an M5A1 light tank belonging to A Company, 4th Tank Battalion, seen here on the island of Roi in the Kwajelein Atoll during fighting on 1 February 1944. It still has the bottom section of its wading stack at the rear, although the rest of the stack has been ditched, probably soon after landing. *(USMC B-23374B via Real War Photos)*

194th Tank Battalions, which had been shipped to Luzon in the Philippines shortly before the Japanese invasion, and formed a Provisional Tank Group under Brig Gen James Weaver. During the fighting that followed, some broke down and had to be abandoned, but the majority were destroyed on the general surrender. Those captured were taken into Japanese service and used against the Americans during the fighting in the Philippines in early 1945, so they were both the first and last M3s to see action in the Pacific area.

The M5 and M5A1 light tanks were the last of the light tanks to be used in the USMC, both being standardised in 1942, after the supply of engines for the M3 light tank had threatened to hold up supply, until Cadillac had suggested using two of their V-8 car engines coupled to their HydraMatic automatic transmissions. Ordnance were somewhat sceptical because the automatic transmission had only been on the market for about a year or so. In response, Cadillac converted a tank and drove it 500 miles to a test ground, which convinced Ordnance and the tank was approved for production. With armour now 58mm thick, the 14.73-ton M5A1 had an enlarged turret with more space for radio equipment. Its hull length was only 14ft 3in, width 7ft 4in and height 7ft 7in. The top speed was 36mph and range 100 miles. The M5s and M5A1s were often the only tanks available, so they saw continual combat on such places as Kwajalein, Saipan, and Tinian in 1944.

Medium Tanks

The major change came, of course, with the arrival of the M4 Sherman medium tank with its 75mm main gun and thicker armour, which made it a formidable

Opposite, above: Hitching a ride! It is difficult to see this Sherman medium tank for the men of Col Victor Bleasdale's 29th Marine Regiment, hitching as they move up to take the town of Ghuta on Okinawa in April 1945. *(USMC 117054 via author's collection)*

Opposite, below: The crew of this Sherman M4A1 will have their hands full, having lost a track, probably to a mine (note also the large crack in the side wooden boards, which are there to prevent the Japanese from attaching magnetic mines). Spare track plates on the front glacis and turret sides also add to protection, since the armour plate is not massively thick. *(USMC M213 via Derrick Wright)*

Below: A covey of flame-throwing tanks assaulting the caves on Mayi Point, Saipan. They include M3A1s, M5A1s and M4A2s, all fitted with flame guns. *(Lt Col Schmidt USMC (Ret.), now deceased, via author's collection)*

opponent for both the light and medium Japanese tanks. Nevertheless, it was still vulnerable to the Japanese 47mm anti-tank gun, especially because of its height, so additional protection (such as track-plates or even sandbags) was often added. One Marine tanker told me, 'We all made various mods to our tanks which weren't authorised by the arsenals, but were very practical, e.g. extra track blocks and bogey wheels carried on turrets and glacis plates and sponsons as added protection; rotating turrets so that the cover opened towards the bow to provide some cover for turret occupants in case they had to bale out. . . . We had 2in × 6in oak planks on our sponsons, with a 2in space between wood and armour – sometimes the space was filled with sand to protect against magnetic mines or to detonate AT shells outside the sponson armor – it worked.'

The wading stacks remain in place on this Sherman, still on the beach. Each tank had its own kit of parts, which was assembled and installed before deep wading began. *(USMC via author's collection)*

Additionally, flame-guns (e.g. the M3-4-3 and E12-7R1 flame-throwers) were fitted in place of the bow machine gun, with a range of about 60yd. Basic details of the Sherman were: crew 5, weight 30 tons, armour thickness up to 76mm, length 19ft 4in, width 8ft 7in and height 9ft. Main armament was the 75mm M3 gun (although a few mounted the M4 105mm howitzer), plus one .50-cal. anti-aircraft MG and two .30-cal. (one coaxial, one bow). Its speed was 24 mph and its range 120 miles. The flame-throwers were most effective, one USMC tanker telling me, 'Our flame-thrower tanks really have been having a field-day for the past three days, burning up caves and pockets of Nips that won't quit.'

Swimming/wading devices. Towards the end of the war, after Tarawa, there was considerable work done on improving both swimming and wading capabilities, to enable medium tanks to 'swim' and to 'wade' ashore. The swimming equipment consisted of detachable pontoons, such as the M19 (Ritchie T-6) Swimming Device; wading gear was improved so that tanks dropped into fairly shallow water could safely wade ashore. Swimming devices were not available until Okinawa, when some twenty tanks were fitted with swimming devices, but no use was ever made of the highly successful DD (Duplex Drive) tanks as developed in Britain and used during the Normandy landings.

Other Armoured Vehicles

The M3A1 White scout car was used as a reconnaissance vehicle in scout companies between 1941 and 1943, when it was phased out and not used in combat, being replaced by Jeeps (see later). For a short period they were replaced in 2nd Marine Division with British-built Bren-gun carriers provided by the New Zealand Army. With a crew of two and carrying up to six passengers, the 5.54-ton White had an armour-plated open-topped body (up to ½in thick on the windscreen shield, but only ¼in at the sides, rear and engine compartment). There were seats in the cab for the crew and seats for the six passengers in the rear compartment. A skate rail ran around the rear compartment that carried one .50-cal. M2 HB flexible and one .30-cal. M1919A4 flexible machine gun. Dimensions were: length 18ft

This bizarre-looking arrangement is an improvised flail tank, constructed by the Seabees in November 1944. The drums rotated and the flail chains set off any enemy anti-tank mines in their path. *(USMC M-151 via Real War Photos)*

6in, width 6ft 8in and height 6ft 6½in. Its top speed was 50mph and range was some 250 miles.

The M3 half-track was one of the basic US half-track personnel carriers and was also used as a command vehicle by the USMC. It could carry up to ten men in the rear compartment, plus its crew of two in the front. Weighing just under 9 tons, it had a top speed of 45mph, a radius of action of 200 miles and its dimensions were: length 20ft 2in (with winch), width 7ft 3.5in (with mine racks) and height 7ft 5in. Armament was one .30-cal. on an M25 pedestal mount as standard; however, additional machine guns could be fitted as necessary. Top speed was 40mph and its range was 175 miles. With modification, this half-track could be used as the chassis for several artillery gun motor carriages (GMC) (see below).

ARTILLERY

Field Artillery

The oldest 75mm gun in service with the USMC was the 'French Seventy-Five', the modernised version of the 75mm gun M1897, known as the 75mm M1897A4, found in regimental weapons companies and artillery battalions until replaced in the former in mid-1942 by 75mm M3 self-propelled guns. The combined gun and its carriage weighed 1.34 tons, and it required a crew of seven to man it. Its maximum effec-

tive range was 9,200yd and its rate of fire between 3 and 6rpm. The prime mover for the 'French Seventy-Five' was the 1-ton truck.

Standardised in 1930 on the M1 carriage (spiked wheels – not used after 1941) and in 1940 on the M8 carriage (pneumatic tyres), the 75mm M1A1 pack howitzer was a most important small field artillery weapon. Although its prime mover was usually a 1-ton truck, it could be broken down into six animal pack loads (for example, for carriage by mules). The total weight of the howitzer, recoil mechanism and carriage in a firing position was just under a ton (2,160lb). It had a maximum effective range of 9,160yd, a crew of six and, in addition to high-explosive ammunition, could fire HEAT (high-explosive anti-tank) and WP (white phosphorous smoke) rounds.

Used alongside the 75mm pack howitzer, until it completely replaced the smaller

The 75mm pack howitzer M1A1 was used in light artillery battalions and usually had a crew of six men. Note the fire controller, minus top and with bare feet. The howitzer could be broken down into six mule packs and was replaced by the 105mm howitzer in 1945. This crew are all wearing one-piece camouflage suits (Army issue) and fatigue hats. *(USMC 127-N-071988 via Do You Graphics, USA)*

howitzer in light artillery battalions in late 1945, was the 105mm M2A1 howitzer. Its weight (gun and carriage) in a firing position was just under 2 tons, its prime mover being either a 1-ton or a 2½-ton truck. With a maximum effective range of 12,330yd and a rate of fire of 2–4rpm, it was carried on the M2A1 two-wheel carriage, with split trail and shield, and had a crew of nine men. Additionally, there were the 105mm M7 and M7B1 self-propelled howitzers, which used the 105mm M2A1 howitzer as their main armament, mounted in the chassis of the M3/M4 medium tank; the M7 used the riveted hull and chassis of the M3 medium tank, while the M7B1 had the cast one-piece nose and chassis of the M4A3 medium tank. Late production M7s and all M7B1s had the M4-type bogies with trailing return rollers. The pulpit-like appearance of the .5-cal. machine-gun compartment on the right-

hand side of this open-topped vehicle caused it to be nicknamed the 'Priest'. Weighing just over 26.6 tons, it had a top speed of 25mph and a range of 85–125 miles. Sixty-nine rounds were carried for the 105mm, while the crew was now seven men.

In the more powerful medium and heavy artillery, there were no fewer than four 155mm guns/howitzers in USMC service – two howitzers and two guns. The first was the 155mm M1918 howitzer, standardised in 1941 and found in limited use within

The crew of this 75mm pack howitzer almost hide it from view as they cluster around during training in Iceland, giving an excellent view of all the personal '782 gear' they had to carry. In the background are two anti-aircraft-mounted .30-cal. Browning HMGs. (USMC 127-N-524206 via Do You Graphics, USA)

This 155mm howitzer belonged to 3rd Marine Division's artillery in action on Iwo Jima. It was just one of the 155mms in USMC service (two guns and two howitzers). *(USMC via Derrick Wright)*

medium artillery battalions. It weighed (howitzer and carriage in a firing position) 3.65 tons and had a crew of eleven. It was mounted on the M1918A3 carriage, with split trail, two wheels and a shield. The towing vehicle was the ubiquitous 2½-ton truck. It had a maximum effective range of 12,295yd and a rate of fire of 1–3rpm. The 155mm M1 and M1A1 howitzer was standardised in 1944 and thereafter found in both the FMF and divisional howitzer battalions. It had a combat weight of 5.67 tons and needed the D-18 dozer/tractor to move it. Like its predecessor, it had a crew of eleven and a rate of fire of 1–3rpm; however, its maximum effective range was now 16,355yd.

The 155mm M1918 M1 gun, a defense battalion weapon, originally of French design and standardised during the First World War, begins the heavy artillery. It had a combat weight of 8.97 tons, and also required a D-18 dozer/tractor as a prime mover, its carriage being the M3 split trail with two-wheel limber and no shield. The crew was eleven, the maximum effective range 20,100yd and its rate of fire 1–3rpm. Last, but by no means least, was the 155mm M1A1 gun, given the nickname of 'Long Tom'. It had a combat weight of 13.4 tons, a maximum effective range of 25,715yd and a rate of fire of 1–3 rpm. Its M1 carriage had a split trail, eight wheels (in pairs), a two-wheeled limber and no gunshield. Its crew was fifteen and the gun was basically an improved M1918 with a longer barrel (just under 4ft longer) and other improvements. Its prime mover was the D-18 dozer/tractor. When used in its sea-coast defense role, it had a pedestal mount (known as the 'Panama' mount).

A 'Long Tom' (155mm M1A1 gun) in action on Guadalcanal. *(USMC B-23322 via Real War Photos)*

Anti-tank Artillery

There were three versions of 37mm anti-tank guns used by the USMC, the oldest being the 37mm M1916 infantry anti-tank gun that saw early service on Corregidor and Guadalcanal and weighed just over 340lb on a wheeled mount, and half that weight on a tripod. It could penetrate only ⅞in of armour plate and was soon replaced by the M3A1 anti-tank gun, standardised in 1939. Its armour-piercing round would penetrate an inch of armour at 1,000yd (2.1in using the APC round), so it was perfectly adequate against most Japanese tanks. Based on the German Rheinmetall gun, but much lighter, it had a maximum effective range of 1,000yd and was used to equip both special weapons battalions and regimental weapons companies. As well as its anti-tank role it was also used against enemy strongpoints because its weight – only 912lb – meant that it could be manhandled over difficult terrain. The M6

self-propelled anti-tank gun consisted of an M3A1 anti-tank gun mounted on a pedestal mount in the rear of a standard ¾-ton 4 × 4 truck. It was standardised in 1942 for use in special weapons battalions, with a crew of four and a combat weight of 3.28 tons. It did not prove a success, mainly as a result of it being very difficult to manoeuvre in close terrain, while most firing had to be done to the rear as full depression could not be obtained to the front of the truck, for obvious reasons. It was phased out in 1943.

The 75mm M3 and M3A1 self-propelled anti-tank guns were the first American self-propelled anti-tank weapons standardised (1941) in the Second World War and were used by regimental weapons companies in the USMC. As the bottom photograph on p. 152 shows, the chassis was that of the M3 half-track, the anti-tank gun being the 75mm M1897A4, giving the weapon a gross weight of almost 9 tons, with a top speed of 45mph and a range of 200 miles. Armament

An excellent photograph of a 37mm anti-tank gun with its crew on Saipan in October 1944. Highly mobile, it weighed just over 900lb in firing order. *(USMC M-159 via Real War Photos)*

This 75mm gun was mounted on an M3 half-track to form the first self-propelled anti-tank gun in USMC service. It was standardised in 1941 and was known as the 'SPM' (self-propelled mount). This one was on Bougainville. *(USMC B-24931 via Real War Photos)*

details were: maximum effective range 9,200yd, elevation −10 degrees to +29 degrees, traverse 19 degrees to the left and 21 degrees to the right, 59 rounds carried (mainly armour-piercing and high-explosive). It had a crew of five.

Anti-aircraft Artillery

Before looking at the AAA weapons individually it is worth appreciating that, in addition to being used in their normal role of providing close-in defense against low-flying aircraft, the light AAA weapons and the heavy machine guns (already described) were also employed flexibly, that is to say, as well as forming weapons groups in defense battalions for the AAA role, they could also be used against ground targets, being landed on the beach with the assault waves. They were therefore designated as being dual-purpose weapons, and used against both air and surface targets, and so were often attached to task-orientated teams.

The Oerlikon 20mm Mk 2 and Mk 4 AA guns were Swiss-designed; although the Oerlikon actually had its origins in Germany, being designed by one Reinhold Becker in 1914. His 20mm gun was originally produced for the German air force by his own firm; he then transferred the design to Seebach Maschinenbau Aktien Gesellschaft near Zurich in 1918. The Marines' version was built in the USA and was exactly the same as those used for anti-aircraft defense on board ships. For use on land, the weapon was mounted on a pedestal with a shield or on a four-wheeled carriage. The gun was gas-operated, had an effective range of 2,000yd and was fed by a sixty-round drum magazine, giving it a rate of fire of 550rpm. Potentially it could also have been an anti-tank weapon, but was never used in this role. It was to be found in

defense and AAA battalions. They were first used on static pedestal mounts, but later were mounted in pairs on wheeled carriages and known as a high-speed 'twin twenty'. Between 1942 and 1944 they accounted for over 30 per cent of enemy aircraft shot down by AAA.

The 37mm M1 Colt/Browning AA gun was a fully automatic air-cooled weapon standardised in 1940 and found in defense battalions. Fed by a ten-shot clip (rate of fire 120rpm), the M3 mount was fixed on a four-wheel carriage without a shield, giving it a weight complete with carriage of 2.7 tons. It was designed by Browning but built by Colt. Its usual prime mover was the 2½-ton truck.

The 37mm M1 was replaced in 1942/3 by the Bofors 40mm M1 anti-aircraft gun, probably the most famous light AA gun of all time, in service all over the world (and still thus). Approval was obtained from the Swedish Bofors Company to allow manu-facture in the USA. Found in defense and

Also photographed on Bougainville is this 40mm Bofors LAA gun. Note that the ammunition is in clips of four rounds. It had a rate of fire of 120rpm. (USMC B-24940 via Real War Photos)

A 90mm M1/M1A1 anti-aircraft gun, seen here on Bougainville beachhead on D-Day. The 90mm had a rate of fire of 30rpm. The M1 was approved for production in March 1940; the later-model M1A1 gun was standardised in May 1941. *(USMC B-24936 via Real War Photos)*

When mounted on the M2A2 'spider' mount and its four-wheeled carriage (no shield), it weighed 7.5 tons. The 3in gun had an effective range of 10,000yd and a rate of fire of 25rpm, and fired both armour-piercing and high-explosive ammunition. It was replaced in 1942 by the 90mm M1 and M1A1 anti-aircraft guns that weighed just over 8.48 tons on its spider mount with its four-wheel carriage, again without a shield. Its prime mover was, as for the 3in gun, the D-9 dozer/tractor. The 90mm gun had a maximum effective range of just over 11,290yd, and a rate of fire of 30rpm. The major difference between the M1 and M1A1 guns was that the former had a hydraulic rammer and the latter a spring-operated rammer.

Coastal Artillery

Used to a limited extent by defense battalions, the sea-coast defense guns had all been removed from ships – the larger the gun, the larger the ship (e.g. 5in from old battleships, 7in from old pre-dreadnought battleships). The 3in/50-cal. Mk 21 Mod 0 sea-coast defense gun was standardised in 1939, and had a pedestal mount with a concrete and wood base and no shield. (The calibre of US naval guns is worked out by dividing the barrel length by the bore diameter, with both measurements being in inches; e.g. 5in/255in = 51-cal.) The maximum effective range of this '3inch navy gun', as it was called, was 14,000yd and its rate of fire 18rpm. Next was the 5in/51-cal. Mk 15 Mod 0 sea-coast defense gun, which

AAA battalions, the original design was kept to, but dimension, threads and clearances were all to US standards to ease manufacture. It was a recoil-operated weapon fed by a four-round clip (rate of fire 120rpm). Mounted on a four-wheel carriage (no shield) it weighed 2.48 tons; the gun on its own was just 356lb. It had a maximum effective range of 5,000yd. The prime mover for the Bofors was once again the 2½-ton truck. The M2 carriage had electric brakes and bullet-resistant tyres and could be towed at up to 50mph. The 40mm Bofors was credited with 50 per cent of the enemy aircraft destroyed by anti-aircraft weapons in 1944–5.

The 3in M3 anti-aircraft gun, found in defense battalions, was similar to the M1 but had a larger-diameter removable liner.

again had a pedestal mount with a concrete and timber base and no shield. Its maximum effective range was 17,100yd and its rate of fire 6–8 rpm. Finally there was the 7in/45-cal. Mk 2 Mod 0 sea-coast defense gun, its pedestal mount having a similar base to the other two (four were emplaced on Midway Island in 1942 then in 1943 replaced by 155mm towed guns). They had a maximum effective range of 16,500yd.

The first defense battalions were equipped with 5in/51-cal. naval guns that had been designed originally for shipboard mounting, then extensively modified for use ashore. Emplaced in static positions, they fired high-explosive, armour-piercing and chemical shells.

Rocket Launchers

A most effective barrage weapon was the rocket launcher, used to launch 4.5in rockets. The initial 4.5in T27E1 rocket launcher was to be found in experimental rocket platoons in 1943 and was only used to a limited extent, but the 4.5in Mk 7 self-propelled rocket launcher that followed in 1944 was a far more sophisticated weapon system, which could be mounted, as the

Rocket-launcher trucks in action. Seen here on Iwo Jima, vehicle-mounted racks of 4.5in rockets unleash their deadly cargo. *(USMC M-224 via Derrick Wright)*

photographs below and at the top of p. 11 show, both seaborne on landing craft, or land-borne on the ¼-ton Jeep in racks. The rockets had a maximum effective range of 1,100yd and a rate of fire (from gravity-fed racks) of 36 rounds in just 4 seconds.

UNARMOURED WHEELED VEHICLES

The USMC has always needed cross-country vehicles and although the outbreak of the Second World War found the US Armed Forces in fairly good shape as far as vehicle standardisation was concerned, the major problem was quantity: there simply were not enough vehicles to go around. Another problem concerned the diesel engine. Although it was widely recognised as being a viable alternative to the petrol engine, War Department policy dictated that the bulk of diesel fuel would go to the Navy for use in seagoing vessels. Consequently, the diesel engine was virtually ignored as a source of power for land vehicles. It is also true to say that it was typical of USMC vehicles of the Second World War era that little or no effort was made to provide weather protection/comfort for the crew; so, for example, in numerous cases, seats were simply mounted on the raised floor of the cab. As far as vehicle serial numbers were concerned, the Marine Corps used the abbreviation 'USMC', or sometimes 'US Marine Corps',

Left: A most useful means of moving ammunition supplies was this two-wheeled supply cart, pulled by 'grunt-power'. *(USMC 118105 via Do You Graphics, USA)*

Below: Having splashed down a landing ship ramp, an example of the ubiquitous Jeep (¼-ton 4 × 4 truck standard) is now being manhandled on to the beach. They were used for a wide variety of tasks, for example to transport Marines or cargo, or to tow guns or ¼-ton trailers. *(USMC B-23994 via Real War Photos)*

before the serial number, to distinguish it as belonging to the USMC (cf. 'USA'/'US Army', 'USN'/'US Navy', and 'USAF'/'US Air Force').

The ¼-ton 4 × 4 truck, popularly called the 'Jeep', was one of the most outstanding automotive developments of the war. Developed by the Quartermaster Corps, it was transferred to the Ordnance Department in August 1942, over 630,000 being built during the war and used all over the world by American forces and their allies, so the USMC had its fair share. Operated by a crew of two, it had space for equipment and additional personnel. Weighing 1.45 tons, it

Above: Marines line up at a water trailer to refill their canteens, just one of the many types of trailer that were vital to the Marines in their island-hopping campaigns. *(USMC B-24752 via Real War Photos)*

Below: This version of the 2½-ton truck was a fuel bowser, seen here on the Guadalcanal in March 1943. *(USMC B-23337 via Real War Photos)*

Unloading from a small landing craft is the equally widely used 2½-ton 6 × 6 lorry, widely known as the 'Deuce and a half' or 'Jimmy'. A vast number of these splendid trucks were used for cargo carrying, or fitted with a wide variety of other bodies for special work, e.g. tankers, operating theatres, dump trucks or mobile workshops etc. *(USMC B-24932 via Real War Photos)*

had a top speed of 65mph, a cruising range of 300 miles on 15gal of petrol, and could tow a variety of guns (e.g. a 37mm anti-tank gun) or a ¼-ton trailer. A tandem hitch made it possible to use two Jeeps for the emergency towing of a 155mm howitzer. A base plate was provided for a .30-cal. or .50-cal. machine gun (either on the dashboard or on a pedestal mount). The Jeep was produced by both Willys-Overland Motors, Inc., and the Ford Motor Co., to identical specifications. Its excellent performance both on and off road made it a winner, as did its adaptability. One interesting version was the ¼-ton amphibian truck (the Model GPA), which was designed for use on both land and water. It weighed just under an additional half-ton and was some 4ft longer than the 11ft land model. It had a land speed of 55mph and a speed in

the water of 5½mph, a crew of four, a payload of 800lb and a towing capacity of 1,000lb. However, the 'Seep' (sea-going Jeep) was never a success and production ceased after some 12,000 had been built. To the best of my knowledge, the GPA was never in service with the USMC.

The 2½-ton 6 × 6 truck, known either as the 'Jimmy' or the 'Deuce and a half', was also built in vast quantities (with a variety of bodies); over 526,000 were built by GMC alone, and some 250,000-plus by other manufacturers. It had a payload of 5,350lb and could tow up to 2,500lb. Power was supplied by a GMC six-cylinder petrol engine. The normal 'Jimmy' had an open-type cab, with a collapsible top and a folding windshield. One truck in each four had a mounting for a .50-cal. heavy machine gun for anti-aircraft protection.

RADIOS AND FIELD TELEPHONES

In general terms the radios used by the Marines tended to be low-power sets, such as the TBX and TBY. Unfortunately the former had insufficient range, while the latter failed when it got wet. The smallest radio was the SCR-536, known as the 'Handie Talkie'.

CHAPTER EIGHT

LANDING SHIPS, LANDING CRAFT AND AMTRACS

A VITAL REQUIREMENT

The safe transportation and equally safe delivery of thousands of troops across the world's oceans was a primary requirement of Allied operations in all theatres of war, but none more important than in the 'island hopping' undertaken in the Pacific theatre in which the USMC played such a major role. Here there were to be a series of amphibious landings on a scale never before contemplated, so that an entire new breed of shipping of all shapes and sizes was required in order to get the troops, their weapons, vehicles, equipment and supplies to the right place at the right time, then help them to assault the enemy-held beaches. Moreover, constant support had to be provided before, during and after the landings, whether they were unopposed or opposed by a tenacious enemy who did not know the meaning of the word 'surrender'. These vessels, which might be manned by personnel of the US Navy, the US Coast Guard, or the US Marine Corps, formed an indispensable part of the amphibious task forces. Therefore it is relevant to look briefly at the various types of shipping involved.

After the debacle of the British and Commonwealth amphibious landings on the Gallipoli peninsula in April 1915, no further large-scale attempts were made operationally, until 1937, when the Japanese began the development of such operations, in which they used cargo landing boats, fitted with bow ramps, in the Shanghai area during their invasion of China. This revolutionary idea allowed their forces to disembark more rapidly than ever before. 1/Lt Victor H. Krulak, then Assistant R-2 of 4th Marine Regiment, witnessed these operations and sent in a report, accompanied by some snapshots, in which he commented, 'these boats [i.e. the ones with bow ramps] were the only ones of the entire group [there were many different types of landing boat being used] which were obviously designed to negotiate surf and shallow beach landings' (see Clifford, *Progress and Purpose*, p. 51, note). The idea soon came to the attention of the Equipment Board and they asked various American shipbuilders to look into it. This led to a New Orleans boat builder, Andrew Higgins, showing them one of his boats that he had developed for use in the swamps and backwaters of the Mississippi river. The Higgins-designed boat, known as the Eureka, would eventually become the first Landing Craft Personnel (LCP), while the Higgins Boat Company would subsequently build over 20,000 landing craft of various types, the majority being the Landing Craft, Vehicle or Personnel (LCVP). Gen Dwight D. Eisenhower, Supreme Allied Commander, Europe, once called the LCVP the most important war-fighting tool of the Second World War, describing Andrew Higgins as the man who had won the war for the Allies.

The principal tactics involved the smaller landing craft (for example, LCPs, LCVPs and LCVs) being carried to the chosen landing area by Landing Ship Tanks (LSTs), or High Speed Attack Transports, such as converted destroyers or destroyer escorts. The larger vessels then lowered the empty, smaller, landing craft into the water, using their cranes or davits. Once safely on the water, they would there be loaded, either with fully equipped assault troops (who would have scrambled over the side of the

landing ship using cargo nets) or with stores and equipment by the landing craft crew who had ridden their vessel down from the deck, so as to ensure full control once it was in the water. The landing vessels would then be assembled line abreast in waves, which would make their way to the allotted beach and carry out their assault landing. Landing ships and landing craft would all be similarly painted, so that the stowed landing craft blended in with the mother ship as far as possible; the two main colours were 'haze grey' or 'Navy blue'.

LANDING SHIPS

Landing Ship Vehicle (LSV)

With a displacement varying between 5,625 tons and 5,875 tons, there were six LSVs built and introduced into service between 1942 and 1943, the main task of these 450+ft long, 20.3kt ships being to transport

Over a thousand of these large Landing Ships, Tank were built during the war. As their draught was only 4ft at the bow, they could be easily beached for unloading during landing operations. Here two LSTs are beached at Cape Gloucester, New Britain, on 24 December 1943. Driving out of LST 202 is a Sherman M4 medium tank; twenty such AFVs could be carried in its tank deck. (USN B-23995 via Real War Photos)

and launch amphibious troop-carrying vehicles at sea. They all had draughts of some 20ft and stern ramps from which to launch amphibians, and had been converted from surplus minelayers or netlayers. They could each carry some 800 fully equipped troops, plus forty-four DUKW (or a mixture of DUKW and LVTs).

Landing Ship Dock (LSD)

A total of twenty-five of these 4,032-ton (7,930 tons seagoing), 15kt ships were built, seven of which were transferred to the UK, leaving eighteen for US service. Each could carry a mixture of LCTs, LCMs, LVTs and DUKWs in their floodable cargo bay, or alternatively, some 1,500 tons of cargo and 240 troops. Their length was 457ft and their draught was only 15ft 10in. They had stern ramps from which to discharge the amphibians while at sea from their large, floodable bays.

Landing Ship Tank (LST)

A staggering 1,052 of these LSTs (328ft long with a displacement of 1,653 tons) were built, which had a range of some 24,000 nautical miles. Their draught was only 4ft at the bow and 10ft aft, so they could be 'beached' during landing operations. First introduced in 1942, many continued to give excellent service after the war; however, a total of thirty-nine were lost in action. Their cargo could be extremely varied, but basic loads were, for example, seventeen LVTs or twenty medium tanks. LSTs were fitted with either an elevator or ramps in order to move AFVs between decks, while over 100 were converted to specialised tasks such as barrack ships, general store issue ships, motor torpedo boat tenders and assault support surgical hospitals. Driven by GM diesels, they earned the nickname 'Green Dragon' because of their camouflage paint scheme.

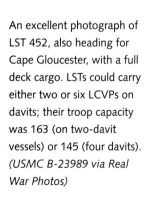

An excellent photograph of LST 452, also heading for Cape Gloucester, with a full deck cargo. LSTs could carry either two or six LCVPs on davits; their troop capacity was 163 (on two-davit vessels) or 145 (four davits). *(USMC B-23989 via Real War Photos)*

Above: A good close-up of the wheelhouse and bridge area of LST 334, showing some of its weaponry, which included 20mm Oerlikon anti-aircraft guns, and .50-cal. and .30-cal. heavy machine guns on anti-aircraft mounts. Note also the sandbags to provide some protection from strafing aircraft. *(USN N-26809 via Real War Photos)*

Below: This LST has been equipped with a catapult for launching the Piper Cub Grasshopper light aircraft, used for reconnaissance purposes. *(USN N-25736 via Real War Photos)*

Landing Ship Medium (LSM)

A total of 525 of these 203ft 6in, 1,095-ton LSMs were built, and 7 were lost in action. They could carry either 5 light or 3 medium tanks, or 6 LVTs or 9 DUKWs, plus 48 troops. Nearly 70 were converted to rocket ships that could carry banks of 4.5in rockets, used to provide fire support during amphibious landing operations.

LANDING CRAFT

Smaller than the landing ships, but equally indispensable were a complete range of other purpose-built craft that could deliver all parts of the assault force on to the beach, that is, the troops themselves, together with their heavy weapons, vehicles, equipment and ammunition – everything that they needed to fight an enemy entrenched in strong defensive positions. For example there were:

Landing Craft, Infantry (Large) (LCI(L))

Displaying 387 tons (laden), these 158ft 6in vessels had gangway ramps on each side, down which the 188 troops descended (an alternative load was 75 tons of cargo). Its draught was only 2ft 8in forward and 5ft aft. Over 1,000 were built, of which 10 per cent

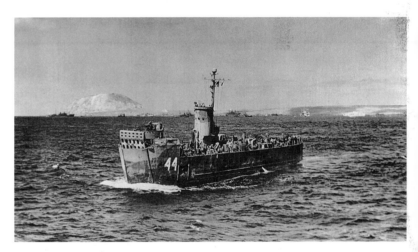

A total of 525 of these Landing Ships Medium were built, their purpose being as a landing ship equivalent of the LCI(L). They could carry six LVTs or nine DUKWs, and forty-eight troops, or up to five light or three medium tanks. This LSM is full of equipment as it approaches Iwo Jima, with the ever-present Mount Suribachi in the background. *(USN N-22082 via Real War Photos)*

Two LSMs, 18 and 51, unloading their cargo at Ormoc Bay, Philippines, on 7 December 1944. Note how different their camouflaged paintwork: LSM 18 is in Measure 31/17L and LSM 51 in Measure 31/15T. *(USN N-6581 via Real War Photos)*

The deadly cargo on this LCI(R) is rocket launchers, the twelve-port launchers being on view. It belonged to 7th Amphibious Force in the Pacific. Note also the 40mm Oerlikon in the forward gun position. *(USN N-26887 via Real War Photos)*

Hitching a ride. LCT 1415 is seen here stowed on the deck of LST 834 (and again in background). The landing craft is itself loaded with vehicles, destined for the invasion of Okinawa (Operation 'Iceberg') on 1 April 1945. *(USN N-26809A via Real War Photos)*

were lost in action. LCIs were adapted to a number of other uses, for example as fire support ships carrying banks of rockets (600 4.5in), 40mm/20mm cannon or machine guns or 3in and 6in mortars; or as smoke-laying vessels to hide the attack force from suicide pilots; or to carry parties of demolition frogmen to clear beaches.

Landing Craft Tank (LCT)

There were two main models of this 280–300-ton vessel: the Mark V, which had only a bow ramp, and the Mark VI, which had both bow and stern ramps. Both could

be carried on board an LST and then launched broadside over the side. Both could carry either four light or three medium tanks, but they were also used for a variety of other tasks, being reclassified as Landing Craft Utility (LCU) after the war.

Landing Craft Vehicle or Personnel (LCVP)

Over 23,300 of these small (35ft 10in long, 10ft 6in wide) boats were built and used to land light vehicles and/or troops. Typical loads were: twelve troops, or 8,100lb of cargo, or a Jeep or a light artillery gun. They were just one type of 'Higgins' Boat to

Right: Marines use a scrambling net to get down the side of their attack transport, the USS *George Clymer*, into an LCVP (PA27-3). A war dog is also being lowered down into the landing craft. *(USMC B-24928 via Real War Photos)*

Below: This Landing Craft Rubber (Large) could carry a party of up to ten reconnaissance/raiding Marines. It was propelled by paddle power as here, or by a 9.5hp Evinrude outboard. Note that the man in the bow has a Browning automatic rifle. *(USMC via Do You Graphics, USA)*

be built in great numbers; others were: Landing Craft Personnel (Ramp), Landing Craft Vehicle, Landing Craft Mechanised.

Landing Craft Rubber

Both large and small rubber boats, plus a rigid inflatable (RIB) were built in consider-able numbers for use by reconnaissance or raiding troops. The former could carry ten or seven troops respectively, while the RIB took fifteen.

AMTRAC

'The development of the amphibian tractor, or LVT, which began in the middle 1930s, provided the solution and was one of the most important modern technical con-tributions to ship to shore operations. With-out these landing vehicles our amphibious offensive in the Pacific would have been impossible' (MajGen Holland M. Smith, 'Amphibious Tactics', *Marine Corps Gazette*, 1946).

There were two versions of these amphibians: the Landing Vehicle Tracked (LVT) and the Landing Vehicle Tracked (Armoured) (LVT(A)). The former were unarmoured amphibious tractors, while the

Two LVT(A)4s race towards the flaming shore of Anguas Island. *(USMC via author's collection)*

latter were strictly armoured fighting vehicles, as they possessed the three main characteristics of a tank: firepower, protection and mobility. While their firepower and protection were important, their mobility was of paramount importance, in that they could get to places which normal tanks could not reach and could do so without the aid of awkward, vulnerable swimming aids such as canvas screens or plastic foam swimming devices which, as we have seen, had to be fitted to M4 Sherman medium tanks to make them amphibious. Both versions were known as amtracs, and given the nickname of 'Alligator' or 'Large Vulnerable Target'. As the second nickname

shows, those who rode in them did not consider that their protection was anywhere near as good as that of a real tank and had the legitimate grouse that they were often required to act as though they were such, despite their vulnerability. Amtracs were not of course unique to the USMC, who operated some 40 per cent of those built, the rest being used by the US Army (55 per cent) and the US Navy (5 per cent).

The LVT concept had originated in the USA after the 'Labor Day' hurricane of 1935 had hit Florida badly. It was John and Donald Roebling, Jr, son and grandson of the builder of the Brooklyn Bridge, Col Washington Roebling, who first had the idea to produce a lightweight, tracked, amphibious 'hurricane rescue vehicle' for use in the Florida Everglades – hence the appropriate nickname 'Alligator'. They completed the first prototype in 1935, but its performance in the water was disappointing. Two years later, when the vehicle had been virtually redesigned, with a better, stronger track system and a much improved performance, the USMC became interested after MajGen Louis McCarty, then commanding the FMF, saw a photograph of it in *Life* magazine. Roebling built an aluminium-hulled prototype (T 24) with the USMC firmly in mind as the potential customer. Despite lukewarm support from the US Navy, the commander of the Atlantic Fleet, Adm Ernest J. King, was persuaded to take a ride in it at Culebra, Puerto Rico, in 1939. Unfortunately the aluminium vehicle broke a track on a reef and the admiral had to wade ashore. However, the following year, Roebling, in conjunction with the Food Machinery Corporation, was contracted to build an all-steel Alligator for the USN and USMC. Ten Roebling tractors were initially ordered; however, after the type was successfully demonstrated, the order was raised to a total of 110. In July 1941, the first production model, the LVT1, was completed and an order placed for 200 of the new vehicles, now officially known as the Landing Vehicle Tracked (LVT). Later, the contract would eventually be increased to 1,225 Alligators, as they were now universally called. At this point it must be emphasised that the amtrac was a logistic, not a fighting, vehicle. However, as Kenneth W. Estes says in his *Marines under Armor*, 'The good intentions of the planners would not survive the exigencies of combat.'

A Need for an Amphibious Armoured Fighting Vehicle

While the LVT1 order was still being completed, the LVT2 was introduced in 1942, being built by the FMC Riverside, California, facility, so that it would not interfere with the LVT1 construction that was still in progress. By late summer 1941, the first USMC tractor battalions were being formed (initial plans were for just one amphibian tractor battalion of seventy-five Alligators per Marine division), to operate the first of over 18,000 Alligators to be built during the war. LVT1 and LVT2 were both made of mild steel only, so could hardly be classed as tanks; they were used for carrying cargo and troops from ship to shore and proved most useful. The quartermaster of the Marine Corps summarised the situation succinctly when he said, 'It is understood that the Amphibian "Alligator" Tractor is not intended for use as an offensive weapon but rather as an amphibious vehicle for the rapid and expeditious transfer of supplies from ship to combat units ashore during a landing attack.' However, it soon became evident that there was a requirement for another type of amphibian that was able to give close, direct fire support to landing troops – in other words an amphibious tank (an 'amphtank' or 'amtank' as they were called). The simplest way of achieving this was to construct an LVT2 using armour plate some 0.25–0.50in thick instead of mild steel, then adding decking plates over the cargo spaces and putting a fully armoured turret on top, equipped with a tank gun. The first of these, designated the LVT(A)1, had the M5A1 light tank turret, complete with 37mm M6 gun and coaxial .30in machine gun. Later, the most successful and widely used armoured variant, the LVT(A)4, would mount the turret from the HMC M8, complete with a 75mm howitzer as its main weapon. Other weapon systems tried in LVT(A) were rocket launchers and flamethrowers. Despite this weaponry, and principally because of the amtrac's light armoured protection, the Marines much preferred to land Sherman M4A2 medium tanks as soon as possible, in order to provide direct fire support for the advance inland from the beach.

Types Built

In all there were nine types of LVT/LVT(A) built. These were:

LVT1

Amphibian tractor; 540 built. The basic Alligator could hold twenty fully equipped men, complete with their personal weapons (plus a crew of three) or 4,500lb of stores. Machine-gun rails were provided on sides and at the rear. Construction was of arc-welded sheet steel. Tracks were unsprung and fitted to the hull. They worked well in the water or on soft ground, but had problems on hard ground. The driver's cab had three windows; the middle one could be opened for ventilation or use as an escape hatch. The LVT1 were first used at Guadalcanal in August 1942, when 1st and 2nd Amphibian Tractor Battalions provided logistical support.

LVT2

Amphibian tractor; 1,355 built. Nicknamed the 'Water Buffalo', the LVT2 was an improved version of the LVT1. It had a new suspension with eleven bogie wheels per track that were sprung on Torsilastic rubber springs which improved track life and made going on harder ground easier. It was constructed of sheet steel with machine-gun rails all around the vehicle. Two escape/ventilation hatches were located in the front for the crew of three or four men, which opened downwards. In the cargo hold, either 6,500lb of cargo or twenty-four fully equipped troops could be carried. The LVT2 entered production in June 1942, but was not used in action until Tarawa in

Amtrac LVT2 'Old Glory' seen here on the beach at Iwo Jima. Note the armoured surrounds to give protection to the machine-gunners. Some 482 LVTs were used in the initial assault. (*USMC M-246 via Derrick Wright*)

LVT4s on the beach at Peleliu begin to move inland. A few LVT(4)s had flame-throwers fitted at the rear of the vehicle behind a large armoured shield. *(USMC B-23417 via Real War Photos)*

November 1943. Just before the battle, all fifty of the LVT2s were modified, with ⅜in boiler plate being installed around the cab for added protection.

LVT3

Amphibian tractor; 2,962 built. This LVT was nicknamed the 'Bushmaster' or 'Beach Buster', and was developed by the Borg Warner Corporation. By the end of the war, it had become the standard cargo LVT. Engines were mounted in side sponsons, allowing a loading ramp to be fitted at the rear, which could be raised and lowered by a hand-operated winch. The ramp had rubber seals around it, while, on board, wooden plugs were carried which could be used to plug holes for on-the-spot repairs to certain parts. It also had improved hydraulic automatic transmission. The driver, co-driver and third crewman were in a cab in front of the cargo area, which could hold twenty-four troops or 12,000lb of cargo.

LVT4

Amphibian tractor; 1,765 built. This was a modified and improved LVT2 with a hand-winch-operated ramp and the engine behind the driver's cab. It could also carry light vehicles or even small field guns (up to a 105mm towed howitzer). There was a mount on each side for .30- or .50-cal. machine guns. It had a crew of three and could carry up to twenty-four fully equipped troops or 8,000lb of stores.

LVT Buffalo

This was the British version of the LVT4. It mounted a 20mm Polsten, plus two .30-cal. machine guns. The 20mm Polsten was designed in Poland, revising the basic Swiss Oerlikon. Further design and manufacture was transferred to the UK when Germany overran Poland in 1939. The Polsten weighed 54.9kg, had a rate of fire of 450rpm and a maximum effective ceiling of 6,630ft when used in the AA role.

Specifications of LVT

Type	Weight (lb)	Crew	Length	Engine	Performance
LVT1	21,800	3	21ft 6in	146hp petrol	75 miles land, 50 miles sea
LVT2	30,900	3–4	26ft 1in	250hp petrol	150 miles land, 75 miles sea
LVT3	26,000	3	24ft 6in	220hp petrol	150 miles land, 75 miles sea
LVT4	28,000	3	24ft 3in	250hp petrol	150 miles land, 75 miles sea

LVT(A)1

This had an M5A1 Stuart light tank turret fitted, the 37mm gun complete with a gyrostabiliser (it was identical to that on the tank except for the deletion of the rear turret radio bustle). There were also 'manholes' at the rear with .30-cal. machine guns installed on scarf rings (the circular ring mounting for machine gun/cannon, usually on a pintle, enabling the weapon to be traversed quickly and easily in any direction). The crew of six also had periscopes for viewing. The engine was between the crew area and the cargo compartment at the rear. There were no doors at the rear, so passengers had to go over the side to exit. The extra armour and turret added about 3 tons to the weight of the amtrac, but this did not matter as no troops or supplies were being carried. In some cases the 37mm gun would be replaced by the E7 flame-thrower.

LVT(A)2

Similar to the LVT2, but with armour plate. It could carry 18 fully equipped troops or 5,900lb of cargo; 450 were built by Roebling and Ford. In total over 3,000 LVT2 and LVT(A)2 were built during the war and proved to be a most valuable asset to the USMC, being responsible for transporting thousands of troops and tons of equipment during the Pacific campaign. The major drawback, of course, was the lack of a ramp, which meant that everything had to be loaded and unloaded over the gunwales.

LVT(A)4

First used at Saipan, this LVT(A) had the open-topped turret from the US Army M8 howitzer motor carriage (HMC), plus a .50-cal. Browning machine gun on top of the turret (as anti-aircraft armament) and a

Water-borne LVT(A)4s head for shore on Okinawa on D-Day (1 April 1945). Note the sandbags and extra side-armour to provide added protection. This first wave was part of A Company, 1st Armored Amphibious Tractor Battalion, 4th Marine Regiment. *(USMC 116103 via author's collection)*

Two LVT(A)4s belonging to 3rd Armored Amphibian Battalion, attached to 1st Marine Division on Okinawa. The LVT(A)4 was armed with a 75mm howitzer, for which 100 rounds were carried. *(USMC 007 0938 81 via author's collection)*

.30-cal. bow machine gun. Later, in 1943, some had the Canadian-built Ronson flame-throwers replacing the 75mm howitzer. The USMC also tried mounting banks of rocket launchers on the sides (either two banks of ten T45 rockets, or twenty T54 rockets).

LVT(A)5

This was as for the LVT(A)4, but with a gyrostabiliser fitted for the main gun. The USMC acquired 128 LVT(A)5s but did not use them in combat. After the war, they became the standard amphibian tank.

Specifications of LVT(A)

Type	Weight (lb)	Crew	Length	Width	Height	Engine	Performance
LVT(A)1	32,800	6	26ft 1in	10ft 10in	8ft 5in	250hp petrol	land 25mph, water 6.5mph
LVT(A)2	35,200 c/w cargo	4	26ft 1in	10ft 10in	8ft 3in	250hp petrol	land 20mph, water 7.5mph
LVT(A)4 and 5	39,460 c/w cargo	6	26ft 1in	10ft 10in	10ft 5in	250hp petrol	land 20mph, water 7.5mph

OTHER AMPHIBIOUS COMBAT VEHICLES

Two other vehicles worthy of mention are both amphibious cargo carriers and well known by their nicknames: the 'Duck' and the 'Weasel'.

The 2.5-ton DUKW-353 Amphibian Truck

The Duck was the amphibious version of the ubiquitous 2.5-ton truck that was known as the 'Deuce and a Half' or, more affectionately, as the 'Jimmy' (see Chapter 7). Its four-letter nomenclature stood for the General Motors model designation: D = year of model (1942); U = amphibian; K = all-wheel drive; W = dual rear axles. It could carry twenty-five troops or 5,000lb of cargo. Its gross weight was 12,400lb. It was petrol-driven, 18ft long and armed with a .50-cal. Browning on a ring mount.

M29C Amphibious Cargo Carrier

The Weasel weighed 6,400lb (gross weight) and could carry 1,200lb of cargo or four troops. The little 16ft vehicle was driven by a petrol engine, its rubber tracks giving it a good performance both in the water and on snow (the 'C' in its nomenclature signifies amphibious conversion). Weasels were first used by the Marines in action at Iwo Jima, to rush forward flame-thrower canisters and to evacuate some of the many wounded.

Another 'maid of all work' was the DUKW. This 2½-ton 6 × 6 amphibious truck could carry up to twenty-five troops or 5,000lb of cargo and was first used by Marines at Eniwetok. This one has been subjected to heavy enemy fire and is badly damaged. *(USMC 111123)*

ANNEXE A
MAIN TYPES OF LANDING CRAFT USED BY THE USMC

Type	Abbreviation	Date From	Length (ft)	Load Carried
Landing Craft Infantry (Large) (early class)	LCI(L)	1942	158.5	188 troops/75 tons cargo
Landing Craft Infantry (Large) (late class)	LCL(L)	1943	158.5	209 troops/75 tons cargo
Landing Craft Tank Mk V	LCT(5)	1942	114.15	4 light/3 medium tanks/150 tons cargo
Landing Craft Tank Mk VI	LCT(6)	1943	119.1	4 light/3 medium tanks/150 tons cargo
Landing Craft Mechanised Mk II Cargo	LCM(2)	1942	45	Light tank/medium artillery gun/55,000lb/55 troops
Landing Craft Mechanised Mk III	LCM(3)	1942	50	Medium tank/medium artillery gun/60,000lb cargo/60 troops
Landing Craft Mechanised Mk VI	LCM(6)	1943	56	Medium tank/medium artillery gun/70,000lb cargo/75 troops
Landing Craft Personnel ('Papa' Boat)	LCP	1938	30	24 troops
Landing Craft Personnel (Large) ('Eureka' Boat)	LCP(L)	1941	36.75	36 troops/up to 8,100lb cargo
Landing Craft Personnel (Ramp) ('Higgins' Boat)	LCP(R)	1942	36.25	36 troops/up to 8,100lb cargo
Landing Craft Vehicle ('Higgins' Boat)	LCV	1942	36.25	light artillery gun/¼-ton and 12 troops/10,000lb cargo or 36 troops
Landing Craft Vehicle or Personnel ('Papa' Boat or 'Higgins' Boat)	LCVP	1942	35.9	light artillery gun/¼-ton truck and 12 troops/36 troops/8,100lb cargo
Landing Craft Rubber (Large)	LCR(L)	1938	up to 16	10 troops
Landing Craft Rubber (Small)	LCR(S)	1938	12.45	7 troops
Rigid Inflatable Boat	RIB	1944	21.5	15 troops

(Source: Rottman, *US Marine Corps World War II Order of Battle*)

CHAPTER NINE

MARINE RAIDERS, PARATROOPERS AND THE GLIDER GROUP

THE RAIDERS

In February 1942, Gen Thomas Holcomb, Commandant of the Marine Corps, ordered the creation of a very special unit; initially known as 1st Separate Battalion, it would soon be called 1st Marine Raider Battalion. Eventually there would be four of these elite battalions and the raiders would earn worldwide fame for the considerable fighting prowess they displayed against the Japanese. However, it has to be said that from the outset there was a strong body of opinion within the Corps that considered it fundamentally wrong to organise such battalions, because, it was argued, every Marine battalion was part of an elite force already. Furthermore, all Marine battalions should be capable of tackling such tasks as those for which this new elite organisation was going to be specially trained and equipped. This was even more difficult to justify at such a critical time, when the USMC, like the rest of America's armed forces, was short of everything, such as weapons, special equipment and landing craft. Nevertheless, many of those who supported the raiders' creation were firmly convinced that guerrilla warfare was going to be the only way to achieve success in the Pacific, especially at a time when Japan was

Cliff-scaling at Camp Pendleton, California. Three Marine raiders practise the art of scaling cliffs during their training in January 1943. They had to be prepared to deal with all types of terrain. Note their weapons: the officer carries a .45 Colt pistol, the platoon sergeant a Thompson SMG (1928 pattern) and the sergeant an M1 rifle. *(USMC 35199 via Do You Graphics, USA)*

in the ascendancy and the war was going badly for the Allies. As Lt Col Jon T. Hoffman explains in his *Marine Raiders in the Pacific War*, these 'other voices' had considerable influence – in other words, 'the ear of the President'. They included, for example, Maj (later Brig Gen) Evans F. Carlson, USMC, and William J. Donovan, a US Army hero of the First World War. Both – entirely independently of one another – were pressing for the formation of a guerrilla force on the lines of the British commandos. Before the war, Carlson had already made a favourable impression on President Roosevelt, and when he was serving in China in 1937, he sent, at the latter's request, weekly letters to the President. One of Carlson's most ardent supporters was Capt (later Lt Col) James Roosevelt, USMC, the President's son, who became Carlson's executive officer in 2nd Raider Battalion, then went on to command 4th Raider Battalion. British commandos had already been in action against the coastline of Europe and British Prime Minister Winston Churchill enthusiastically supported the concept of such raiders to the President, despite the fact that some of their operations had not been entirely successful. However, commando training was clearly a focus of considerable interest in the USMC and they welcomed the opportunity to send Marines to the UK to observe and take part in such training (attended also by some members of the London detachment who guarded the embassy there).

The eventual outcome was that when their creation was approved, two very different battalions took shape. The 1st Raider Battalion was created and commanded by Lt Col (later MajGen) Merritt A. Edson, known as 'Red Mike'; 2nd Raider Battalion was created and commanded by Lt Col Evans F. Carlson. Both were, in their

own way, outstanding officers, having shown themselves in pre-war operations to be aggressive, daring small-unit commanders. Additionally, another senior officer who played a major part in the raiders' formation was MajGen Holland M. Smith, who, when commanding 1st Marine Brigade during fleet landing exercises in the Caribbean in 1940, had first-hand experience of the lack of adequate landing craft that made it impossible quickly to build up adequate combat power on a hostile shore. This made the initial assault elements vulnerable to counter-attack and even defeat, while the rest of the amphibious force were still on board their transports, powerless to help because they had no means of getting ashore. Part of 'Howlin' Mad' Smith's solution to this problem, which he tried out during the next round of manoeuvres in 1941, was to embark 1st Battalion, 5th Marine Regiment, in six 'destroyer transports' (see below), make them into an independent command reporting direct to his HQ, and attach to them the Marine division's only tank company, as well as its sole parachute company. Instead of using this force to lead the assault, he landed it two days later on a beach well to the rear of the enemy. With air support, this mobile force moved swiftly inland, surprised and destroyed the enemy reserves and took control of key lines of communication. Smith described its action as being 'a spearhead thrust around the hostile flank'. This was precisely the type of operation that he envisioned the raiders performing.

Destroyer Transports

The newly developed 'destroyer transports' (known by the designation 'APD') were destroyers modified by the removal of all torpedo tubes, one gun, two boilers and their stacks (funnels). This created a hold amidships for both cargo and troops. In total there were initially six APDs; however, before the war ended, a further 133 destroyers and destroyer escorts would be converted into destroyer transports. These ships helped to solve the inherent problems of a lack of adequate transport and of immediate fire support, although the shortage of any on-board amenities in these vessels was initially a major drawback (e.g. no ventilation, no bunks and just 4 washbasins for all the 143 raiders that one APD could carry), only rectified after a high-level investigation. As the raiders moved out into the Pacific, so did the APDs, becoming their primary means of transportation for long-range movement. The raiders' chosen assault landing craft, which they would use once they had arrived in the target area, was the ten-man rubber boat, the Landing Craft Rubber (Large) (LCR(L)).

Raider Battalions: Organisations

The raider battalions were given top priority for men and equipment within the Corps, and they had no problem in attracting volunteers, especially as they promised to be the first to take the fight to the Japanese. However, as already mentioned the two battalions were organised very differently.

1st Raider Battalion Organisation

Edson's battalion was based upon the eight-man squad, as laid down by HQ USMC, with a squad leader, two BAR men, four riflemen armed with Springfield M1903 rifles, and one sniper, again with a Springfield rifle but this time mounting a telescopic sight. (He would later give his support to the four-man 'fighting team' that was credited with enabling small-unit leaders to continue with their missions, despite a loss of communications and the unit' being under heavy fire. This four-man fire team would

become standard for all Marine infantry by the end of March 1944.) Companies contained three rifle platoons and a weapons platoon, while the weapons company provided additional light machine guns and 60mm mortars. An 81mm mortar platoon would also be added to the HQ Company by the Commandant, but would never be deployed overseas.

2nd Raider Battalion Organisation

Carlson implemented an important change to the raider organisation that had been promulgated by Washington: he created a ten-man basic squad, comprising a squad leader and three fire teams of three men each (one Thompson sub-machine gun, one BAR and one Garand M1 semi-automatic rifle). In order to keep manpower within the limits of the carrying capacity of the APD, each rifle company had just two rifle platoons and a weapons platoon.

Training

Initially, training was carried out within the two newly formed units, because the official Raider Training Centre did not come into existence until late 1942/early 1943. Like the two unit organisations, training methods were equally dissimilar, being based upon the ideas of their battalion commanders, as Col Hoffman explains:

The 2nd Raiders set up their pup tents at Jacques Farm in the hills of Camp Elliott, where they remained largely segregated from civilisation. Carlson rarely granted liberty and sometimes held musters in the middle of the night to catch anyone who slipped away for an evening on the town. He even tried to convince men to forego leave for family emergencies, though he did not altogether prohibit it. Training focused heavily on weapons practice, hand to hand fighting, demolitions and physical conditioning, to include an emphasis on long hikes. As the men

Right: Marine raiders had to be able to handle all sorts of knives. Here, two practise knifeplay with scabbarded M1917 bayonets, but note that they are wearing raider stilettos on their hips. *(USMC 35200 via Do You Graphics, USA)*

Below: More training at Camp Pendleton, in January 1943. Here, Marine raiders build up speed and stamina on their mountainside obstacle course as they charge up a slope with their weapons at the ready. *(USMC 35184 via Do You Graphics, USA)*

grew tougher and acquired field skills, the focus shifted to more night work. . . . Carlson's system of organisation and training was designed to create a force suited 'for infiltration and the attainment of objectives by unorthodox and unexpected methods'. He and Roosevelt (his executive officer and son of the President) were developing the guerrilla unit they had envisioned. . . . Training was similar [in 1st Battalion] to that in the 2nd Raiders, except for more rubber boat work due to the convenient location of Quantico on the Potomac River. The 1st also strove to reach a pace of seven miles per hour on hikes, more than twice the normal speed of infantry. They did so by alternating periods of double timing [running] with fast walking. Although Red Mike [Lt Col Edson] emphasised light infantry tactics, his men were not guerrillas. Instead they formed a highly trained battalion prepared for special operations as well as more conventional employment. Edson's style of leadership contrasted starkly with that of his counterpart. He encouraged initiative in his subordinates, but rank carried responsibility and authority for decision-making. He was a quiet man who impressed his troops with his ability on the march and on the firing ranges, not with speeches. His Raiders received regular leave and he even organised battalion dances attended by busloads of secretaries from nearby Washington. The two raider battalions bore the same name, but they could hardly have been more dissimilar. What they did have in common was excellent training and a desire to excel in battle.

In Carlson's battalion everyone was inculcated with an unconventional military philosophy that was, as Hoffman explains, 'an admixture of Chinese culture, Communist egalitarianism and New England town hall democracy. Every man would have the right to say what he thought and their battle cry would be "Gung Ho!" – Chinese for "work together". Officers would have no greater privileges than the men, and would lead by consensus rather than rank.'

Checking weapons, Guadalcanal, April 1943. After spending a long time in the jungle, these Marine raiders are checking their weapons and equipment before the next operation. Note the 'dog tags' (identity discs) around the neck of the right-hand man. *(USMC 54416 via Do You Graphics, USA)*

Initial Raider Operations

By the summer of 1942, both raider battalions were in the field, preparing for the types of missions they had been trained for – 1st Raider Battalion going ashore at Tulagi during the Guadalcanal landings, and 2nd Raider Battalion carrying out a diversionary raid on Makin Island. The initial landing on Tulagi on 7 August, spearheaded by Companies B and D, 1st Raider Battalion, was most successful; the enemy was not expecting a landing at that point because of the heavy coral outcroppings there, so it was unopposed. Japanese opposition did build up during the night and would follow a pattern that would be repeated during many similar engagements that were to follow during the Pacific war, the enemy launching a series of separate attacks against the Marine lines, occasionally making small penetrations, but in each case failing either to consolidate their gains or to exploit them. By nightfall on 8 August, Tulagi was secure.

The Makin Island operation followed on 17/18 August, 2nd Raider Battalion being brought in by two transport submarines. From the outset there were problems: the heavy swell caused great difficulties during

the launching of the raiders' rubber boats, while outboard motor failures also dictated further last-minute changes. Events did not improve when they reached the shore, where they were bombed and strafed heavily, but nevertheless continued with their mission and killed most of the Japanese on the island. The raid, however, was unsuccessful in taking any prisoners or destroying any important facilities, apart from a store of 1,000 barrels of aviation gas which they blew up. The raid was scheduled to end at 1930 hr, but relaunching the rubber boats through the heavy surf proved exceptionally difficult and only one-third of the original raider force managed to return to the submarines on schedule, minus most of their weapons and equipment. Total raider dead numbered thirty, of which fourteen were killed in action, seven drowned and nine tragically left behind, who were taken prisoner and then later beheaded. The raiding force returned to Pearl Harbor, disembarking on 25 August 1942. After a short rest it embarked for the new permanent raider base camp at Espiritu Santo, one of the islands of the Vanuatu group in the south-west Pacific.

After these mixed fortunes, the debate as to whether more raider battalions should be formed as an integral part of each Marine regiment or kept as division/corps troops, continued unabated. Adm Nimitz, for example, was opposed to their being anything but corps troops, forcibly stating, 'The Commander in Chief, US Pacific Fleet is of the opinion that Raider Battalions are specialised troops and should be reserved for appropriate tasks . . . and that extemporised organisation of Marine Forces should be made only in the case of dire necessity.' This view was supported by the Marine Corps Commandant, Gen Holcomb, who opposed the formation of added raider battalions, principally because all available

personnel were required for the three new Marine divisions then in process of forming. However, in August 1942, it was directed that provisional raider battalions would be formed in 2nd, 7th and 8th Marine Regiments. This order was soon to be countermanded as opinion swung the other way, but not before Provisional Raider Battalion, 2nd Marine Regiment, had begun to be raised on Espiritu Santo (activated 29 August 1942).

Two More Battalions Formed

Nevertheless, in the light of this controversy, the newly forming Provisional Raider Battalion, 2nd Marine Regiment, was disbanded within two days of the arrival of the authentic 2nd Raider Battalion at Espiritu Santo. Two further Marine raider battalions were created that autumn. The 3rd Raider Battalion was formed in Samoa on 20 September 1942, under the command of Lt Col Harry B. Liversedge (whose nickname was 'Harry the Horse'). He was a former enlisted Marine and a champion shot-putter who had represented the USA at both the 1920 and the 1924 Olympics. Volunteers came from many of the Marine units in Samoa, while small contingents were posted across from the two existing raider battalions. A month later, on 23 October 1942, 4th Raider Battalion was activated in southern California under the command of Major James Roosevelt. Both of the new battalions arrived in Espiritu Santo in February 1943. A month later, on 15 March 1943, 1st Raider Regiment was formed, also on Espiritu Santo and put in command of all four raider battalions, with Col Liversedge (now a full colonel) as regimental commander. A week later, Lt Col Alan Shapley took over command of 2nd Raider Battalion from Carlson. Hoffman describes him as being a straightforward line officer who had no interest in 'gung-ho' and swiftly turned the unit into a more orthodox battalion.

Lt Col Michael S. Currin, another officer with orthodox views, would take over 4th Raider Battalion from Roosevelt. Regimental headquarters now enforced a common organisation among all four battalions, based upon a mixture of Edson's and Carlson's ideas. Each battalion had a weapons company and four rifle companies (each with one weapons platoon and three rifle platoons). The regiment's employment was now, however, to be based more on Edson's concept than Carlson's, namely to create a highly trained, lightly equipped force that used conventional methods to accomplish special missions, but that still could, when necessary, replace a line battalion. No longer were guerrilla tactics required for success.

This change of emphasis fortunately suited the changing thrust of the war in the Pacific. Future Marine divisions would primarily be involved in assaulting Japanese forces 'holed up' in tight perimeters or on small isolated islands. This change reflected the remarkable development of the amtrac and other sophisticated weapons, and of the landing craft, doing away with the need for light assault units that would have suffered because they lacked the firepower and numbers of a normal line unit.

Raider Battalion Structure as at 24 September 1942 (total strength 901 all ranks)
Headquarters company: 139 all ranks
  Battalion headquarters: 91 all ranks, with two LMG and four Boys anti-tank rifles
  Communications platoon: 23 all ranks
  Quartermaster and motor transport platoon: 36 all ranks
Four rifle companies: each 135 all ranks
  Company headquarters: 18 all ranks
  Weapons platoon: 30 all ranks, with two .30 LMG, two Boys anti-tank rifles and two 60mm mortars

Three rifle platoons: each 29 all ranks
Weapons company: 211 all ranks
  Company headquarters: 33 all ranks
  Demolition platoon: 76 all ranks, with two anti-tank rifles
  60mm mortar platoon: 36 all ranks, with three 60mm mortars
  Two machine-gun platoons: each 33 all ranks, with four .30 light machine guns

Raider Regiments and Training Establishments
Following the activation of 1st Raider Regiment at Espiritu Santo in August 1943, 2nd Raider Regiment (Provisional) was activated on 12 September 1943, in New Caledonia, to control 2nd and 3rd Raider Battalions of 1st Raider Regiment for I MAC's forthcoming Bougainville operation. It would be disbanded on 26 January 1944 at Guadalcanal.

As already mentioned, the Raider Training Centre did not get started until late 1942, when the Commandant authorised a slight increase to the establishment of the newly formed 4th Raider Battalion: two officers and twenty-six enlisted men, who became the cadre for the centre at Camp Pendleton, California. The Raiders Replacement Training Company formally came into being at Camp Pendleton on 5 February 1943; six months later it was redesignated Raider Training Battalion. Its purpose was to train new men up to the standards expected of all raider personnel, so that there would be a pool of qualified replacements immediately available for the battalions overseas. Courses lasted for eight weeks and initially contained much of the type of training aimed at producing the Carlson/Roosevelt 'guerrilla'. For example, there were classes in 'individual cookery', which was a 'fetish' of Carlson's, who considered that regular infantry relied far too much on vulnerable, bulky field kitchens. There were also rubber boat operations, a week-long tactical exercise in which the students were divided into a main body and two guerrilla bands, which acted as aggressors. The course also spent a lot of time on individual skills and small-unit tactics, such as marksmanship, scouting, patrolling, physical conditioning and individual combat, including hand-to-hand knife fighting. Deactivated in January 1944, the Raider Training Battalion personnel were reassigned to 5th Marine Division.

Raiders' Specialised Clothing and Equipment

The raiders were the first Marine Corps personnel to adopt camouflaged clothing as their main uniform. Initially, however, it was a question of self-help, with individuals using black dye, together with brown and green paint, to camouflage their existing green uniforms and webbing personally. They also made their own helmet covers out of hessian and camouflage netting. The first official-issue jungle uniform was the one-piece M1942 suit, which opened down the front and fastened by means of a full-length zipper, plus a single press-stud at the collar. It had two large breast pockets and two

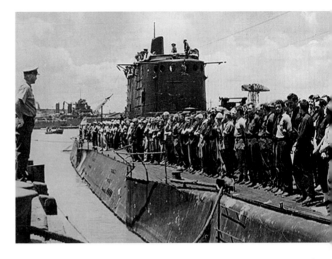

Above: Returning to Pearl Harbor, 26 August 1942. Men of 2nd Raider Battalion line the deck of one of their transport submarines as they return after a raid. Note that some wear borrowed naval uniforms and others are still dressed in their black-dyed khaki, which was a feature of raider operational dress at the time, prior to the issue of camouflage-pattern uniforms. *(USMC 200151410475 via Do You Graphics, USA)*

Below: Another group of raiders; these are members of a scout/sniper platoon. Note the mixture of dress, especially the black two-piece uniforms (dyed by the individuals concerned) ostensibly for night work. *(USMC 83767 via Do You Graphics, USA)*

181

A tough-looking group of raiders pose during a lull in the battle, next to one of the Japanese dugouts that they cleared on Cape Torokina, Bougainville on 1 November 1943. They are all wearing P1942 camouflaged uniforms (one with a camouflaged helmet cover). Note also the weapons carried: the two in front have Springfield M1903 rifles, while the rest Garand rifles or carbines. Some also carry grenade-launchers, while the cardboard tubes on the back of the leading Marine are probably for the carriage of rifle grenades. *(USMC 2147 via Do You Graphics, USA)*

even-larger hip pockets, all four being held closed by two press-studs each. Internally, the uniform had built-in braces which were intended to help take up some of the weight of the normally well-filled hip pockets. However, these braces were often removed by the wearer as they were uncomfortable and cut into the tops of the shoulders. Made of herringbone twill, the uniform was in four colours and designed to be reversible, one side being browns and greens, the other browns only (light and dark); the wearer could then choose the side that suited his background best (e.g. jungle or beach). The major problem with the M1942 jungle uniform was that of defecating. In order to do so, the wearer had to undress almost completely, dropping all his webbing in the process and, inevitably on occasions, soiling his own clothes when 'taken short'. I understand that many cut an 'escape hatch' in the rear to try to get over this problem, which will be entirely understood by any British tank crewman who has had to wear 'one piece denims'.

Far preferable was the two-piece utility HBT camouflage P1942 uniform, which was initially only issued to raider units and snipers. However, by late 1943, it was generally available to all Marines. Reversible and camouflaged on both sides, the jacket had just one top pocket (left breast) and one patch pocket (right side). The USMC insignia was stencilled on the breast pocket. There were two patch pockets on the trousers (both sides), while the fly had four press-studs (a weakness that did not stand up to field conditions). Lack of pockets was a disadvantage, however, as Jim Moran explains in his excellent book on *USMC Uniforms and Equipment*: 'A common Raider trait was to cut through the green sides of both the jacket and trousers to gain access to the pockets on the brown sides.' There was a modified version of this suit issued in 1944, in which some of the problems (such as the shortage of pockets) were addressed. However, the persistent problems with the camouflaged uniforms was that they were hot to wear and liable to fade. Another major drawback was that, although the mottled pattern certainly blended with the foliage, the lighter colours were particularly noticeable when the wearer was on the move. Other available camouflaged items were helmet covers (made of the same material as the camouflaged uniforms), ponchos and shelters (each Marine carried a 'shelter half'). The helmet covers were also reversible and there were special ones for snipers with built-in face veils.

With the following notable exceptions, the rest of the raider uniform and personal equipment was standard Marine Corps 782 gear:

raiders' boots – there were cases of special boots being made and worn by certain raider battalions. These were high leg boots made of brown leather that were more robust than the normal-issue 'boondockers'.

knives – specially designed 'gung-ho' sheath knives were adopted by Carlson's 2nd Raider Battalion, while others favoured a stiletto, modelled on the British commando-type fighting knife.

Above: Marine raiders with their war dogs, used, for example, for scouting or for message carrying. They are on their way up to the front lines on Bougainville in November/December 1943. *(USMC 237-T via Do You Graphics, USA)*

Right: On parade in Guadalcanal, 12 February 1944. Officers and men of the Marine raider battalions march past their commanding general, MajGen Roy S. Geiger, after being designated to disband and reactivate as 4th Marine Regiment. The 1st, 4th and 3rd Battalions became 1st, 2nd and 3rd Battalions, 4th Marine Regiment, while 2nd Raider Battalion became the regimental weapons company. *(USMC 72979 via Do You Graphics, USA)*

Disbandment

The change of emphasis to a more conventional approach was brought about by both the 'institutional opposition to elite forces' that I have already touched upon and the realisation that, although there were now some half-million Marines, there would never be enough manpower available to create all the 'special units' that some wanted, if the primary aim of having six fully equipped and manned Marine divisions was ever to be achieved. For these reasons the 'writing was on the wall' as far as the disbandment of the raiders was concerned. This step had already begun by mid-December 1943 and was promulgated on 8 January 1944, thus giving HQMC the extra manpower it so desperately needed. However, the raiders did not just completely disappear. On 1 February 1944, 1st Raider Regiment was redesignated 4th Marine Regiment, 1st, 3rd and 4th Battalions becoming 1st, 3rd and 2nd Battalions respectively of 4th Marine Regiment, while 2nd Raider Battalion became the regimental weapons company. Almost 6,000 Marines and naval medics had served in the raiders before they were disbanded. As Col Hoffman says at the close of his short history of the raiders, 'The commanders in the Pacific Theatre may not have properly used the Raiders, but the few thousand men of these elite units bequeathed a legacy for courage and competence not surpassed by any other Marine battalion.'

THE PARATROOPS

Breaking the Deadlock of Trench Warfare

Although the parachute had been invented in the eighteenth century, it was not used by service pilots until towards the end of the First World War and its potential for landing airborne troops was not realised until the inter-war period, even though Col Billy Mitchell, who commanded the US Army Air Corps in France in 1918, had suggested using aircraft to break the deadlock of trench warfare. He had proposed that aircraft carry an attacking force over the trenches to be dropped by parachute behind the enemy lines. The idea was shelved, then forgotten. Throughout the 1920s parachutes did become more commonplace as aircraft became more widely used, but parachuting as a hobby was confined to a small body of enthusiasts – everywhere that is apart from the USSR, where parachute towers were erected in many large cities and anyone who showed any interest was encouraged to learn how to jump. America was no different from the rest of the world, parachuting being confined to a small number of amateurs. However, these included a few Marines. Then, on 24 September 1927, five Marine and four Navy 'jumpers' took part in a test drop at the Naval Air Station, Anacostia, Washington, DC – the very first military troop parachute jump in the world. It would be another ten years before a second USMC military parachute jump took place, during the fleet landings exercises of 1937, when another small group of enthusiasts took part, dropping on to an island off California. However, the size of the Marine Corps precluded a major involvement and it would be a few more years before the emergence of 'Jumping Leathernecks'.

The Second World War

Despite the fact that by the mid-1930s the Red Army was able to attempt drops of thousands of specialised paratroops, who were not only highly trained soldiers but also skilled saboteurs, it was Germany that was first to put such troops to good use at the start of the Second World War, when they used both paratroops and glider-borne forces in their assaults on Denmark,

Norway, the Netherlands and Belgium in 1940. The successes of these troops had a considerable effect upon the Allies and both the USA and UK began training their own specialised airborne forces. In America, this included the Marine Corps. The defining moment came when large numbers of German paratroopers of Gen Student's II *Fliegerkorps*, which contained the 7th Airborne (*Fallschirmjaeger*) Division supported by 5th Mountain (*Gebirgs*) Division, made a daring assault on the British-held Mediterranean island of Crete in May 1941. After two weeks of heavy fighting, the parachute and glider-borne troops successfully captured the island – but not without suffering heavy losses, especially severe among Hitler's elite paratroopers. While their undoubted success caused the Allies to decide to invest heavily in airborne forces, the considerable casualties they had sustained (nearly 50 per cent of the 13,000 paratroopers were killed or wounded and 350 aircraft were destroyed) convinced Hitler that the opposite conclusion was the correct one. He therefore decided that airborne assaults were too risky and in consequence never launched another major airborne operation again.

Plans are Launched

As far as the USMC was concerned, the opposite conclusion had already been reached, in that just a few days after the initial German successes of 1940, the acting director of the Division of Plans and Policies at HQ Marine Corps issued a memorandum to his staff, the opening sentence of which read, 'The Major General Commandant [Thomas Holcomb] has ordered that we prepare plans for the employment of parachute troops.'

Volunteers were called for and it was not long (October 1940) before the first small group of would-be paratroopers reported for training, graduating some five months later in February 1941. The first-ever primary training centre was located at Naval Air Technical Training Centre, Lakehurst, New Jersey. Lakehurst was chosen because it was the USN's Parachute Materiel School (where sailors and Marines were trained to pack parachutes for pilots) and just 20 miles from Highstown, New Jersey, where there were two 150ft parachute towers belonging to the Safe Parachute Jump Company. The company had earlier built a popular parachute tower at the New York City World's Fair in 1939 as an amusement ride. After a lean period, Lakehurst eventually had the necessary facilities built, so as to be able to train 100 men at a time on a five-week course (often stretched to six weeks or more as a result of weather delays). Total number of fully qualified parachutists trained was intended to be 700 per year.

The art of parachute packing had to be carefully taught, because mistakes would be fatal. Each paramarine had to pack his own parachute under the supervision of a certified rigger. This packing session was at San Diego, in 1942. *(USMC 402908 via Do You Graphics, USA)*

Above: Three paramarines help two of their fellow paratroopers with their parachutes prior to a practice jump at Camp Gillespie on 12 May 1943. *(USMC 41030 via Do You Graphics, USA)*

Below: Learning to become parachute riggers. These WRs are being taught the basics of adjusting parachute harness at the New River, North Carolina, training school on 17 May 1943. *(USMC 5432 via Do You Graphics, USA)*

Unfortunately, even this output could not be maintained, and by mid-1941, they were two months behind schedule. In July 1941, it was proposed that an additional parachute training facility should be established at the Marine base in New River, North Carolina, but this did not happen immediately. Instead, HQMC had sensibly decided to move the primary parachute school to San Diego, where the weather was better (hence reducing the delays), and the Marine aviation units were nearby. This move took place between April and May 1942, to the existing Camp Elliott; however, purpose-built barracks were quickly erected at nearby Santee, with jump towers, mock-up planes and airfields – in other words, everything that was needed to train paratroopers. All parachute training was moved there at the end of August 1942, the new camp being called Camp Gillespie.

During 1942, they also set up another training facility at Hadnot Point, New River, and in June, 1st Parachute Battalion transferred an officer and thirteen NCOs there to form a cadre of instructors. The new school opened on 10 August and, although its first class of fifty-four students was delayed by shortages of parachutes and the need to erect jump towers etc., they eventually passed out on 13 October. Thereafter, classes were of seventy-five, with a new class starting every week from the end of 1942 onwards. When working to full capacity, the Marine parachute programme could produce 135 new paratroopers every week, although actual numbers trained were never that high. Finally, there was one other source of trained paratroopers: during 1st Parachute Battalion's initial rest and recuperation period ('R&R') following fighting on Gavutu and Guadalcanal, they had difficulty in obtaining qualified reinforcements, prompting the CO, Lt Col Robert H. Williams, to set up his own 'informal' training establishment. Despite lacking towers and most other facilities, it still managed to produce 100 trained 'jumpers' out of volunteers from other units serving in New Caledonia.

In May 1940, when the Plans and Policy Division of HQMC had made its initial request for a parachute programme, the planners had suggested a notional organ-

isation of a single infantry battalion, with support from a platoon of pack howitzers, plus some anti-tank and anti-aircraft weapons. By late October 1940, it had been decided that every infantry regiment would train one of its battalions as 'air infantry', with one company of each of these battalions able to conduct parachute operations. It was further estimated that some 750 paratroopers would be needed to man these battalions, but that these men would have to be prepared to be normal infantry as well, principally because of chronic shortages in line units. However, this first level of commitment did not last for long as the enthusiasm for parachute operations increased and the Corps soon began talking about 'multiple battalions specialising in parachute operations'.

The first organisational table for a parachute battalion was issued in March 1941, authorising a battalion of three line companies and an HQ unit. Each line company had a weapons platoon (three 60mm mortars and three LMGs) and three rifle platoons, each consisting of three ten-

More training in parachute rigging for these WRs at New River in May 1943. *(USMC 5434 via Do You Graphics, USA)*

man squads (armed with six rifles, two BARs and two Thompson SMGs), as compared with the then normal infantry squad of nine men (eight rifles and one BAR). However, the normal infantry battalion was considerably larger than the parachute battalion (34 and 832, as opposed to 24 and 508), the main difference being the former's heavy weapons company. The paratroopers lacked the larger supporting weapons, but made up for them, in theory, by having a larger proportion of individual automatic weapons.

Once the USA entered the war, there were further changes to the organisational tables, a 1942 amendment, for example, doing away with the weapons platoons, distributing one 60mm mortar to each rifle platoon and scrapping the three LMGs. This was not such a drastic change as may have appeared at first, because each rifle squad was authorised to have three Johnson LMGs, while the remaining riflemen would be armed with Reising SMGs. This supposedly gave the squad tremendous firepower. Unfortunately, however, as we saw in Chapter 7, the Johnson took far too long to reach battalions in any quantity, while the Reising SMGs proved unreliable. The following year, the major change was to create a regimental structure, complete with an HQ and service company and a weapons company. The latter had some 7 officers and 172 men and boosted the firepower of the lightly armed battalions. The weapons company was large: 4 81mm mortars, 12 .30-cal. Browning LMGs, 12 .30-cal. Browning heavy MGs (water-cooled), 2 .50-cal. Browning heavy MGs, 2 bazookas and 8 rifle grenade launchers. The battalion was now 23 officers and 568 (replacing 24 and 508). The additional manpower was all in the HQ company, 33 of whom formed a demolitions platoon. I MAC also allowed battalions to re-establish their weapons companies, composed exactly like those that had been done away with in 1942, thus increasing the strength of battalions by a further 3 and 87. The new rifle squad (11 men) was supposed to have the considerable firepower of three Johnson LMGs, three Johnson rifles and five Reising SMGs; however, by then the parachute regiment had adopted the fire team concept of a squad leader and three three-man teams.

1st Marine Parachute Regiment, 1943
Headquarters and service company
Weapons company
Four parachute battalions: each 583 all ranks
  HQ company: 106 all ranks
  Company headquarters: 15 all ranks
  Battalion headquarters: 57 all ranks
  Demolition platoon: 34 all ranks
  Three parachute companies: each 159 all ranks
  Company headquarters: 42 all ranks
  Three parachute platoons: 39 all ranks, with one 2.36in rocket launcher and one 60mm mortar

Clothing and Equipment
During their short existence, the Marine paratroopers were issued with a number of items of clothing and equipment that were unique within the USMC. For example, there were at least three different patterns of jump smock, worn during training but never on operations because, of course, there were no combat jumps, although they did fight with distinction as infantry during the campaign in the Solomons.

Marine paratroopers were each equipped with two parachutes: the main chute on their backs and the reserve chute on their chests. When jumping from transport aircraft, the main chute was opened by means of a static line that was attached to a cable running along the length of the cargo compartment. Once the jumpmaster gave the signal, the paratrooper crouched in the doorway and made his exit dive, pulling his knees up to his chest, with his arms wrapped around the chest chute. If he did not feel the shock of his main canopy opening almost immediately on leaving the

aircraft, he had to pull the ripcord and deploy the reserve chute. Descent speed depended upon weight, hence the desire to carry as little as possible (e.g. light weapons only); the ideal speed was 16ft/sec, but even then the jumper had to fall and roll when he hit the ground, so as to spread the shock beyond his leg joints.

The Marine paratroopers had decided, like the raiders, to opt for camouflaged uniforms, so the utilities and the jump smocks that were worn on top of them were all made of camouflaged material. As with the raiders, there were a number of different patterns, which gradually improved; for example, trying to produce a completely reversible jump smock proved to be an insuperable tailoring problem. One of the most useful specialised items of equipment was the basic 'kit first aid paratrooper' that

Below, left: Front view of a paramarine, also taken at New River, NC, in October 1943. He is wearing a camouflage parachute smock on top of a very smart collar and tie, so this was clearly a training session. On his chest is a USN MAB radio in a carrying bag (thought to have been made by the USMC Depot QM Dept). The radio was designed to furnish a very compact single-frequency radio link between paratroop forces. *(USMC 5885 via Do You Graphics, USA)*

Right: Side view of a paramarine. *(USMC 5880 via Do You Graphics, USA)*

was standard issue to all paratrooper corpsmen (that is, medics). To supplement the basic Marine Corps 782 gear, there were a few items of equipment unique to the paratroopers:

drop bags – both khaki and camouflaged, to carry weapons and ammunition, usually strapped to hang under reserve chutes.

jump boots – in dark russet leather, taller than normal boondockers and probably more robust.

drop knives – mainly for use to cut oneself free of entangled rigging lines on landing and thus carried in a special external pocket on the jump smock, where it was readily available.

camouflaged leg bag – designed to hold the Reising 55 sub-machine gun.

leather jump helmet – obtained from USN sources, where it was worn by their dive-bomber rear-gunners; ideal to be worn underneath the M1 steel helmet.

Tactical Units

The first tactical unit to be formed was 1st Platoon, 2nd Parachute Company, on 10 March 1941 at San Diego, and on 1 May it was redesignated A Company, 2nd Parachute Battalion. Four weeks later, on 28 May 1941, A Company, 1st Parachute Battalion was raised at Quantico; despite being attached to 1st Provisional Marine Brigade that was at the time en route for Iceland, it remained at Quantico and was redesignated B Company, 1st Battalion on 20 September 1941. The original plan was for battalions to be organic within divisions, like reconnaissance troops and raiders, but this was never fully developed, although parachute battalions were assigned to 1st, 2nd and 3rd Marine Divisions. Although initially all parachute battalions had their rifle companies lettered A, B and C, when 1st Parachute Regiment was formed in 1943, they were relettered in sequence throughout the battalions, hence: 1st – A, B and C;

2nd – E, F and G; 3rd – I, K and L; 4th – N, O and P (the missing letters D, H, M and Q were kept in the event that the weapons companies would be authorised).

The Formation of I Marine Amphibious Corps Parachute Group

In March 1943, I Marine Amphibious Corps (I MAC) Parachute Group was formed at Noumea, New Caledonia, comprising the three existing battalions (4th Battalion, although it was part of the regiment, never actually joined it overseas, nor ever fully completed its training). When activated the following month, at Camp Kiser, Tontouta, New Caledonia, this group became 1st Marine Parachute Regiment, but remained attached to I MAC. During the defense of Cape Torokina, Bougainville, the regiment also formed the Provisional Parachute Battalion, from elements of their regimental headquarters and I Company, 3rd Battalion.

Although parachute operations were planned for July and October 1943, the parachute battalions never actually made any combat jumps, primarily because of the lack of suitable aircraft. At the time only six squadrons of transport aircraft were available to the Marines for parachute operations and this was only sufficient to drop a single battalion. Additionally, tactical opportunities and the vast distances involved were adverse contributing factors, which affected Army paratroopers equally badly. Gordon Rottman also quotes examples of small numbers of Marine parachutists who served with the OSS (Office of Strategic Services) in north-west Europe, and were inserted by parachute for missions in France and north China.

Formal Doctrine

It was the then Commandant of Marines, Gen Thomas Holcomb, who in May 1940 had written to the Chief of US Naval Operations, requesting help from naval attachés to gather information on foreign parachute programmes. Their efforts in London and Berlin produced some valuable leads and subsequently the staff at HQ USMC looked closely into the sort of missions that a Marine parachute unit might perform. These were: raids, reconnaissance, the seizing of airfields, aerial envelopment of enemy rear areas, and the occupation of key terrain in advance of the main force. The last two of these missions were specifically linked by some observers to the conduct of amphibious operations. However, the Marine Corps did not develop a formal airborne doctrine until late in 1942, when a manual was published entitled *Parachute and Air Troops*. It contained the belief that airborne forces could 'constitute a paralysing application of power in the initial phase of a landing attack'. It also claimed that paratroops could seize crucial points, such as airfields or bridges, and also operate behind enemy lines in small groups to gather intelligence and carry out sabotage. The doctrine acknowledged that such actions could be limited to small objectives and that these could be held for only short periods, so establishing the vital necessity to link up swiftly with the seaborne or overland forces following up. The manual envisaged the formation of an air brigade composed of one regiment of paratroops and one of air infantry (presumably glider-borne), while basic tactics were worked out in conjunction with Marine transport pilots who would carry the troops. Approach flights would be at low altitudes (as low as 50ft), with a last-minute ascent to several hundred feet, at which the paratroopers jumped from the aircraft. All commanders would have been briefed thoroughly beforehand (using maps, aerial photos, terrain models and so on) so that

they knew exactly what to do as soon as they hit the ground. They would carry folding weapons (e.g. the Johnson or Reising) plus basic personal equipment (including ammunition), while heavier weapons and supplies would be dropped using cargo parachutes.

A Change of Heart

Unfortunately there was a lack of both training facilities and suitable aircraft to complete paratroop training for the embryo airborne force and so the Commandant directed that they should look at using paratroops for secondary missions, such as rubber boat operations, reconnaissance, demolitions and other such special missions that required only small forces that did not necessarily need airborne insertion – in other words, just the sort of missions undertaken by Marine raiders. As Col Jon T. Hoffmann says in his *Silk Chutes and Hard Fighting*, 'In many respects the Marine Corps had moulded the parachutists and raiders into carbon copies of each other, with the parachutists' unique ability to enter battle being the only significant difference between the two special units.' Maj Merle T. Cole, in his article 'The Paramarines', quotes four reasons given by a Corps historian as to why the Marines never jumped into combat:

1. The lack of lift capacity. No more than six transport squadrons could be concentrated by Marine Corps aviation for a single operation, thus limiting air transport to one reinforced battalion.
2. Lack of shore-based staging areas for mass flights.
3. The long distances between objectives.
4. USMC objectives were generally small in area and thus densely defended, making them unsuitable for mass parachute landings.

First into Action

Despite not being used as paratroops, the highly trained and motivated paratroops would see a considerable amount of action, the first being 1st Parachute Battalion under Maj Robert Williams, who left the USA in June 1942, then, after training in Fiji, participated in the assault landings on the Solomon Islands as part of 1st Marine Division, fighting alongside the raiders in the first American offensive of the war. It proved to be a prolonged and bloody operation. Similar operations would follow during 1943–4, involving 1st, 2nd and 3rd Battalions and 1st Parachute Regiment.

Reductions and Deactivation

Inevitably, for the reasons explained, the requirement for trained paratroopers waned and by the spring of 1943, training quotas were first reduced, then the inevitable orders were given to deactivate all parachute units. The 1st Marine Parachute Regiment was first concentrated at San Diego and then deactivated at the end of February 1944. Most of the 3,000 parachutists, both officers and enlisted men, were reassigned to the newly raised 5th Marine Division at Camp Pendleton. As Col Hoffman says at the close of his history of the USMC parachute units in the Second World War, 'The marine parachute units of World War II never jumped into combat, but they did make an indelible impression on the history of the Corps.'

THE END OF THE 'ELITE OF THE ELITE'

Thus both these elite forces, the raiders and the paratroopers, were disbanded well before the war ended. Both left a lasting impression upon the Corps, but at the same time their disbandment undoubtedly proved, if such an obvious truth needed proving, that they were unnecessary luxuries within an already elite force. All that was ever really required was 'a few Marines'.

THE GLIDER GROUP

Before closing on airborne operations, mention must also be made of a force that might have had the potential to rival the German *Gebirgs* (mountain) troops, which were used as glider-borne support of their paratroopers in the successful capture of Crete in May/June 1941, as already indicated. The Marine Corps had been approached in 1930 by a firm who had offered to develop a radio-controlled glider filled with explosives as a type of guided bomb. However, no serious studies into the use of gliders took place until after the German capture of Crete. The Corps's renewed interest in gliders was closely associated with its parachutist programme, Gen Holcomb having indicated that one battalion of each Marine regiment would be designated as 'air troops', with, as already explained, one company of paratroopers, the remainder being air-landed. It was the way in which this 'air-landing' would be achieved that fostered Marine interest in gliders, principally because they were more economical than powered aircraft and would also allow landings to take place on terrain where normal aircraft could not land or take off. Accordingly, a call was made inviting volunteers (preferably second lieutenants) to apply for glider pilot training, to be followed later by NCOs as co-pilots. At the same time the Bureau of Aeronautics (BuAer) was looking into glider development, but, as Charles L. Updegraph comments in his survey of USMC special units of the Second World War, they were 'somewhat less than enamoured with the whole idea'. The USN had experimented with gliders at Pensacola Naval Air Station in 1933, as a way of using them in primary flight training, but had come to the conclusion that they were of little use, provided adequate numbers of powered aircraft were available.

Nevertheless, the Marine Corps went ahead with their planning, the initial requirement being for seventy-five twelve-man gliders, each with a pilot and co-pilot, to transport one 'air infantry battalion'. At the time, the largest glider built in the USA was only large enough to hold four people, including crew, and there was little expertise in either glider construction or pilot training. To assist the BuAer in its studies, the Marine Corps set out its 'desirable features' for a transport glider:

- a capability to take off from land or water
- a capability to transport equipment, including light cars, 37mm anti-tank guns and if possible light tanks
- a capability to include a static line for parachute jumping
- machine-gun mounts for airborne defense
- a transport capacity of at least twelve men (based upon 250lb per man)

(Source: Charles L. Updegraph, Jr, *Special Marine Corps Units of WWII*)

Actual training of four Marine Corps officers, led by Lt Col Vernon M. Guymon, began in November 1941 at the Motorless Flight Institute, while a further eight volunteers went to the Lewis School for glider pilot training, all graduating by mid-December. Events continued apace, and by mid-March 1942, one- and two-man gliders had been delivered and were in use. More importantly, the delivery of the first twelve-man glider was expected shortly, and the size of the glider organisation had been increased. On 16 March, the Commandant

requested the approval of the Chief of Naval Operations to form Glider Group 71, to be initially composed of HQ and Service Squadron 71 and Marine Glider Squadron 71 (VML-711). Approval was granted and, with effect from 24 April 1942, the group came into being with an establishment of 20 officers and 218 enlisted men (9/64 in the HQ and Service Squadron, 11/154 in VML-711), transferring to the Marine Corps Air Station at Parris Island and being assigned to the FMF.

Training continued during the spring and early summer using both powered aircraft (such as the Grumman J2F-3 'Duck' amphibian) and two-man gliders. However, the CO (Lt Col Guymon) considered most of the training to be a waste of time as the would-be glider pilots were all already trained naval aviators. Transitional training on to gliders was what was really needed, but this could only be accomplished when the twelve-man gliders were available. During the summer of 1942, reconnaissances were made to find suitable sites for the development of glider bases, the first to be chosen being at Eagle Mountain Lake, Texas. Unfortunately, even when Glider Group 71 arrived there, in November 1942, none of the twelve-man gliders had been delivered.

It was soon clear that the glider programme was now being given a lower priority. By February 1943, it was ordered that no further steps should be taken, until more pressing matters facing the Marine Corps in the Pacific had been dealt with. It was by now also clear that gliders were unsuitable for war in the Pacific, being impractical to use except in the most favourable conditions. After securing the approval of the Secretary of the Navy, the Commandant therefore ordered the termination of the Marine glider programme with effect from 24 June 1943.

Chapter Ten

MARINE AVIATION

A Great War Beginning

Marine Corps aviation began during the First World War with the organisation, in spring 1918, of 1st Marine Aviation Force, based at Miami, Florida. Then, on 30 July 1918, this fledgling force sent three squadrons to France, with a fourth following three months later. They became the Day Wing of the Allied Northern Bombing Group, flying numerous successful operations against German submarines and their bases. By the end of the war, the force numbered 2,500 all ranks and some 240 aircraft.

Between the wars, there were considerable changes, such as the beginnings of flying off ships, which they embraced wholeheartedly, two Marine squadrons becoming part of the fleet air organisation and seeing service on board two aircraft carriers.

Director of Marine Corps Aviation

In June 1935, responsibility for aviation within the Marine Corps was taken from the Division of Operations and Training at HQMC and established as a separate and independent section under the Major General

MajGen Roy S. Geiger. Having commanded a squadron in France in the First World War, he was promoted to brigadier-general in September 1942 and sent to command 1st Marine Aircraft Wing in Guadalcanal. He was then given command of all Marine Corps aviation as a major-general. His next promotion was to command I Marine Amphibious Corps. He also briefly took control of Tenth US Army when Gen Buckner was killed. Geiger's final wartime command was the Fleet Marine Force, Pacific. *(USMC)*

Commandant. A year later, on 1 April 1936, the Officer in Charge, Aviation, became the Director of Marine Corps Aviation, with divisional status. The Director served as the Commandant's adviser on all aviation matters and as the liaison officer between the USMC and the US Navy's Board of Aeronautics. Marine aviation remained dependent upon the Navy for its aeroplanes and for all other aviation equipment.

Probably the most important pre-war development was the establishing of the Fleet Marine Force in the 1930s, bringing about many changes in the organisation of Marine Corps aviation. For example, Aircraft Squadrons, East Coast Expeditionary Forces, was renamed Aircraft One, Fleet Marine Force, and Aircraft Squadrons, West Coast Expeditionary Forces, became Aircraft Two, Fleet Marine Force. (The actual redesignation of the forces on each coast as wings, did not happen until 1941.) When

they were detached for operations, the forces took the name of the organisation with which they were operating, for example 'Aircraft, 2nd Marine Brigade'. Mobilisation certainly benefited Marine aviation, as did President Roosevelt's obsession with air power. The Navy Department had asked for some 15,000 new aircraft and this was approved in 1940, the Marine Corps's share being about one-tenth, i.e. thirty-two squadrons. However, this would mean that the Corps had to provide thousands of pilots and ground crew, which was not at all easy when one appreciates that at the end of 1940 they had only 425 pilots and under 3,000 enlisted men (see growth table at Annexe C to this chapter). To make things more difficult, the aviation personnel needed special ability, which took away some of the 'cream of the crop' from those joining up.

Directors of USMC Aviation During the Second World War

11 Mar. 39–29 Mar. 1943	Brig Gen Ralph J. Mitchell
30 Mar. 43–12 May 1943	Col Clayton C. Jerome (Acting Director)
13 May 43–15 Oct. 1943	MajGen Roy S. Geiger
16 Oct. 43–17 Jul. 1944	Brig Gen Louis E. Woods
18 Jul. 44–24 Feb. 1948	MajGen Field Harris

THE MISSION OF MARINE AVIATION

The mission and organisation of Marine aviation, as directed by the Secretary of the Navy on 18 January 1939, was as follows:

Grumman F3F-2s, the last biplane produced for the USMC; they served in the FMF from 1937 to 1941. These three were stationed near San Diego, California, at North Island, Coronado. (USN 83924)

1. Marine Corps aviation is to be equipped, organised and trained primarily for the support of the Fleet Marine Force in landing operations and in support of troop activities in the field; and secondarily as replacement squadrons for carrier-based naval aircraft.
2. The organisation, personnel complement, and other details of Marine Corps aviation are to conform as closely as practical to similar naval aviation organisations.
3. The Bureau of Aeronautics is to exercise supervision over their respective activities connected with Marine Corps aviation in the manner provided for similar naval aviation units.

(Source: Rottmann, *US Marine Corps World War II Order of Battle*)

As I have said, Marine aviation was dependent upon the USN for its aircraft and associated equipment, and in June 1940 they took delivery of a new dive-bomber, the Douglas SDB-1 Dauntless, which proved to be one of the most important American combat aircraft of the war. It was a most successful machine that continued to give outstanding service until 1944, long after its

The Douglas SBD Dauntless dive-bomber was one of the most successful US dive-bombers of the war. Initially they operated out of Guadalcanal and the Russell Islands. *(USMC 81420)*

contemporaries had all but disappeared from the scene. In fact it was responsible for sinking more Japanese shipping than any other Allied aircraft and for stopping the Imperial Japanese Navy at Midway in June 1942 and played a leading role in the Solomons campaign.

EXPANSION

After Congress had approved funds for the additional aircraft, major expansion plans were now possible, the target being for four groups, each of eleven squadrons. Although this sounds ambitious, it was estimated that an amphibious landing by even a division-sized force would require the support of at least twenty-six squadrons of aircraft – 12 fighter, 8 bomber, 4 utility and 2 observation. However, progress towards achieving this goal was slow. When, in February 1941, the major USMC expansion took place and the

A typical fighter strip hacked out of the jungle; this one was at Torokina on Bougainville. Photographed in December 1943, the parked aircraft are mainly Corsairs, while an SBD Dauntless dive-bomber is landing close to a grading machine that is still hard at work levelling the runway. *(USMC 74672)*

brigades became divisions, their air support groups were redesignated 1st and 2nd Marine Aircraft Wings (MAW-1 and MAW-2). At the time of the Japanese pre-emptive strike on Pearl Harbor, there was only one single group in each wing, with a total of just over 250 aircraft and 700 pilots in the entire Marine aviation. As well as the grievous loss of ships, the Japanese bombing of Pearl Harbor also saw the destruction of 188 aircraft, including 47 of the 48 Marine aircraft of Marine Air Group 21 that was stationed there. At that time there was an urgent need to get aircraft out to the outer defenses and two carriers (USS *Lexington* and *Enterprise*) were already ferrying Marine aircraft, the former en route to Midway with part of VMSB-231, the latter on its way back from Wake, having flown off twelve F4F Wildcat fighters of VMF-211 to reinforce its

defenses on 4 December. Fortunately neither carrier was attacked; however, Wake was subsequently bombed and eight of the Wildcats destroyed on the ground, together with their main 25,000-gallon fuel tank. There were further air raids, followed by a major Japanese amphibious assault, but this was turned back by the remaining four Wildcats and the shore-based Marine artillery (six 5in guns and twelve 3in anti-aircraft guns), the Japanese losing two ships and some 700 men. However, further, better-organised enemy assaults inevitably followed and, although the garrison held out for a further two weeks, it eventually had to surrender.

The fall of the Philippines would follow, during which most of the American Far East Air Force would be completely destroyed, most aircraft being on the ground when the Japanese made their major strike on 8 December. For the minimal loss of a handful of aircraft, the Japanese destroyed over 100 American aeroplanes. There was nothing to prevent even further success, the policy of forward defense having proved a failure. There was now a wide buffer zone between the opposing sides that undoubt-

An F4U Corsair fires eight 5in rockets at an enemy position on Okinawa. *(USMC 80-G-435693 via Compendium Publishing)*

edly favoured the Japanese. Nevertheless, they had by no means defeated the Americans, as would be proved when the USA had harnessed its vast economic and industrial potential. The first evidence of this happening were the naval battles of the Coral Sea (7–8 May) and Midway (4–7 June), the latter being the real turning point in the Pacific war.

Although the battle was won mainly by carrier-borne aircraft that sank three Japanese carriers and crippled a fourth, the Marine squadrons on Midway played their part; this was Marine Air Group 22, com-prising VMSB-241 (flying SBDU Vindicators and SBD-2 Dauntless) and VMF-221 (Buffaloes and Wildcats). Leading one of the two striking units of VMSB-241 was Maj Lofton R. Henderson, whose name would be immortalised in the name given to the jungle airstrip on Guadalcanal – 'Henderson Field'. Over 100 Japanese dive-bombers and torpedo bombers attacked Midway in the early hours of 4 June and within minutes all the aircraft had been scrambled. They had only time for a single pass at the enemy bombers before they were counter-attacked by swarms of Japanese

Zeros which outclassed the elderly Marine aircraft, shooting down nine of the twelve Marine Corps fighters.

In May 1942, the enemy invaded the island of Tulagi, then by the end of the month had landed more troops on nearby Guadalcanal, where they began to build an airstrip (between Tenaro and Kukum). The 1st Marine Division assaulted both Tulagi and Guadalcanal in August 1942, and the leathernecks were subjected to constant air raids while they endeavoured to construct Henderson, plus two subsidiary strips. This was achieved by 20 August, using heavy equipment which the enemy had aban-doned, and MAW-1 flew in two squadrons – VMF-223 (F4F Wildcats) and VMSB-232 (SBD Dauntless). These were the first elements of what soon became called 'The Cactus Airforce', 'Cactus' being the codename for Guadalcanal. During the months of September to November 1942, many units served in the 'Cactus Airforce',

F4F-3 Grumman Wildcats from VMF-211 flew off the deck of the USS *Enterprise* to Wake Island's new, but still unfinished, airstrip. From the strip they would defend Wake against the Japanese. *(National Archives 127-N-29309)*

whose kills included 20 enemy ships sunk and a further 14 damaged. A total of 260 enemy aircraft were also destroyed. Cactus lost some 101 aircraft from enemy action, some of them during a devastating shelling by two Japanese battleships on the night of 13/14 October, when over 900 shells were fired from their 14in guns. Most of the shells landed on Henderson Field (where 41 all-ranks were killed and 31 of the 38 SBDs on the strip were destroyed), but fortunately not on the fighter strip, which was virtually unscathed, as were 29 of their Wildcats. Later attacks did more damage; however, in one remarkable effort the Cactus Air Force managed to put twelve SBDs and eight F4Fs into the air, plus a Catalina flying boat rigged to carry two torpedoes. The Catalina, flown by the General's aide, Maj Jack Cram, scored a direct hit with one of its torpedoes on an enemy troop transport.

CLOSE SUPPORT

During the New Georgia campaign, Marine aviation developed a very good close support technique, using air liaison parties on the ground in Jeeps equipped with radios on which to call down highly accurate air strikes. These not only made their strikes far more effective but also lessened the chance of casualties among friendly troops, always a danger in these conditions. It was also at this time that the Marines started to receive the Vought 4FU Corsair, which quickly proved its superiority over the enemy Zeros; when in use with the USN/USMC in the Pacific they were credited with 2,140 victories for the loss of only 189 Corsairs, undoubtedly the most outstanding carrier-based fighter to be deployed operationally during the war. However, because of teething problems with the Corsair's landing ability on carriers, all early deliveries went to the shore-based Marine squadrons, most notably to Maj 'Pappy' Boyington, CO of VMF-214, who was the war's top Marine Corps fighter ace and a Medal of Honor winner to boot. The Corsair also went on to show its ability as a dive-bomber that could deliver its 1,000lb bombs and its fire from six 0.5in Browning machine guns accurately on to enemy targets.

Marine aviation went on supporting the Army, Navy and the Marine Corps as the Pacific war drew to its successful conclusion.

199

Maj Gregory 'Pappy' Boyington was a leading Marine Corps ace, in command of the 'Black Sheep' Squadron, VMF-214. Shot down near Rabaul and seriously wounded, he was taken prisoner but survived to be liberated, and was promoted to lieutenant-colonel and awarded the Medal of Honor, which was presented by the President. Here, he briefs his pilots at the Turtle Bay strip. *(USMC N-24880 via Real War Photos)*

Scramble! Pilots leave the parachute loft and race to their aircraft, which stand ready for action close by. The aircraft are Corsair F4Us of VMF-214. *(USMC N-24884 via Real War Photos)*

As the table in Annexe C shows, at its peak the air arm comprised some thirty-one groups with a total of 145 squadrons. It had downed 2,355 enemy aircraft, the top-scoring unit being VMF-121 with 208 victories. They had also, to quote Sherrod, 'pounded Japanese airfields, shipping and bases from the Solomons to the Western Pacific . . . flown night fighters, reconnaissance aircraft, transport and observation planes, anti-submarine and long range patrols, but did so more in support of the general aerial campaign rather than in support of amphibious operations.' Is it any wonder that one USN admiral signalled, 'Three Cheers for the Leathernecks!'?

FLIGHT CLOTHING AND EQUIPMENT

Flight clothing was considered to be just as much naval equipment as purely Marine Corps uniform, because, as originally explained, the Navy was the source of all such functional items, which included leather boots, leather gloves, goggles, cloth helmets (containing headphones) and a one-piece cotton khaki flying suit. Capt John M. Foster, USMC, flying from Munda, said that he wore a flying suit, then slung a 'leather shoulder holster containing my 45-caliber automatic over my neck and buckled the belt, strung with my hunting knife, first aid kit, extra cartridges and canteen around my waist'. In addition, he also wore a baseball cap and carried his flying helmet, goggles and gloves, while all pilots also carried in their aircraft a further 65lb of parachute, rubber raft and jungle pack.

BASIC ORGANISATIONS

The smallest unit was the flying squadron, which one could compare in size to a battalion-sized command. Squadrons usually operated as part of a group, and even though they were able to operate independently for limited periods, they needed additional service personnel from their parent group for this. The normal squadron (irrespective of role/aircraft type) contained the following elements:

Squadron headquarters
Operations and intelligence
Communications
Engineering and material (i.e. aircraft maintenance)
Transport
Ground defense (ideally, a platoon-sized force)
Three or four aircraft divisions of six aircraft

For example, a fighter squadron would normally have 18 fighter aircraft, 40 pilots, 10 ground staff officers and about 250 enlisted men. The high ratio of pilots to planes meant that squadrons could fly almost 'around the clock' if necessary. Selected ground staff officers and pilots performed special duties such as executive, operations, intelligence, communications, radar, construction and maintenance, ordnance, engineering, *matériel*, transportation; additionally, they served as mess officers, adjutants and doctors (flight

Ground crews like these, pictured hard at work on Marine aircraft, were the unsung heroes of the air war. It was their efforts that ensured that squadrons maintained such high numbers of aircraft operational. *(USMC Capt Elton A. Barnum collection)*

surgeons). Squadrons with aircraft that needed crews (in addition to pilots), such as scout-bombing or torpedo-bombing planes, would have enlisted men as aerial gunners. Larger, multi-engine aircraft (such as bombers, utility/transport or photographic aircraft) would have up to sixty officers flying, including (as well as pilots) co-pilots, bombardiers and navigators. They would also have more enlisted men (up to 460 in bombing squadrons) as aerial gunners, flight engineers, and radio operators. They would also have additional mechanics, as there would be more engines to service and more gun turrets, bombsights and other aircraft equipment to maintain.

Later on in the war, the size of fighter and scout-bomber squadrons was increased to twenty-four aircraft, so that the overall number of squadrons could be reduced, and some deactivated. Rottmann quotes the following, by way of example, for Marine Aircraft Group 13, based in the Samoa and Ellice Islands in August 1943:

Squadron	Location	Aircraft
HS-13	Tutuila	two PBY-5A, three J2F-5, two R4D, two SNJ
VMF-111	Funafuti	twenty-six F4F-4
VMF-441	Nanomea	twenty F4F-4
VMSB-151	Funafuti	nineteen SBD-4
VMSB-241	Tutuila	twenty-one SBD-4

Awards to Marine Aviation Units

In total there were seventy-eight Presidential Unit Citations (PUC), fifty-two Navy Unit Citations (NUC) and one Distinguished Unit Citation (Army) (DUC) awarded to Marine aviation units, broken down as follows:

HQ squadrons	13 PUC, 7 NUC
Service	9 PUC, 7 NUC
Fighter	32 PUC, 13 NUC, 1 DUC
Scout-bomber and torpedo-bomber	9 PUC, 15 NUC
Medium bomber	2 NUC
Transport and photo	3 PUC, 3 NUC
Observation	6 PUC, 3 NUC
Air warning	6 PUC
Air support control units	1 NUC
Separate commands	1 NUC

MEDAL OF HONOR RECIPIENTS

Name	Squadron	Place	Date(s) of action
*Bauer, Lt Col Harold W.	VMF-212	Guadalcanal	28 Sept., 3, 16 Oct. 1943
Boyington, Maj Gregor	VMF-214	Solomons-Rabaul	12 Sept. 1943–3 Jan. 1944
DeBlane, Lt Jefferson J.	VMF-112	Solomons	31 Jan. 1943
*Elrod, Capt Henry T.	VMF-211	Wake	8–23 Dec. 1941
*Fleming, Capt Richard E.	VMSB-241	Midway	4–5 Jun. 1942
Foss, Capt Joseph J.	VMF-121	Guadalcanal	9 Oct. 1942–25 Jan. 1943
Galer, Maj Robert E.	VMF-224	Guadalcanal	Aug.–Sept. 1942
*Hanson, Lt Robert M.	VMF-215	Rabaul	1 Nov. 1943, 24 Jan. 1944
Smith, Maj John L.	VMF-223	Guadalcanal	21 Aug.–15 Sept. 1942
Swett, Lt James E.	VMF-221	Guadalcanal	7 Apr. 1943
Walsh, Lt Kenneth A.	VMF-124	Solomons	15, 30 Aug. 1943

* awarded posthumously

The F6F Hellcat night-fighter represented a new and very successful weapon for the Marine Corps. *(USMC 92399)*

Corsair F4Us on Turtle Bay fighter strip, Espiritu Santo, New Hebrides. They wait on stand-by while ground crews carry out last-minute checks. *(USMC N-24888 via Real War Photos)*

WRs attach depth bombs to an aircraft's bomb rack during a course at the Ordnance School, USMC Air Station, Quantico, in August 1944. *(USMC via author's collection)*

Above: One of the smallest aircraft in operational use with the USMC was the tiny Piper AE-1B Grasshopper, used for the speedy evacuation of wounded when the situation demanded. *(USMC 80-G-498161 via Compendium Publishing)*

Below: The Piper NE-1B Grasshopper was used for observation, as here over Naha, the capital city of Okinawa, in May 1945. *(USMC 127-GR-106-121116 via Compendium Publishing)*

TYPES OF SQUADRONS (SEE ALSO ANNEXES A & B FOR AIRCRAFT DETAILS)

Marine Fighting Squadron (VMF)

Most numerous squadron type. Multi-role, used for air-to-air combat, combat air patrols, anti-ship attack, bomber escort and close air support (CAS) as fighter-bombers, to support amphibious assault and ground operations. Main aircraft types: F4F Wildcat, F4U-2 Corsair and F6F Hellcat.

Marine Night Fighting Squadron VMF(N))

Equipped and trained to conduct interdiction of enemy aircraft still en route to their targets, and enemy shipping. Equipped with IFF, VHF radio and short-range radar. Main aircraft types: F4U-2 Corsair and F6F Hellcat (also PV-1N Ventura patrol bomber used early on, and F7F Tigercat at end of war, but the latter did not see action).

Marine Scout Bombing Squadron (VMSB)

Dive-bombing and long-range patrol/scouting. Main aircraft used: SBD Dauntless and SB2C Helldiver.

Marine Fighter-Bombing Squadron (VMBF also sometimes VMFB)

Equipped with ground attack versions of standard fighters. Main mission was CAS, also ship attack.

Marine Torpedo Bombing Squadron (VMTB)

Created by redesignating scout-bombing and fighter-bombing squadrons. Used mainly for low-/high-altitude bombing. Main aircraft: TBF-1C Avenger torpedo-bomber.

Marine Bombing Squadron (VMB)

First combat mission was not until May 1944, then used for low-/high-altitude horizontal bombing, long-range ship attack and reconnaissance. Main aircraft: B-25 Mitchell.

Marine Scouting Squadron (VMS)

The only unit to operate under this designation was VMS-3 in the Virgin Islands, equipped with the J2F-2A Duck armed amphibian, until replaced by OS2N-1 Kingfisher and later SBD Dauntless.

Paratroopers leaving a Douglas R4D Skytrain in a practice paradrop near San Diego in 1942. This maid of all work (civilian nomenclature Douglas DC-3) was used for a wide variety of missions by MAG-25, the South Pacific Combat Air Transport Command (SCAT) but not for parachuting. *(USMC 402924)*

Marine Observation Squadron (VMO)

Equipped with light observation aeroplanes and later camera-equipped fighters. Used for directing artillery and naval gunfire, also liaison flights; photoreconnaissance fighters conducted long-range photo- and visual reconnaissance.

Marine Photographic Squadron (VMD/VMP)

Equipped with long-range patrol bombers (e.g. Liberators or Privateers) and photoreconnaissance fighters. Conducted long-range, very-high-altitude photo-reconnaissance.

Marine Utility/Transport Squadron (VMJ/VMR)

Equipped with C-47 Skytrain twin-engined transports, and later C-46 Commando transports. Conducted cargo and troop transport, resupply, parachute drops and medical evacuation.

Marine Target Towing Detachment (VMTD/VMJ)

First formed at Ewa in October 1944. Mission was to tow aerial targets for anti-aircraft gunnery and radar tracking practice by Marine anti-aircraft artillery battalions, using B-26C Marauders and C-46 Commandos.

GROWTH OF USMC AVIATION PERSONNEL

Date	Officers					Enlisted Men				
	Pilots	Student Pilots	Ground	Women	Total	Pilots	Student Pilots	Ground	Women	Total
31 Aug. 1939	185	20	16	nil	221	47	4	1,111	nil	1,162
30 Jun. 1940	200	11	17	nil	228	45	6	1,581	nil	1,632
31 Dec. 1940	385	22	20	nil	427	40	17	2,573	nil	2,630
30 Jun. 1941	453	nil	27	nil	480	52	1	3,050	nil	3,103
31 Dec. 1941	610	28	41	nil	679	49	67	5,672	nil	5,788
30 Jun. 1942	1,284	63	282	nil	1,629	85	98	15,140	nil	15,323
31 Dec. 1942	2,240	52	1,191	nil	3,483	131	135	33,515	nil	33,781
30 Jun. 1943	4,898	91	2,322	10	7,321	132	135	51,857	86	52,210
31 Dec. 1943	8,266	56	3,356	169	11,847	93	53	72,706	2,885	75,737
30 Jun. 1944	10,416	67	4,339	318	15,140	41	248	90,998	6,199	97,486
31 Dec. 1944	10,355	78	5,036	345	15,814	86	92	94,598	7,440	102,216
31 Jan. 1945	10,349	88	5,059	345	15,841 (peak)	63	88	101,805	7,365	109,321 (peak)
30 Jun. 1945	9,998	107	4,970	328	15,403	43	94	96,116	7,065	103,318
31 Aug. 1945	10,005	104	5,055	334	15,498	44	116	93,858	7,112	101,130

MARINE AIRCRAFT CARRIER UNITS

Initially Marine aviation managed to carry out their primary mission of supporting the FMF using land-based aircraft, rather than carrier-borne, because there were enough land bases in range during the campaigns in the Solomons and New Britain. However, later on (from 1944 onwards), it was a different matter. Carrier-based aircraft were essential, but by that time, as Gordon Rottmann puts it, 'Marine aviation had become enamored with shooting down enemy airplanes, a principal USAAF mission, while carrier-based Navy aviation provided much of the support to Marine ground units. As the Fleet Marine Force battled through the Marshalls and the Marianas, supported by the Navy and USAAF, much of the Marine aviation was relegated to endlessly bombing bypassed Japanese-held eastern Marshall and Caroline Islands into coral dust.' However, things began to change from the summer of 1944 onwards, with the Marine Commandant, Gen Vandegrift, lobbying hard to get Marine fliers on board carriers. It was also the case that the ground forces needed more-specialised close air support than could be provided from within the Navy, which led to the use of Marine squadrons to fill the gaps on fleet carriers, the first being assigned in February 1945.

Marine carrier-based units were deployed on board two types of aircraft carrier: fleet carriers (CV) and escort carriers (CVE). Those on the fleet carriers were subordinate to the Navy carrier air group (CVG), but on escort carriers they were the only unit aboard. The first Marine unit to fly combat missions from an aircraft carrier was Detachment Flight Echelon VMO-155 when it flew off USS *Nassau* in support of the Army's May 1943 Attu landing. They were the only FMF unit to operate in the North Pacific area (flying three F4F-3P photo-reconnaissance fighters). Marine air combat operations took place off the following CVs:

USS *Essex* (CV-9), USS *Franklin* (CV-13), USS *Bunker Hill* (CV-17), USS *Wasp* (CV-18) and USS *Bennington* (CV-20).

Marine fighting and torpedo-bombing squadrons flying off CVEs had the single mission of directly supporting ground units and were designated 'CVS' for carrier squadron. It was originally hoped that eleven CVEs would be provided to the Marine Corps, but only six had been made available by VJ Day. Those operating from fleet carriers retained their standard organisation and were not redesignated as CVS.

MARINE AVIATION GROUND UNITS

Marine aviation ground squadrons and other units that provided direct support to ground combat units included barrage balloons (see Chapter 5), air warning and landing force air support control units, while others provided service and administrative support to aviation units in such areas as headquarters, service, air regulating, air depot and repair/salvage. The air warning squadrons were initially organised to provide radar air warning only, but later they were equipped to provide ground control intercept (GCI) and fighter direction centres. The need for ground control of close air support (CAS was defined as being within 1,000yd of the front line) had become apparent on Guadalcanal, with inexperienced infantry officers endeavouring to direct strike aircraft using inadequate tactical radios.

ANNEXE A

MAIN TYPES OF AIRCRAFT USED BY THE USMC

Fighters (F)

Brewster Buffalo F2A-2 and F2A-3	1940	Land-/carrier-based interim fighter. Small quantity only. First USMC fighter to see action. Used by VMF-211 and VMF-221 on Wake. Known as the 'Flying Coffin'.
Grumman Wildcat F4F-3 and F4F-4	1941 (F3); 1942 (F4)	Land-/carrier-based (F4F-3 land only). Mainly used as land-based by USMC despite F4 having folding wings. VMF-211 gained special honours for its defense of Wake with just four F4Fs.
General Motors Wildcat FM-1 and FM-2	1943	Land-/carrier-based (FM-1 land only). Built by General Motors, so that Grumman could concentrate on F6F Hellcat. Used by VMF 114, 115, 218 and 225.
Chance Vought Corsair F4U-1, F4U-2, F4U-4	1943	Land-based (F4U-2 night-fighter). First used by VMF-124 and 213 aboard USS *Essex*. F4U-2 used first by VMF(N)-532. F4U-4 was improved close air support fighter.
Brewster F3A1, Goodyear FG-1 and FG-1D Corsair	1942	Manufacturers' variants of Chance Vought F4U-1. Many were used by USMC as land-based fighters in lieu of the F4U-1.
Grumman Hellcat F6F-3 and F6F-5	1943 (F-3); 1944 (F-5)	Land-/carrier-based. F6F-3 replaced the Wildcat. F6F-5 adapted for close air support role.

Scout Bombers (SB) and Torpedo Bombers (TB)

Curtiss Helldiver SBC-4	1940	Observation and command transport. Developed as a scout bomber; one of the few biplanes deployed overseas. Replaced by SBD-1 in 1943.
Douglas Dauntless SBD-1 and SBD-4	1941	Most successful US dive-bomber in terms of its longevity and achievement in blunting the might of the Imperial Japanese Navy. (Also later, SBD-5 and SBD-6 scout bombers introduced in 1943 and 1944, replaced by F4U-4 in late 1944.)
Vought-Sikorsky Vindicator SB2U-3	1941	Dive-bomber. Used only by VMSB-131 and SBD-3, then became a trainer, replaced operationally by the Dauntless.
Brewster Buccaneer SB2A-4	1942	Scout bomber. Originally built for the Netherlands as a light bomber, then taken over by USN/USMC. Equipped first night-fighter squadron, VFM(N)-531.

Curtiss Helldiver SB2C-1A	1942	Scout bomber. Difficult to handle, transferred from USAAF, used as trainer. (Also SB2C-3 dive-bomber introduced in 1944, but saw only limited use.)
Grumman Avenger TBF-1C	1942	Torpedo-bomber. Ungainly appearance, nicknamed 'Turkey'. Variant made by General Motors, TBM-1Cs, used by USMC. (Also General Motors TBM-3E Avenger introduced in 1944, an upgraded version of TBF-1C built by General Motors.)

Patrol Bombers (PB) and Other Patrol Aircraft

Consolidated Catalina PBY-5A	1941	Patrol bomber. Amphibian command aircraft. Also search and rescue. Only three examples in service.
North American Mitchell PBJ-1C, PBJ-1D, PBJ-1H and PBJ-1J	1943	Patrol bomber. 1C and 1D were virtually identical. 1J was locally modified as night attack version.
Consolidated Liberator PB4Y-1	1943	Patrol bomber. Photoreconnaissance patrol bomber. Fought with USMC every step of the way over the islands to Japan.
Consolidated Privateer PB4Y-2	1944	Land-based maritime patrol bomber.
Lockheed Vega Ventura PV-1N	1943	Patrol aircraft. Developed from Lodestar transport. Used by VMF(N)-531.

Utility (U), Observation-Scout (OS) and Observation Aircraft (O)

A wide range of utility aircraft were impressed into service. These were the most widely used among them: Curtis CNC-1 Falcon trainer; Grumman J2F-5 Duck utility; Naval Air Factory OS2N-1 Kingfisher observation and scout aircraft; Piper NE-1B Grasshopper observation aircraft; Piper AE-1 Grasshopper evacuation aircraft; Consolidated OY-1 Sentinel observation aircraft (known as 'Flying Jeep').

Transports (R)

Douglas R3D-2	1940	Carried 16 troops or 22 paratroopers; 2,400lb cargo.
Douglas R4D-1 Skytrain	1941	Nicknamed 'Gooney Bird'. Carried 28 troops or 18 stretchers; 6,000lb of cargo. Military version of DC-3 Dakota.
Curtiss R5C-1 Commando	1943	Carried 40 troops or 33 stretchers; 15,000lb cargo. Replaced R4D series.

(Source: Rottmann, *US Marine Corps World War II Order of Battle*)

ANNEXE B
USMC AVIATION AIRCRAFT STATISTICS

Name	Weight (empty, lb)	Powerplant	Speed (mph)	Range (miles)	Armament
Fighters					
F2A Buffalo	6,321	1 × 1,200hp	321	965	4 × .50in MG, 2 × 100lb bombs
F4F-4 Wildcat	5,758	1 × 1,200hp	318	770	6 × .50in MG, 2 × 100lb bombs
F4U Corsair	9,205	1 × 2,450hp	446	1,005	6 × .50in MG, 2 × 1,000lb bombs or 8 × 5in rockets
F6F Hellcat	9,153	1 × 2,000hp	380	1,530	6 × .50in, 2 × 1,000lb bombs or 6 × 5in rockets
Bombers (Scout and Torpedo)					
SBC Helldiver	4,841	1 × 950hp	237	590	2 × .30 MG, 1 × 500lb or 1 × 1,000lb bomb
SBD Dauntless	6,535	1 × 1,350hp	255	773	2 × .50in MG, 2 × .30in MG, up to 1,600lb bombs plus 650lb bombs under wings
SB2U Vindicator	5,634	1 × 825hp	243	1,120	2 × .50in MG plus up to 1,000lb bombs
SB2A Buccaneer	9,924	1 × 1,700hp	274	1,675	2 × .50in MG, 4 × .30in MG, plus up to 1,000lb bombs
SBC Helldiver	4,841	1 × 950hp	237	590	2 × .30in MG, plus 1 × 500lb or 1 × 1,000lb bombs
TBF Avenger	10,700	1 × 1,750hp	267	1,130	3 × .50in MG, plus 1 × .30in MG and up to 2,000lb bombs, torpedoes, etc.
Patrol Aircraft and Medium Bombers					
PBY Catalina	20,910	2 × 1,200hp	179	2,545	2 × .30in MG, 2 × .50in MG, up to 4,000lb bombs/depth charges
B-25 Mitchell	19,480	2 × 1,700hp	272	1,350	12 to 18 × .50in MG, 8 × 5in rockets and up to 3,000lb bombs
B-24 Liberator	36,500	4 × 1,200hp	290	2,100	10 × .50in MG plus maximum 12,800lb bombload (normal 5,000lb)
PB4Y Privateer	37,485	4 × 1,350hp	237	2,800	12 × .50in MG plus up to 12,800lb bombs
B34/PV Ventura	17,275	2 × 2,000hp	315	950	2 × .50in MG, 6 × .30in MG, plus 2,500lb bombs

Utility and Observation

JF Duck	4,400	1 × 900hp	190	750	None (excluding depth charges)
L-4 Grasshopper	730	1 × 65hp	75	190	None

Transports

C-47 Skytrain	16,970	2 × 1,200hp	229	1,500	None
C-46 Commando	32,400	2 × 2,000hp	269	1,200	None

(Source: Mondey, *The Concise Guide to American Aircraft of World War II*)

ANNEXE C
GROWTH OF USMC AVIATION

Date	Wings	Aircraft Groups	Aircraft Squadrons
31 Aug. 1939	Nil	2	9
31 Dec. 1940	Nil	2	10
30 Jun. 1941	Nil	2	11
31 Dec. 1941	2	2	13
30 Jun. 1942	2	10	31
31 Dec. 1942	4	10	41
30 Jun. 1943	4	20	60
31 Dec. 1943	4	21	88
30 Jun. 1944	5	28	130
31 Dec. 1944	5	31	145 (peak)
31 Jan. 1945	5	32	135
30 Jun. 1945	5	32	131
31 Aug. 1945	5	29	132

CHAPTER ELEVEN

USMC WOMEN'S RESERVE

A NEW BEGINNING

The most significant date as far as the formation of the Marine Corps Women's Reserve (MCWR) was concerned was 7 November 1942, when President Franklin D. Roosevelt gave his assent to a women's reserve being placed in the Division of Reserve of the then Adjutant Inspector's Department, bringing to an end the somewhat unseemly wrangling that had gone on before as to whether or not women should be allowed to become Marines. Of course this had happened in the past, there being some 300 'Marinettes' working in the Headquarters, Marine Corps, during the First World War, so as to free male Marines to go to fight in France. (Moreover, some would claim that there had been a female Marine many years before; a small pamphlet appeared in some towns in New England in the summer of 1815, entitled 'The Female Marine', purporting to tell the life story of one Lucy Brewer of Plymouth County, Massachusetts, who had served on the USS *Constitution* during the War of 1812. See 'Lucy Brewer, Leatherneck or Liar?' in G. Forty and A. Forty, *Women War Heroines*.) However, there had been considerable opposition to the formation of the MCWR in the Second World War, as Col Mary V. Stremlow, USMCR (Ret.) explains in her *Free a Marine to Fight:*

Women Marines in World War II. She opens her pamphlet (one of the USMC Commemorative Series), by recounting a story, now clearly part of Marine Corps folklore, in which she tells how the portrait of Archibald Henderson, 5th Commandant of the Marine Corps, crashed from the wall during a dinner party on 12 October 1942, after Maj Gen Commandant Thomas Holcomb had announced his decision to recruit women: 'the Commandant was asked, "Gen Holcomb, what do you think about having women in the Marine Corps?" Before he could reply the painting of Archibald Henderson fell.' Col Stremlow's wry comment is, 'We can only surmise how Archibald Henderson would have reacted to the notion of using women to relieve male Marines "for essential combat duty". On the other hand, Gen Holcomb's opposition was well known. But in the fall of 1942, faced with the losses that were suffered during the campaign for Guadalcanal – and potential future losses in upcoming operations – added to mounting manpower demands, he ran out of options.'

This is not the place to go into the pros and cons of the arguments that raged; however, it was clear that once the Navy Bill (Public Law 689) was signed on 30 July 1942, establishing both the Navy Women's

The WRs Colour Guard passes in review at Camp Lejeune, North Carolina, in November 1943. *(USMC 6067 via Do You Graphics, USA)*

Reserve (WAVES) and the Marine Corps Women's Reserve (MCWR), and was followed, as already mentioned, by the President's seal of approval, then the matter was settled once and for all. Targets could now be set, the plans calling for 500 officers and 6,000 enlisted women to be recruited within four months, and a total for the MCWR of 1,000 officers and 18,000 enlisted women as the target to be achieved by June 1944. The plan for rank and grade distribution would follow the same pattern as for the men, with only minor differences. For officers, for example, there would be one major and thirty-five captains, the rest being first and second lieutenants. However, later, when the senior woman in both the USN and USCG was promoted to naval captain rank, so the senior officer in the MCWR became a colonel. The first lady to hold the post was Col Ruth Cheney Streeter (see photograph at bottom of p. 256) who was sworn in by the Secretary of State for the Navy on 29 January 1943 and commissioned in the rank of major. In fact she was not the first woman on active duty; Mrs Anne A. Lentz, a civilian clothing expert loaned from the WAAC by the Army, and who had

been helping to design uniforms for the then embryo MCWR, had been commissioned in the rank of MCWR captain. Following on from these two, six more women were recruited for the following 'critical posts': MCWR Public Relations, MCWR Training Programme, MCWR Classification and Detail, MCWR rep for west coast activities, MCWR Recruit Depot and, finally, the Assistant to the MCWR Director.

Of course the public and press had dreamt up all kinds of catchy names for the MCWR, but Gen Holcomb, despite his initial opposition to using women, stated his views very strongly in an article in *Life* magazine (issue 27, March 1944), when he said, 'They are Marines. They don't have a nickname and they don't need one. They get their basic training in a Marine atmosphere at a Marine post. They inherit the traditions of Marines. They are Marines' (quoted in Stremlow, *Free a Marine to Fight*).

STRINGENT TESTING

Initially the qualifications needed were the same for both officers and enlisted women, which were United States citizenship; not married to a Marine; either single or married but with no children under 18; height not less than 5ft; weight not less than 95lb; good vision and teeth. For enlisted women ('general service' as it was called), the age limits were 20 to 35 and an applicant had to have attended high school for at least two years. Officers had to be between 20 and 49, and either a college graduate or have a combination of two years' college and two years' work experience. Later, some of the regulations were relaxed so that, for example, wives of enlisted Marines were allowed to join, while enlisted women could marry after 'boot camp' (primary training). Black women were not specifically barred, but none were knowingly enlisted. Recruiting for the MCWR was almost too successful; for example, thousands of women volunteered within a month of the coming into existence of the MCWR. Women working in war industries had to be discouraged from enlisting, but some were very insistent. Consequently, the MCWR met its targets on schedule and by 1 June 1944 had reached its target strength of 18,000. Recruiting then ceased for four months and, when resumed on 20 September 1944, was only ever continued on a very limited basis.

October 1943. Not 'Little Boy Blue come blow up your horn', but rather 'Pfc Betty Blue come blow your bugle!' One of the two original field musicians first class in the Marine Corps Women's Reserve, Pfc Betty Blue blew all the morning and evening calls – colours, tattoo and taps – at the WR School, Camp Lejeune, Ca. *(USMC 6263 via Do You Graphics, USA)*

OFFICER TRAINING

Mount Holyoke

Thanks to an early agreement to share training facilities with the Navy, officer training was able to start when the MCWR had been in existence for only a month. The Navy's Midshipmen School for women officers had been established at Smith College in Northampton, Massachusetts, and later branched out into nearby Mount Holyoke College in South Hadley. Enlisted women were trained at Hunter College in the Bronx, New York City. Undoubtedly the distinguished reputations of these institutions enhanced the public image of both the WAVES and MCWR. The first group of seventy-one Marine officer candidates arrived at Mount Holyoke on 13 March 1943

and were formed into companies, under command of a male officer. Officer candidates joined as privates and, after four weeks, if successful, were promoted to officer cadet (thus earning the right to wear the coveted silver OC pin).

Initially there was a shortage of uniforms, and recruits were given very precise instructions on what to bring with them, e.g. raincoats, rainhats (no umbrellas), lightweight dresses or suits, a plain bathrobe, soft-soled bedroom slippers, easily laundered underwear, play suit/shorts for PT (no slacks), comfortable dark-brown, laced Oxfords (because experience had proved that drill tended to enlarge the feet). During the first four weeks the curriculum was identical to that of the WAVES, except for drill. Col Stremlow comments that the DIs were 'reluctant male drill instructors transferred to Mount Holyoke from the Marine Corps Recruit Depot, Parris Island, S. Carolina'. The recruits studied naval organisation and administration, naval personnel, naval history and strategy, naval law and justice, ships and aircraft. The second phase of training was devoted to Marine Corps subjects taught by male Marines (and WR officers once they had been trained). This second phase took place separately from the WAVES and covered such subjects as Marine Corps administration and courtesies, map reading, interior guard, safeguarding military information and physical fitness.

History was made on 4 May 1943, when the very first women became commissioned officers in the Marine Corps. Thereafter, the Marine Corps section of the school operated on a two-part overlapping schedule, with a new class arriving every month, the first three classes each receiving seven and a half weeks of training. In all, 214 MCWR officers were trained at Mount Holyoke.

Camp Lejeune

Meanwhile, plans were afoot to consolidate all MCWR at Camp Lejeune, New River, North Carolina, by 30 June 1943. The women who made up the fourth officer candidates' class were the first to go to Camp Lejeune; having started at Mount Holyoke on 5 June and been promoted to officer cadets on 29 June, they then boarded a troop train for the two-day trip to Camp Lejeune on 1 July, and finally graduated on 7 August.

ENLISTED WOMEN

'Boot Camp' for the enlisted women was the US Naval Training School (Women's Reserve) at Hunter College in the Bronx, New York City, the first 722 volunteers arriving between 24 and 26 March 1943, and being billeted in nearby apartment houses. They began their training with the WAVES and graduated on 25 April. The curriculum was largely geared to the Navy, so that some subjects had to be changed, and once again Marine drill instructors (still reluctant) had to be obtained from Parris Island. Training sessions varied between three and a half and five weeks, with time being allotted for issue and fitting of uniforms, drill, PT, lectures on customs and courtesies, history and organisation, administration, naval law, map reading, interior guard, defense against chemical attack and air attack, aircraft identification and the safeguarding of military information.

Transfer to Camp Lejeune

Between 26 March and 10 July 1943, six classes of recruits (each of approximately 525) arrived every two weeks. Of the 3,346 women who began training at Hunter College, 3,280 graduated. The staff there included the only woman Marine officer (commissioned directly from civil life) together with subject instructors (10 officers and 23 enlisted men), plus 15–20 male drill instructors. Just as with the officer cadet training, the training of enlisted women was transferred to Camp Lejeune, where in total some 19,000 became Marines during the war. One month before the new schools opened, the MCWR Director requested that weapons demonstrations should be made part of the syllabus, which was approved, and from then on WRs attended two half-day demonstrations which included hand-to-hand combat, use of mortars, bazookas, flame-throwers and small arms, and amtracs and landing craft, making them the only American servicewomen to receive such combat training during 'boot camp'.

If this was a step in the right direction, then the harassment, the use of derogatory nicknames and even worse were something that the newly arrived MCWRs had to put up with from many of the male recruits. In the end it was necessary for the Commandant to write to unit commanding officers, fixing responsibility for a major change of attitude firmly on their shoulders. Although it took some time for change to take effect, Col Stremlow says that by mid-

1944 'open hostility gave way to some sort of quiet truce and it wasn't long before the women's competence, self-assurance, sharp appearance and pride won over a good many of their heretofore detractors. . . . And, in time, Marines could be counted on to take on soldiers and sailors who dared harass WRs in their presence.'

Commissioning Enlisted Women

A most significant change happened in July 1943, when it was decided to open the opportunity for commissioned status to enlisted women, thus taking advantage of their experience and at the same time building morale and *esprit de corps*. To be eligible, they had to have at least six months' service, be recommended by their CO, and be selected by a board of male and female officers at HQ USMC. From then on, the majority of newly commissioned officers came from the ranks. This led to the creation of the Reserve Officer Class (ROC), who attended a four-week course designed to broaden the students' perspective, for example the ROC staff teaching them that firmness and motivation were far better than toughness and threats. Eventually, 975 women were commissioned into the Marine Corps Reserve.

SPECIALIST TRAINING

From the outset, members of the MCWR, both officers and enlisted women, had to attend a wide variety of specialist schools,

Annie Oakley in khaki! 1/Lt Ruth N. Telander got a score of 308 – 2 points above the expert's rating – firing the M1 Garand rifle. She also scored 96 per cent with the .45 Colt automatic pistol – 10 points above the expert's qualification. August 1944, San Diego. *(USMC 37559–A via Do You Graphics, USA)*

A WR 'carves the fatted calf' under instruction at Camp Lejeune, August 1943. A grand total of 18,460 WRs were on duty just before the war ended, all doing worthwhile jobs and thus releasing male Marines for combat overseas. *(USMC 5734 via Do You Graphics, USA)*

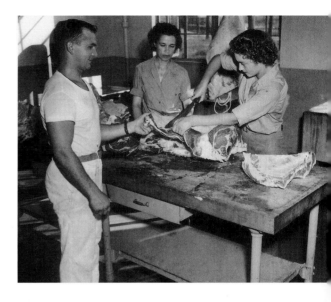

some thirty in all, where they were taught a diverse range of different trades including, for example, those of paymaster, first sergeant, parachute rigger, aerographer, control tower operator, motion picture operator/technician, aircraft instruments technician, radio operator, radio material teletype-writer and automotive mechanic; in addition, they were trained in clerical skills, signals, celestial navigation, aviation supply and photography, and for work in post exchanges and uniform shops. They were thus well-trained specialists before they were posted to their units. Although some 50 per cent of the WRs were employed in clerical duties, as the list of trades shows, many new areas were explored and women proved how willing they were to try new technical fields; this was especially so in the field of aviation.

CLASSIFICATION

In 1945, when looking to the future, Col Streeter classified jobs for MCWRs into four classes, namely: Class I – those tasks which women could do more efficiently than men; Class II – those in which women were as good as men and could replace them on a one-for-one basis; Class III – those jobs in which women were not as good as men, but could be so employed if the need was vital; Class IV – those tasks in which women were definitely not to be used.

UNIFORMS

From the outset the Commandant had decreed that the women should be dressed in traditional Marine forest green, with red chevrons of the same dimensions as those worn by the men. A special uniform unit was created in June 1943 and of course Mrs Anne Lentz, who has been mentioned earlier, played a major role in the design of the new uniforms, the first ones being approved in official uniform regulations published in August 1943. These regulations would not be altered until April 1945, when Uniform Regulations, US Marine Women's Reserve 1945 were issued, reflecting numerous sensible changes, modifications and additions. Officers received a $250 uniform allowance, enlisted women $200 in order to buy the following items: two winter uniforms, hats, shoes, summer outfits, a purse, a wool-lined raincoat, specified accessories and underwear. Great care was taken to ensure that the carefully designed uniforms met the Corps's high standards, mirroring what was worn by the men, both in colour and style. However, it was cut from a lighter-weight cloth and there were some

This group of WRs are wearing summer uniforms and hats (two types). Note also their green purses and white gloves. The photo was taken in Washington, DC, in June 1943, at a 'Free a Marine to fight' recruiting drive. *(USMC 127-N-10825 via Do You Graphics, USA)*

small differences. In general terms, officers and enlisted women both wore the same-styled uniforms made of the same fabric. Perhaps the most easily recognised item of clothing that was unique to the MCWR was their visored, bell-crowned hat, trimmed with 'lipstick red' cord, so different from those hats worn by all the other women's services. For winter, they had heavy green overcoats, khaki trench coats with a detachable lining, and a red scarf (always worn in winter). Anne Lentz had specially selected the two-piece green and white seer-sucker or plissé summer service uniform, for both its comfort and ease of laundering. When it was realised that the officers' rank insignia would not show up sufficiently on the striped dress, green shoulder boards were added. However, the favourite uniform of all was the short-sleeved, V-necked, white twill summer uniform, worn with gilt buttons on the jacket and cap, dress emblems and white pumps. As Col Mary Stremlow comments, 'The stiffly starched uniform never failed to evoke compliments.'

CLASSIFICATION – DETAIL – TRANSFER

As Col Stremlow explains, 'In 1943 the country desperately needed women power, but almost no one knew for certain just how far the limits of tradition could be stretched or, more likely, breached.' This was the problem facing the MCWR along with the entire USA, because, as one might have expected, at that time not many women drove buses or vans – and fewer mended them. Also, they did not work at trades such as electrician or plumber, and rarely, if ever, supervised men. 'Society had long since deemed certain jobs too dirty, too dangerous, too strenuous, or for unspecified reasons, just not suitable for women.' So this was the social climate in which the Marine Corps had to select, train, classify and assign the 18,000 eager, newly recruited young women, at a rate of some 1,000 a month, working to the Director's philosophy that they would try anything except 'heavy lifting and combat'. This called for a considerable change of heart by everyone and also fundamental changes of emphasis. For example, the men were generally posted from their 'boot camp' in large troop drafts, based on the theory that most military skills had to be learned by everyone. Women, however, were individually posted into previously identified job vacancies, because many possessed individual, unique skills. This required considerable cooperation to ensure, initially anyway, that skills were recognised and the right person put into the right job. Nevertheless, Col Stremlow quotes an example of a woman trained and classified as a telephone operator arriving at a post where she was assigned as a 'soda jerk' in the PX (post exchange).

ACCOMMODATION

The assignment of WRs to posts needed special consideration, their welfare, morale and reputation being just as important as the needs of the Marine Corps. Initially, women were only posted to locations in which their services had been asked for, and then only where suitable accommodation was available. Additionally it was standard practice not to assign one WR on her own – no fewer than two was the rule – while enlisted women could not be assigned to a post unless there was a woman officer in the vicinity. It was also customary to assign women officers to units with twenty-five or more WRs. In general terms, the quality of barrack living was extremely high among the WRs, and immaculate WR barracks were undoubtedly the norm and became a source of great pride to all.

DISCIPLINE

Fortunately there were few serious disciplinary problems because, as Col Stremlow points out, 'Because of their intense desire to be accepted by Marines and approved of by the general public, women Marines were their own severest critics and peer pressure to walk a tight line proved very effective.' Records show that out of the 18,000 enlisted women, only 36 were ever court-martialled. The most common infractions were unauthorised absence – usually less than ten days – and violations of regulations (most commonly on dress, fraternisation, etc.). Marriage was not considered as a reason for either discharge or punishment, while pregnancy was considered to be a medical rather than a disciplinary case. However, it is true to say that at times and in certain locations, disciplinary matters were treated

Boarding a train in San Diego, bound for the docks and overseas, are a group of WRs. They wear their winter service uniform, complete with raincoats and scarves (scarlet). Note also that they are carrying camouflaged musette bags (presumably for their travelling necessities and spare uniform), to which are attached shelter halves/blanket rolls. *(USMC 127-N-402433 via Do You Graphics, USA)*

Left: Photographed on the wooded shores of New River at Camp Lejeune are three Native American Marines, who were now under training. They all wear the very smart forest-green winter service uniform, complete with handbags and gloves. *(USMC 5834 via Do You Graphics, USA)*

Below: Close-up of the WR winter uniform. The three-button coat had four pockets and open-notched lapels on which were the standard Marine Corps collar dogs. The coat was worn over a khaki shirt (blouse) and tie. The skirt was a standard six-panel design, extending below the knee. Badges of rank were as normal. *(USMC 501984 via Do You Graphics, USA)*

in an old-fashioned way and 'mature women were often treated like school girls'. For example, a rule that was never challenged was the fact that women on a base could not have a car, despite the fact that this was permitted for men of equal rank (giving a certain allure to jobs in the motor pool.)

OVERSEAS POSTINGS

Although Army WACs were able to serve in all theatres of war, this had raised considerable disquiet among some members of Congress that American women might be located too close to combat, and they argued for tighter restrictions. Taking the opposite stance, there were Marine and naval commanders who insisted that WRs should be used at Pearl Harbor so as to allow men to be released for combat, and this request was quantified as a figure of 5,000 naval servicewomen (WAVES and WRs) being needed. This led to Public Law 441, being signed on 27 September 1944, amending an earlier law of 30 July 1942, by providing that 'Members of the Women's Reserve shall not be assigned to duty on board vessels of the Navy or in aircraft while such aircraft are engaged on combat missions, and shall not

Right: Cpl Trude May Quick was a qualified mechanic and welder for the MT Division at the San Diego Base, thus relieving a fighting Marine for combat service. *(USMC 36280 via Do You Graphics, USA)*

Below: Working on fitting a reconditioned engine into a USMC bus are two WRs, both graduates of the MT School attached to the post garage at Camp Lejeune, in October 1943. *(USMC 6265 via Do You Graphics, USA)*

be assigned to duty outside the American Area and the Territories of Hawaii and Alaska, and may be assigned to duty outside the continental United States only upon their prior request.' The first contingent of 5 officers and 160 enlisted women arrived on 28 January 1945, disembarking in Honolulu while the Pearl Harbor Marine Band played 'The Marines' Hymn', 'The March of the Women Marines' and 'Aloha Oe'. A contingent of WAVES who had also been on board the SS *Matsonia* (as well as Marines, sailors, military wives and ex-POWs) went ashore first, dressed in their best uniforms. They were followed by the WRs in dungarees, boondockers and overseas caps, much to the delight of the crowd of curious Marines who had gathered to welcome them to Hawaii.

In Hawaii, most of the women worked in clerical jobs; however, some came from the Marine Corps Air Station, Cherry Point, North Carolina, so they were soon hard at work helping to service aircraft. WRs also ran the Motor Transport section at Pearl Harbor, serving nearly 16,000 people a month, working around the clock and with an excellent safety record. They received high praise from the Deputy Commander HQ FMF for their efficiency, attitude and enthusiasm. Eventually by the summer of 1945, there were a total of just over 1,000 WR in Hawaii (55 officers and 946 enlisted women).

Above: This WR was on her way to Hawaii in January 1945. She is leaning against a Navy-issue lifejacket and wears a summer uniform short-sleeved green shirt, slacks and the WR garrison cap. *(USMC 107299 via Do You Graphics, USA)*

Centre: The War is Over! Wearing summer white twill uniforms with gilt buttons and white pumps (this was the 'hands-down' favourite WRs' uniform of the war), an excited group of WRs listen to the announcement of the Japanese acceptance of the Allies' surrender terms, in the Navy Annex (HQ MC) on 14 August 1945. *(USMC 902189 via Do You Graphics, USA)*

Below: 'Time to go home.' These were the first seven WRs to be discharged – no wonder they are looking so happy! *(USMC 463252 via Do You Graphics, USA)*

WOMEN'S RESERVE BAND

Perhaps the most colourful and well-travelled unit of the MCWR was the MCWR Band, formed in September 1943. Based at Camp Lejeune and trained by members of the Marine Corps Band, Washington, DC, it comprised forty-three musicians, a drum major (Audre Fall) and a Director of Music (Master Sergeant Charlotte Plummer). As well as playing at reviews, formal guard mountings, passing-out parades and the like, it entertained both on and off bases throughout the USA during the war, and gave many hospital concerts, playing especially to the wounded and maimed Marines. They also played for the President and Adm Chester W. Nimitz and, at special request of the Treasury Department, made a number of War Bond and Victory Loan tours to such cities as Chicago, Pittsburgh, Philadelphia and Cleveland. Their official march was entitled 'The March of the Women Marines', music and words by Louis Saverino and Emil Gasser, both of the US Marine Band.

Hard at work taking an inventory of spare parts is Pfc Jean Melody, another WR who has replaced a male Marine, in San Diego in January 1945. *(USMC 39393 via Do You Graphics, USA)*

THE FINAL BREAKDOWN

Towards the end of the war, just two and a half years after its formation, there were 18,460 women on duty with the USMC Women's Reserve – 820 officers and 17,640 enlisted women. They were working in 225 specialities when the war ended, in 16 out of 21 functional fields, filling 85 per cent of the enlisted jobs at HQ Marine Corps and comprising a half to two-thirds of the permanent personnel at all large USMC posts and stations. Undoubtedly they had fulfilled their *raison d'être* brilliantly.

Women's Reserve Employment (As at 1 June 1945)

The breakdown of occupations was as follows:

Professional/Semi-Professional

Scientific	76
Personnel	338
Artistic (musical)	306
Misc. (e.g. teachers)	622
Total	1,342

Clerical

Clerks, general	1,764
Clerks, typist	2,982
Stenographer	1,129
Special clerical	1,182
Clerical supervisory/admin	498
Clerical communications	661
Clerical supply	1,936
Clerical office machine ops	127
Total	10,279

Sales

Total	741

Service

Personal service	438
Protective service	149
Total	587

Mechanical

Aviation	1,086
Non-aviation	285
Total	1,371

Skilled Trades

Aviation	83
Non-aviation	261
Total	344

Semi-Skilled Jobs

Aviation	143
Non-aviation	1,162
Total	1,305

Unskilled Jobs

Total	14

Students

Total	35

General Duty (not classified elsewhere)

Total	1,648
Grand Total	17,666 *

*six unaccounted for

(Source: Stremlow, *Free a Marine to Fight: Women Marines in WWII*)

'. . . I'VE CHANGED MY MIND'

Col Mary V. Stremlow closes her concise history of the MCWR in the Second World War with two quotations, the first being an extract from a treasured message received by the MCWR on 13 February 1944 (their first anniversary) from President Franklin D. Roosevelt which read, 'The nation is as proud of you as of your fellow Marines – for Marine women are upholding the brilliant traditions of the Corps with a spirit of loyalty and diligence worthy of the highest admiration of all Americans. You have quickly and efficiently taken over scores of different kinds of duties that not so long ago were considered strictly masculine assignments; and in doing so, you have freed a large number of well-trained, battle-ready men of the corps for action.'

High praise indeed. However, as she says, 'standing out among all the beautifully worded accolades bestowed on the women Marines of the Second World War, is a simple statement made by General Holcomb, the Commandant so opposed to having women in the Marine Corps in the beginning who wrote, "Like most Marines, when the matter first came up I didn't believe women could serve any useful purpose in the Marine Corps. . . . Since then I've changed my mind."'

Molly Marine. This statue stands outside the Marine Corps Research Centre at the USMC Base, Quantico. It is a bronze replica of the original standing on the corner of Elk and Canal Streets in New Orleans, that was dedicated on 10 November 1943. *(USMC 2003317123757 via Do You Graphics, USA)*

CHAPTER TWELVE

THE DIVISIONS AT WAR

ACROSS THE PACIFIC

The divisions of the US Marine Corps fought their way across the Pacific in one island-hopping campaign after another – Guadalcanal, Tarawa, the Gilberts, the Marshalls, the Marianas, Iwo Jima, Okinawa and all the rest on their way to mainland Japan – proving themselves to be just as courageous, resourceful and tough as their forefathers had been in so many battles over the years since their formation in 1775.

1st Marine Division, 'The Old Breed' (also called the 'Big One')

Activated on 1 February 1941 from the existing 1st Marine Brigade, the strength of 1st Marine Division when the Japanese bombed Pearl Harbor eleven months later was only 518 officers and 6,871 enlisted men. Thus, for their first battle, which would be on Guadalcanal in August 1942, they needed to be reinforced, and were so,

with troops from 2nd Marine Regiment (one of the regiments of 2nd Marine Division), 1st Raider, 1st Parachute and 3rd Defense Battalions, plus miscellaneous other units, the entire invasion force eventually numbering some 19,546 all ranks. This first battle came after spending several months training in New Zealand, followed by an all-too-brief period of intensive preparation, during which the men of the division had to work night and day to reload their shipping. This was so that the cargo and troops were in the right places for a beach landing, because of

Two Marines take a 'time out' for a smoke during the bitter fighting on Peleliu, in September 1944. Note the .30-cal. Browning MG held by the Marine on the right and the 'USMC' and 'bird on a ball' emblem stencilled on his pocket. *(USMC 874 via Compendium Publications)*

course when they had left the USA, some months previously, cargo had merely been put aboard in a way to make the most economical use of space; that is to say, the ships were not tactically loaded. Other major problems that had to be overcome included a lack of knowledge of the topography of Guadalcanal (there was not even one detailed map available), while they had no idea what defenses the Japanese had built to defend it or the neighbouring islands. Information had to be gleaned from former traders who had visited the islands before the war, and from aerial recon-naissance – not easy when everywhere was covered in thick jungle. However, it was vital that the battle should be a success for a number of reasons, in particular because it would be the first offensive against an enemy who had seized the initiative at Pearl Harbor and continued to conquer every where they went in the Far East, building up a fearsome reputation that the Americans would have to match. The question was, how would the supposedly 'soft' Americans

size up to the highly disciplined and ruthless Japanese? More realistic perhaps, was the view held by Gen Tadamichi Kuribayashi, tough martinet commander of Iwo Jima, who had served as an attaché in the USA during the late 1920s. During this period, he had written in a letter to his wife, 'The United States is the last country in the world that Japan should fight. Its industrial potential is huge and fabulous and the people are energetic and versatile. One must never underestimate the Americans' fighting ability.'

Unexpectedly, there was no opposition on the beaches when 1st Marine Division landed on the morning of 7 August; the enemy had been surprised by the intensity

Leaving Guadalcanal. After months of bitter fighting during Operation Watchtower, Marines of 1st Marine Division leave by truck and on foot. These men were in the first landings and were the last to leave, when relieved by US Army troops in early December 1942. (USMC B-23323 via Real War Photos)

of the naval bombardment and fallen back into the hills. This was an unexpected bonus and allowed the Marines time to get some of their more awkward loads on shore. However, simultaneous landings on the adjoining islands of Tulagi, Gavutu and Tanambogo were not going as well and there was heavy fighting, especially during the first night. 'Here for the first time,' the official history of the campaign notes, 'a curious weakness in Japanese tactics could be seen . . . an inability . . . to exploit . . . advantages. Time after time he succeeded in coming through our lines . . . accomplishing no more than nuisance or harassing activities' (McMillan *et al.*, *Uncommon Valor*). Much of the fighting was hand-to-hand, but the Marines gradually got the better of their tenacious enemy.

Then, on 9 August, a Japanese naval task force slipped undetected into the waters off Guadalcanal and, in under a quarter of an hour, sank or badly damaged five American cruisers, causing the remainder of the fleet to withdraw, leaving the Marines stranded, without any resupply. Instead of being able to mount an offensive to clear the islands, all they could do now was to 'hunker down' and set up a static perimeter around the airstrip (Henderson Field). From then on, until mid-November, when American naval superiority was at last re-established, the Marines stubbornly defended their perimeter, launching only limited offensive actions but fighting non-stop to prevent the enemy from breaking through. The Japanese on the other hand, mounted four major offensives, which were all beaten back, as *Uncommon Valor* explains: 'There are battles in which a few men distinguish themselves, and there are battles in which every man must fight with distinction or die.' They were writing about the Battle of the Ridge, which in many ways was the crucial engagement of the Guadalcanal

campaign. In commending 1st Raider Battalion, 1st Parachute Battalion and 11th Marine Artillery Regiment (the Division artillery), the divisional commander, MajGen Vandegrift, called them 'the best fighting troops that any service could hope to have'. They would continue to hold off all comers until they were relieved on 9 December. The 1st Marine Division (Reinforced) was awarded the Presidential Unit Citation 'for courage and determination . . . of an inspiring order', while 5 men were awarded the Medal of Honor, 113 the Navy Cross, 304 the Silver Star, 4 the Distinguished Service Medal, 3 the British Distinguished Service Order and 2 the Conspicuous Gallantry Medal.

After Guadalcanal, 1st Marine Division spent some nine months recuperating in Australia; 90 per cent had contracted malaria, all were physically exhausted and 40–50 per cent were hospitalised during their stay near Melbourne, while many were sent home to pass on their first-hand battle experience at Marine Corps training camps. Gen Vandegrift, who was awarded the Medal of Honor, would eventually become Commandant of the Marine Corps, being replaced as CG of 1st Marine Division by William H. Rupertus on 8 July 1943. During the latter part of the nine months, rigorous training began for an assault on their next objective, which was to be Cape Gloucester in south-west New Britain. The 1st Marine Division was then serving in MacArthur's Sixth US Army and would fight a bitter battle, securing the flank as Sixth US Army made its advance to Hollandia (east Indonesia, on the northern coast of New Guinea). Cape Gloucester airfield was the objective of this, their second jungle battle; the Japanese were using it to mount bombing strikes on New Guinea. The operation was in three phases: first, a drive westwards from the landing beaches to the airfield;

Men of 1st Marine Division prepare to embark for New Britain on 24–6 December 1943. Note the line of waiting landing ships drawn up on to the beach with their bow doors open as the vehicles and men get ready. *(USN Photo N-26820B via Real War Photos)*

Men of 1st Marine Division wading ashore from their landing craft on to New Britain, 24 December 1943. Note the tractor pulling an artillery piece, followed by a gaggle of leathernecks, who are making sure to keep their weapons out of the surf. *(USMC B23996 via Real War Photos)*

then a second advance eastwards to capture Hill 660, which dominated the airfield perimeter; and third, a series of aggressive patrols and amphibious operations to destroy the enemy and an advance towards Rabaul. Phase 1 was completed and the airfield secured by 2 January 1942; Hill 660 fell two weeks later, after bitter fighting and heavy casualties. Final mopping-up of the enemy then followed. The third phase was completed by mid-March. What made the New Britain operation worse than Guadalcanal was the mud caused by the monsoon rainfall (100in in three months – 8in in a single night.)

This time they 'recuperated' at Pavuvu, one of the Russell Islands, which was practically deserted apart from masses of coconut palms and a copra-drying plant. After a difficult period with only minimal comforts (not made any better by the fact that they had expected to go back to the delights of Australia again), training began seriously in June 1944 as they prepared for their next operation. This would be Peleliu, where they would suffer enormous casualties: 2,000 on the first day, the total (7,079) being higher than during any other major amphibious assault in the Pacific, and equalled only by Iwo Jima. A quick, easy battle had been expected; instead it took twelve days of vicious fighting, from 15 to 27 September, before the Stars and Stripes were raised in front of what was left of the airfield administrative buildings. Fighting in other parts, such as Bloody Nose Ridge, went on longer, but eventually the remaining enemy were dealt with. The division then returned to Pavuvu, where much had been done to improve the living conditions and general facilities. They also now had a new CG – MajGen Pedro A. del Valle.

Once again they had another island to take. This time, it was Okinawa, which had, in the area that 1st Marine Division fought, more elaborate and better coordinated defenses than Peleliu, and the division would pay the price: 8,653 casualties, of which 2,234 were killed. However, initially, the Marines had a reasonable time with just the lightest opposition. Then everything changed, the enemy counter-attacked in early May (3–5), during which they landed a sizeable force behind 1st Marine Division lines. The 6th Marine Division then moved into a flank position and both divisions reverted to III AC. This brought 1st Marine Division right into the centre of the line that was trying to break through the Japanese main defenses in extremely difficult terrain. During the heavy fighting that followed, tank–infantry teams proved most successful, especially the more destructive flame-thrower tanks.

To add to the leathernecks' problems, the monsoon rains came during the last week of May, making any movement exceptionally difficult. Nevertheless, they continued to winkle out the remaining Japanese, and on 21 June the island was declared clear. The 1st Marine Division had optimistically hoped that they would be sent to Hawaii to recover from two years of fighting, but it was not to

be. Their 'rest' area was to be the north end of Okinawa, where isolated Japanese were still being killed. The war ended while they were encamped on the Motobu peninsula, but instead of going back to the USA they were sent to north China, the leading elements landing there at the end of September 1945. The division command post was at Tientsin and their first mission was to concentrate, disarm and repatriate all Japanese in the area, while assisting in the redistribution of Chinese Nationalist forces to areas formerly occupied by the Japanese.

2nd Marine Division, 'Silent Second'

Formed from 2nd Marine Brigade, 2nd Marine Division came into existence on 1 February 1941, its initial commander being MajGen Clayton B. Vogel, their first station Camp Elliott, near San Diego, California, and their first wartime task, as part of the Western Defense Command, the defense of the Californian coast from Oceanside to the Mexican border, additionally being responsible for manning the anti-aircraft defenses around San Diego. Once it was clear that there would be no immed-iate Japanese invasion, the division was concentrated at Camp Elliott for intensive training. It would be some time before they would fight at Tarawa. Nevertheless, various elements of the division were already overseas; for example, one of their three Marine infantry regiments (6th Marine Regiment) was serving in Iceland and would not rejoin the division until March 1942, while two companies of their engineer battalion were at Pearl Harbor, the very spot where the Pacific war began. Also, during late 1941, 2nd Marine Brigade was formed from 8th Marine Regiment, 1st Battalion, 10th Marine Regiment and other elements of 2nd Marine Division, sailing for Samoa on

6 January 1942.

February 1942 saw 9th Marine Regiment activated as a new regiment of 2nd Marine Division, but after training the regiment was detached to become a unit of the Amphibious Corps, Pacific Fleet. The 2nd Marine Regiment was also detached, sailing for the south-west Pacific area in late June; by 7 August they had reached Guadalcanal and would soon go into action with 1st Marine Division as already explained. Also, on the same day, one of its companies landed on the island of Florida, just to the north of Guadalcanal, to cover a landing on Tulagi and Gavutu islands. This was the very first landing made against the enemy by US forces in the Second World War and it would take two days of bitter fighting to overcome the Japanese garrison.

Mid-October saw 6th Marine Regiment on their way to New Zealand, soon to be followed by the rest of 2nd Marine Division. They had been training hard and were anxious to get into the fight, despite the fact that they were not fighting as a complete division. The 2nd Marine Regiment would remain virtually in contact with the enemy for the next thirty months, their first action being the provision of covering fire to the landing force of 1st Marine Regiment on Guadalcanal. This was followed by the first serious fighting on 9 and 10 November, with little progress being made against stiff Japanese resistance.

The hard battles on Guadalcanal have already been recorded, but what has perhaps not been properly covered were the other hardships that had to be faced, such as malaria, jungle rot and malnutrition. Both 2nd Marine Regiment (which had fought for six months non-stop) and 8th Marine Regiment (fighting for three months) had to be given a chance to recuperate from their ordeals, so were sent to New Zealand (Wellington) while the rest of the division remained on the island for the final battles.

Tarawa was, like Guadalcanal, another great gamble. 'All that preceded Tarawa was a mixture of fortune, of good luck and bad, of seasoning in strife. Tarawa was the line of departure for the Second Marine Division as a division.' So wrote C. Peter Zurlinden, Jr, in *Uncommon Valor* (McMillan *et al.*), and he goes on to explain how the methods that the Marines used to overcome each new situation helped them to set a pattern for further offensive action, all the way to Okinawa. They also had a new CG, MajGen Julian C. Smith, for an assault that had been preceded by naval and air bombardments, intended to destroy the intricate defenses on Betio, the main island of the group and the target for 2nd Marine Division.

The assault began before dawn on 20 November, and was met by a heavy salvo from the Japanese shore batteries, which continued until silenced by the guns of the

Using hand grenades and their rifles/carbines, a Marine infantry squad takes on a cave in the jungle-like woods of Saipan on 6 August 1944. *(USMC B-23519 via Real War Photos)*

Tanks and infantry working together to take enemy positions on Tinian in August 1944. *(Lt Col R.K. Schmidt, USMC, now deceased, via author's collection)*

naval escort and dive-bombers from the Pacific Fleet. During the next seventy-six hours, one of the fastest and fiercest battles of the war was fought, with over 3,000 casualties, nearly one-third of whom were killed, died of their wounds or were missing in action. At 1312 hr on 23 November, the battle ended and Betio was officially declared taken. The following day, the battered 2nd and 8th Marine Regiments boarded their troop transports for the new divisional camp in Hawaii, while 6th Marine Regiment mopped up on Betio and the other islets, before rejoining their comrades in Hawaii, to prepare for the next island battle. This time it would be Saipan-Tinian on the Marianas – a long thrust, close to the mainland of Japan, bypassing other Japanese-held islands to enable American land-based aircraft to reach the enemy heartland. The 2nd Marine Division would be joined by 4th Marine Division, under MajGen Harry Schmidt, and 27th Infantry Division to form V AC, commanded by Lt Gen Holland M. Smith, USMC (see Chapter 3).

The battle for Saipan opened on 15 June 1944; 2nd Marine Division was now commanded by MajGen Thomas E. Watson, with Col 'Red Mike' Merritt Edson as his second in command. Edson had won the Medal of Honor at Guadalcanal with the raiders. The 2nd and 4th Marine Divisions would land abreast, with 2nd Marine Division in the north. Despite a heavy pre-assault bombardment, the enemy defended stubbornly; there were some 20,000–30,000 on the island, with the protection of intricate defenses, including the many caves.

However, as the Japanese were pushed back into the last few miles of the island, they became more and more desperate, making many 'banzai' charges in order to die 'honourably'. Saipan was all but cleared by 13 July, and a week later 4th Marine Division, together with 2nd and 8th Marine Regiments of 2nd Marine Division, were ready to embark to take on Tinian, the smallest of the Marianas. Fortunately, opposition was initially fairly light until 1 August, but then stiffened. It took until mid-November finally to clear up the last remnants. The greatest reward after the Marianas was the promise that any veterans with two years' service, from Guadalcanal to Tinian, would be sent home once ships were available, and this was achieved. Total divisional losses in the entire Saipan–Tinian campaign were 1,363.

Okinawa was the next campaign (for Iwo Jima, 2nd Marine Division was area reserve), where they were part of Task Group 512 and were only used as a diversion along the south-east coast at the same time as the main landings on 1 April 1945. Early June saw both the capitulation of Okinawa and the capture of Iheya and Aguni in the Ryukyu group by 2nd Marine

Division. The 8th Marine Regiment was also used on the eastern flank of the main fighting in southern Okinawa, before the island was declared secure on 21 June. This was followed by a final embarkation and debarking on Japan, where they initially occupied Nagasaki.

3rd Marine Division, 'The Fighting Third'

'On the day Iwo Jima was secured a corporal in E Company, 21st Marines of the Third Division, was sitting in the sand figuring out his record: "Left New Zealand July 1943. Landed on Guadalcanal. From the 'Canal to Bougainville. Back to the 'Canal. On to Guam. Mopped up Guam. On to Iwo Jima. Now it's March 1945. No liberty in almost two years. No civilisation. Jungle all the time except for Iwo." He stopped short, but he might have added one thing. He was the only man in his outfit who had been through all three battles without a wound. In general, that was the story of every outfit that made up the Third Marine Division' (McMillan *et al.*, *Uncommon Valor*).

Called by some 'The Workhorse Division', 3rd Marine Division was formed in New Zealand in June 1943, although its major units had been organised in the USA in September 1942 (at Camp Elliott, California, and at New River, North Carolina), the two echelons going overseas separately. The 3rd Marine Regiment was the first major unit to go abroad, on 1 September, bound for American Samoa, where they took over the defense of Tutuila and underwent rigorous jungle training. Then, in May 1943, they moved to New Zealand to join the newly forming 3rd Marine Division under MajGen C.D. Barrett, for more training. In July 1943 they embarked for 'up north', their first stop being Guadalcanal, where they had to deal with enemy stragglers and experienced their first enemy air raids. In September,

MajGen Barrett became commander of I MAC; he was later killed in an accident and replaced by MajGen A.A. Vandegrift, CG 1st Marine Division. MajGen Allen Hal Turnage took over the division, and would command them during their assault on Bougainville.

The invasion of Bougainville was an important step towards dealing with the major Japanese base of Rabaul, some 200 miles to the west. There were two main enemy enclaves on the island; the Buka area, with airfields and some 20,000 enemy, located on the north-west end of the island; and the Kahili–Shortland area on the south-east end, where there were about 15,000 enemy. After an amphibious landing at Empress Augusta Bay on the southern coast, the Marines would establish and hold a deep beachhead in which airstrips would be constructed. From these, Marine aircraft would first destroy the two Japanese bases, isolate the island and then neutralise Rabaul. After full-scale landing rehearsals in the New Hebrides, the convoy sailed north. D-Day would be 1 November.

On D-6 a New Zealand brigade took Treasury Island, just south of Bougainville, to be used as an advanced staging base, while 3rd Marine Division convoy headed for Kahili in a feint assault. Then, in the middle of the night, they turned seawards, then north towards Empress Augusta Bay, where H-Hour for the main landing would be 0715 hr. There was heavy enemy resistance on the right flank around Cape Torokina, but this was eventually dealt with, and the next day a beachhead had been established some 1,500yd deep. Just as soon as any remaining enemy had been mopped up, the Seabees went to work building roads through the swampy ground and started to build a fighter strip. In a few weeks, they had achieved the impossible and, just

Taking a 'time out' for a conference. During an attack near Adelup Point on Guam, on 6 August 1944, Marine tank crews dismount and pause for a smoke, while their tank commanders confer. Their Shermans are parked behind the crews in a semi-circle. *(USMC B-23520 via Real War Photos)*

twenty-one days after they had begun, Marine fighter planes were using the Bougainville airstrip. The Japanese endeavoured to make a counter-landing, but the enemy convoy was intercepted at sea and four Japanese cruisers were sunk.

The division would go on fighting on Bougainville until the end of the year, when they were relieved by US Army units, withdrawn just before Christmas and sent back to Guadalcanal for rest and retraining. The next operation planned for 3rd Marine Division was an attack on Kavieng, New Ireland, in March 1944. This was revised, however, when both Rabaul and Kavieng were isolated and thus made ineffective; 3rd Marine Division was prepared instead for an operation thousands of miles closer to Tokyo – namely the Marianas – to seize Saipan, Tinian and Guam. It was decided that, as already explained, 2nd and 4th Marine Divisions, supported by 27th Infantry Division, would land on the island; 3rd Marine Division would be held offshore as a floating reserve. If all went well, they would be used two days later, together with 1st Provisional Marine Brigade, in an assault on Guam. However,

delays occurred and the division found itself waiting off Guam for more than fifty days, until a new D-Day was set for 21 July. Two beachheads were chosen, 3rd Marine Division, under MajGen Turnage, landing three combat teams abreast on a long, curving beach between Adelup and Asan Points. It was estimated that there were some 30,000 Japanese on Guam, in perfect defensive positions among the hilltops and ravines. The fighting was bitter, the enemy having to be winkled out of their intricate clusters of caves with flame-throwers and demolitions, while their nightly 'banzai' attacks threatened the Marine positions all through the battle area.

Eventually the Marines began to get the upper hand, overrunning the main Japanese command post on Guam and pushing the enemy into the northern end of the island, where the last act of the battle was fought by a group of seven dug-in and well-camouflaged Japanese tanks that had to be knocked out one by one. The island was secure by 11 August, but there remained some 10,000 disorganised enemy stragglers in the northern part of the island who had to be mopped up; there would still be hostiles on Guam until after VJ Day more than a year later.

January and February 1945 saw 3rd Marine Division training for yet another operation, this time Iwo Jima, as part of V AC. Lying only some 750 miles from Tokyo, the small, 8-square-mile island was garrisoned by some 23,000 enemy, who had created many underground fortifications and were bound to put up a fierce fight. D-Day was 19 February and the fighting was every bit as tough as had been expected, with heavy casualties on both sides. The island was not secured until 17 March – D+26.

Now the division began training for the final assault – Operation 'Olympic', the initial invasion of Japan itself. Fortunately it never came off; as *Uncommon Valor* (McMillan *et al.*) comments, 'It would have been a rough operation – maybe the worst of all. But the outcome would never have been in doubt.'

4th Marine Division

Existing units and cadres from 3rd Marine Division began to assemble in various bases in early 1943, being split between the East and West Coast Echelons. The 23rd Marine Regiment was initially assigned to 3rd Marine Division, but then reassigned in February 1943, to 4th Marine Division, even though the division was yet to form. In May, 23rd Marine Regiment was split in half to form 25th Marine Regiment as well, while the rest of the divisional units also came into existence. On 16 August 1943, all the parts came together and 4th Marine Division was formally activated, with a total strength of 17,831 all ranks. Six months' training followed and on 13 January 1944, the division sailed from San Diego, the first and only division to go directly into combat from the USA. Ten days later the convoy arrived at Kwajalein and the first waves hit the beach at noon on 1 February, hitting both the islands of Roi and Namur simultaneously. Roi was soon secured, but Namur was very different and resistance was heavy. Tanks came ashore to support the attack in the afternoon, but progress was slow, because most enemy, although scattered and disorganised, did not retreat or surrender, so had to be killed.

The capture of Kwajalein Island a few days later gave the task force control over all the Marshall Islands, four individual Marines of 4th Marine Division being awarded the Medal of Honor during the first twenty-four hours of fighting – an all-time record unmatched by any other division in the Second World War. The taking of Roi–Namur pushed the American Pacific frontier almost 2,500 miles west of Pearl Harbor. After the battle, the division went to Hawaii to rest and retrain for the next operation; this would be the invasion of Saipan and Tinian on the Marianas, a further 1,000 miles west of the Marshalls.

The 4th Marine Division spent the next few months training on the island of Maui and enjoying the generous hospitality of the islanders, until May 1944, when they embarked for Saipan as part of V AC, while III AC was involved in the capture of Guam. Altogether over 165,000 troops were assembled for the two operations, the largest number ever under Marine command, while Fifth US Fleet, supporting the assault (over 800 ships), was the largest assemblage of warships ever known in the Pacific. Saipan was the HQ of the Japanese Central Pacific Fleet and defended by nearly 23,000 soldiers, plus a further 20,000 inhabitants.

D-Day was 15 June, with two Marine divisions (2nd and 4th) landing abreast on a 4,000yd beach along the western shoreline. Almost complete surprise was initially achieved, but then enemy resistance stiffened. By nightfall, the beachhead was about 1,500yd deep. However, the enemy had all the advantages of observation and terrain and were determined to make the Marines pay a heavy price for every yard of ground, which was studded with natural caves and prepared bunkers and provided excellent defensive positions for artillery and smaller weapons, while tangled undergrowth and fields of sugar cane hid snipers. Fighting continued until early August, despite steady progress, the enemy being reduced to passive defense from a rugged terrain of coral-limestone caves. Nevertheless, they defended stubbornly and withdrew in good order, usually by night. Towards the end, many committed suicide rather than be captured, including some of the civilian population. The successful capture of Tinian followed, 4th Marine Division being awarded the Presidential Unit Citation for their part in the landing there, after its performance on Saipan.

Iwo Jima, only 650 miles from Tokyo, was the next target, vitally important as a fighter base from which to escort the B-29s flying from Saipan. There was no opportunity for a surprise assault, the 23,000 Japanese garrison being subjected to a non-stop seventy-two-day aerial bombardment, followed by a three-day naval bombardment. Nevertheless, many of the garrison still remained to be dealt with in an assault during which personal bravery was unsurpassed in the Marine divisions that bore the brunt of the landings, Adm Nimitz commenting that 'uncommon valor was a common virtue'. The battle was in four phases: the fighting on the beaches, the capture of the two airfields in the centre of the island, the conquest of the high ground on Iwo's northern half, and the final annihilation of the enemy in the caves along the rocky coast. All this had to be achieved against an enemy that had well-prepared positions, and was determined, fanatical, well armed and well directed. It was undoubtedly 4th Marine Division's toughest battle; it took them thirteen days of fighting to break the Japanese line and the division alone suffered 6,591 casualties in those two weeks – and the battle was still far from over. The fourth and final stage of the battle was probably the worst; for example, many Japanese would charge by night suicidally into the Marine positions, with landmines strapped to their chests. Nevertheless, by the evening of 16 March, the island was declared secure. Over 22,000 enemy had been killed by the three Marine divisions, 8,982 being counted in 4th Marine Division's area alone. But the victory had been costly: 9,090 Marines had been killed or wounded, or were listed as missing.

Following Iwo Jima, the 4th Marine Division returned to Camp Maui to prepare for Operation Olympic and were still there when Japan surrendered. In September 1945 they returned to the USA and were the first Marine division to be deactivated. They had been overseas for twenty-one months, taken part in four invasions in thirteen months and spent five months aboard ship. Neverthess, as David Dempsey says in *Uncommon Valor* (McMillan *et al.*), 'Perhaps no division saw more violent combat in such a short space of time. Sixty-three days of fighting accounted for the highest casualty rate of any Marine Division. During the four operations in which the Division was engaged, 81,718 men saw action one or more times. Of these 17,722 were killed, wounded, or missing in action – over 21%.'

5th Marine Division, 'Spearhead'

In 1944 it was not easy to find spare manpower within the Marine Corps. With four divisions already deployed in the Pacific and 6th Marine Division forming on

Above: One man armed with a Thompson SMG stands guard while others collect 'dog tags' from Marines killed on the beach at Tinian on 1 August 1944. *(USMC B-24745 via Real War Photos)*

Below: M4A3 Sherman tanks of C Company, 4th Tank Battalion, and Jeeps are seen here on the beach at Iwo Jima. Note again the wooden planking on the tank sides (protection against magnetic mines) and the grids over the tank periscope housings.
(Lt Col R.K. Schmidt, USMC, now deceased, via author's collection)

Guadalcanal, they were hard-pressed to find the men to fill another division, yet they managed to do so, and to include over 40 per cent of veterans. As *Uncommon Valor* explains, 'There were paratroopers who had never had a chance to make a combat jump but nevertheless proved their mettle as infantrymen in the Solomons. There were Marine Raiders, disbanded as a unit like the paratroopers, who had raided Makin and fought the Japanese behind his lines on Guadalcanal when the war was young.' The new division was activated at Camp Pendleton, California, on 21 January 1944, its first CG being a veteran artilleryman, MajGen Thomas E. Bourke. However, he soon had to move on to another appointment and was relieved by MajGen Keller E. Rockey, who would command the division in the bloodiest battle in Marine Corps history.

By the summer of 1944, 5th Marine Division was complete and ready to sail. By 1 October it had settled down in its new 'home' at Camp Tarawa, Hawaii. They continued their training there and in late January 1945 left to assault Iwo Jima, D-Day being 19 February. The 5th Marine Division's role in the operation was twofold:

first, to land 28th Marine Regiment on the southernmost stretch of the eastern beach and secondly, take the dominant Mount Suribachi (a 556ft extinct volcano). The 27th Marine Regiment would land on their right, cut across to the western side of the island and drive northwards. The 26th Marine Regiment was to be held in reserve, ready to support either of the other two regiments. The enemy, who defended every inch of the island, firmly believed that Mount Suribachi was impregnable and would never be taken. It was an artilleryman's 'dream' observation post, as it commanded a view over two-thirds of the island. It was eventually taken by 28th Marine Regiment after several days of vicious fighting, much of which was at close quarters, and during which the division suffered over 1,000 casualties. The summit was finally reached on the morning of 23 February. The Stars and Stripes were raised on the top – first a tiny flag, then a much larger one (4.5ft by 9ft) that could be seen all over the island and by the men in the ships which lay offshore. (It was of course the subject of Joe Rosenthal's famous photograph. Of the eight men who raised the two flags, three were later killed, three wounded and only two were unscathed.)

However, the battle for Iwo Jima was still far from over; the core of the enemy cross-island defense in 5th Marine Division's sector was Hill 362, which proved just as tough a nut to crack as its slightly taller mate, Hill 382, which cost 4th Marine Division so many casualties that they called it the 'Meat Grinder'. Everywhere, the hills were covered in caves and pillboxes from which the enemy had to be blasted; Hill 362 fell on D+10. The Marines made full use of all their weapons, the most successful being flame-throwing tanks, against which the enemy had no defense. They were accustomed to dealing with ordinary tanks, using satchel charges, but the flame-throwing tank 'spewed forth great bursts of flame . . . and struck terror into his heart. Once an armoured bulldozer had scraped out a road for a flamethrower, the tank could make short shrift of any enemy position.'

Sometimes the Japanese attacked from the rear, waiting until night-time to emerge from bypassed caves and tunnels. Sometimes they would wear uniforms taken from Marine dead. They would also deliberately shoot to maim rather than to kill, so that they would have more targets when the wounded man's comrades went to his aid.

The fighting continued until 26 March, when, thirty-five days after they had first landed, 5th Marine Division fought its last battle – a short one, but bitter in its intensity. As *Uncommon Valor* (McMillan *et al.*) explains, 'Slowly, methodically, and with the disinterested air of men to whom death was an old, old story, the Fifth Division squeezed the enemy into ever-smaller pockets.' It had eventually taken almost as much ground away from the enemy as two other divisions combined and in doing so had lost more men than any other division in Marine Corps history.

Iwo Jima would be the 5th's first and last campaign, and it had fought from Iwo's southernmost tip (Mount Suribachi) to the island's north-east corner. Now they were going back to Hawaii to lick their wounds and train for the invasion of Japan. Gen Rockey left to command III Amphibious Corps, his place taken by their first CG, MajGen Thomas E. Bourke. But the invasion never happened, and in August 1945, 5th Marine Division sailed for Japan, going ashore at Sasebo on 22 September without a shot being fired. In January 1946,

Raising the Stars and Stripes on Mount Suribachi. This historic photograph, taken by the late Joseph Rosenthal on 23 February 1945, became one of the most evocative photographs to be taken during the Second World War and will forever typify the heroism of the leathernecks. *(USMC 80-G-413988/SI 1221 via Compendium Publishing)*

the division returned to the USA and was deactivated on 5 February 1946 at Camp Pendleton.

6th Marine Division, 'Striking Sixth'

The 'Striking Sixth' was the only Marine division to be formed overseas, being activated at Tassafaronga, Guadalcanal on 7 September 1944. Its core was 1st Provisional Marine Brigade, formed a few months earlier for the Guam operation, together with 4th and 22nd Marine Regiment. Its commander throughout would be MajGen Lemuel C. Shepherd, Jr. As with 5th Marine Division, 6th Marine Division had more than just a smattering of men who had been in the thick of the fighting almost from the start of the Pacific war. Its shoulder patch explained everything, the encircling border containing the names of Melanesia, Micronesia and Orient, as *Uncommon Valor* explains: 'The first two were for Tulagi, Guadalcanal, Makin, New Georgia, Bougainville, Parry, Engebi, Eniwetok, two dozen land dots in the Marshalls, Emirau, Saipan, Guam. "Orient" stemmed from the old days of 4th Marine Regiment in Shanghai and from the defense of Bataan and Corregidor, and pointed to the future – in China once more and in Japan itself.' The traditions of 4th Marine Regiment went all the way back to the original 4th Marine Regiment who had been in China in 1927. Now, the reborn 4th, for the very first time in Corps history, would assume the title and colours of a regiment not formally disbanded, while the

Heavily laden Marines pass through a small village on Okinawa, trudging past enemy dead. *(USMC 127-G-119485 via Compendium Publishing)*

men of the new 4th were not 'raw boots' but rather prime experts from the raider battalions, whose 'gung-ho' spirit had made them legendary. Their first mission as a separate regiment was the invasion of Emirau Island in the Bismarck Archipelago in March 1944. It was a bloodless coup, but there were tougher days ahead.

The other infantry regiment was the 22nd Marine Regiment, activated at Camp Elliott, California, in June 1942; the following month the unit sailed for Samoa to relieve other units bound for the offensive in the Solomons. They would remain there for the next year, training, then move to Hawaii, before joining in the campaign against the strongly fortified Marshall Islands (a double chain of coral atolls, 32 islands and 867 reefs that the Japanese had fortified). Of these, the most important were Engebi (with a large airfield), Parry and, south of Engebi, Eniwetok. The fighting was very tough but, moving three battalions abreast, 22nd Marine Regiment swept across Engebi and by nightfall had just about completed its task. Eniwetok

was next, and by the evening of 23 February (the operation began on 17 February) Parry, too, had been taken. Then, using Kwajalein as its base, 22nd Marine Regiment proceeded to seize twenty-nine other islands in the Marshalls in the next month.

The division's units assembled on Guadalcanal on 15 March 1944, then rendezvoused with III AC at Ulithi Atoll in the Carolines. It assaulted Okinawa on 1 April 1945 and fought there until 21 June, when Okinawa was declared secure. In that eighty-two-day period, 6th Marine Division had:

- captured part of Naha, once a city of 60,000 inhabitants, the largest city to be occupied by the Marines during the war;
- captured Naha airfield on Oruku, an important ferrying stop for the Japanese flying southwards towards the Indies, Formosa, Malaya, the Philippines and China;
- captured Yontan airfield, the second major airbase on Okinawa;
- captured Unten Ko midget submarine base, together with vast stores of equipment and supplies;
- seized more than two-thirds of the physical land area of Okinawa;
- killed more than 20,000 Japanese troops and captured more than 2,800;
- broken the Naha–Shuri–Yonbaru Line, won the vital battle of Sugar Loaf and smashed the last line of defense at Mezado Ridge.

In achieving all this, the division had suffered 8,226 casualties. This figure is for Okinawa only and does not include the losses that the component units suffered on

Men of 6th Marine Division flush Japanese defenders from the coral rock of Okinawa's coastline in May 1945. (USMC B-23496 via Do You Graphics, USA)

Next stop Tokyo! A boatload of 4th Marine Regiment troops landing on Japanese soil for the very first time, on 30 August 1945. *(USMC 80-G-338350 via Compendium Publishing)*

Eniwetok, Saipan, Guam and in other actions. Over 1,700 were killed in action.

On the day the war ended, 6th Marine Division was at Guam, in the middle of training for the assault on Japan. However, even before peace was declared, the 4th Marine Regiment 'took off' and were the first Marines to land in Japan in the Second World War, at the Kurihama naval base on 30 August 1945, in the Yokusaka defense area, less than 500yd from where Adm Perry and a Marine detachment had landed ninety-two years earlier. The rest of the division sailed to Tsingtao and Chefoo in northern China, operating in Shantung Province until deactivated in Tsingtao on 31 March 1946, without setting foot in the United States.

ANNEXE A

COMMANDING GENERALS (CG) OF USMC DIVISIONS DURING THE SECOND WORLD WAR

Division	Rank	Name	Date From	Date To
1st	MajGen	Holland M. Smith	1 Feb. 1941	13 Jun. 1941
	MajGen	Phillip H. Torrey	14 Jun. 1941	22 Mar. 1942
	MajGen	Alexander A. Vandegrift	23 Mar. 1942	7 Jul. 1943
	MajGen	William H. Rupertus	8 Jul. 1943	1 Nov. 1944
	(Brig Gen Oliver P. Smith temporary CG 9 May – 20 Jun. 1944)			
	MajGen	Pedro A. del Valle	2 Nov. 1944	8 Aug. 1945
	MajGen	DeWitt Peck	9 Aug. 1945	10 Jun. 1946
2nd	MajGen	Clayton B. Vogel	1 Feb. 1941	7 Dec. 1941
	MajGen	Charles F.B. Price	8 Dec. 1941	1 Apr. 1942
	MajGen	John B. Marston	2 Apr. 1942	30 Apr. 1943
	MajGen	Julian C. Smith	1 May 1943	10 Apr. 1944
	MajGen	Thomas E. Watson	11 Apr. 1944	22 Jun. 1945
	MajGen	LeRoy P. Hunt	22 Jun. 1945	10 Jul. 1946
3rd	MajGen	Charles D. Barrett	16 Sept. 1942	14 Sept. 1943
	MajGen	Allen H. Turnage	15 Sept. 1943	14 Sept. 1944
	(Brig Gen Alfred H. Noble acting CG 15 Sept.–13 Oct. 1944)			
	MajGen	Graves B. Erskine	14 Oct. 1944	21 Oct. 1945
4th	(Brig Gen James L. Underhill acting CG 16–17 Aug. 1943)			
	MajGen	Harry Schmidt	18 Aug. 1943	11 Jul. 1944
	MajGen	Clifton B. Cates	12 Jul. 1944	deactivation
5th	Brig Gen	Thomas E. Bourke	21 Jan. 1944	3 Feb. 1944
	MajGen	Keller E. Rockey	4 Feb. 1944	24 Jun. 1945
	MajGen	Thomas E. Bourke	25 Jun. 1945	15 Dec. 1945
6th	MajGen	Lemuel C. Shepherd, Jr	7 Sept. 1944	24 Dec. 1945
	(promoted from Brig Gen on 12 Sept. 1944)			

ANNEXE B

MARINE CORPS DIVISIONAL BATTLE STARS

Division	Battle Star	Remarks
1st	Guadalcanal	Two stars
	New Britain	
	Peleliu	
	Okinawa	
2nd	Guadalcanal	
	Tarawa	
	Saipan–Tinian	
	Okinawa	One Regiment only
3rd	Bougainville	
	Guam	
4th	Iwo Jima	
	Marshalls	
	Saipan–Tinian	
5th	Iwo Jima	
6th	Makin	Only one battalion, 4th Marine Regiment
	Solomons	Part of 4th Marine Regiment only
	Bougainville	Part of 4th Marine Regiment only
	Marshalls	Only 22nd Marine Regiment
	Saipan	Only one battalion, 29th Marine Regiment
	Guam	1st Provisional Brigade
	Okinawa	

'Old Glory' flies proudly, while a Corps linesman rigs communications from the beachhead at Tinian on 2 August 1944. Note also the amtrac in the background. *(USMC B-23521 via Real War Photos)*

ANNEXE C

MAJOR BATTLES AND DEPLOYMENTS OF THE SECOND WORLD WAR (7 DECEMBER 1941 TO 15 AUGUST 1945)

Pearl Harbor–Midway	7 Dec. 1941
Guam	8–10 Dec. 1941
Wake Island	8–23 Dec. 1941*
Bataan and Corregidor	26 Dec. 1941–6 May 1942*
East Indies (Badoeng Strait)	19 Feb. 1942
Coral Sea	4–8 May 1942*
Midway	3–6 Jun. 1942*
Guadalcanal–Tulagi landings	7–9 Aug. 1942*
First Savo (air and naval)	9 Aug. 1942
Capture and defense of Guadalcanal	10 Aug. 1942–8 Feb. 1943
Makin Island	17–18 Aug. 1942*
Eastern Solomons	23–5 Aug. 1942
Cape Esperance (naval)	11–12 Oct. 1942
Santa Cruz Island (air)	26 Oct. 1942
Guadalcanal (naval and air)	11–15 Nov. 1942
Tassafaronga (naval)	30 Nov. 1942–1 Dec. 1942
Komandorski Island (Aleutians)	26 Mar. 1943
New Georgia–Rendova–Vandunu occupation	20 Jun. 1942–31 Aug. 1943
Kula Gulf (naval)	5–6 Jul. 1943
Kolombangara (naval)	12–13 Jul. 1943
Vella Lavella occupation	15 Aug. 1943–16 Oct. 1943
Cape Gloucester (New Britain)	26 Dec. 1943–1 Mar. 1944*
Green Islands landing	15–19 Feb. 1944
Treasury Island landing	27 Oct. 1943–6 Nov. 1943
Choiseul Island diversion	28 Oct. 1943–4 Nov. 1943
Cape Torokina occupation and defense	1 Nov. 1943–15 Dec. 1943
Tarawa (Gilbert Islands)	20 Nov. 1943–8 Dec. 1943*
Kwajalein and Majuro Atolls (Marshalls)	31 Jan. 1944–8 Feb. 1944
Eniwetok Atoll (Marshalls)	17 Feb. 1944–2 Mar. 1944
Saipan, capture and occupation	15 Jun. 1944–10 Aug. 1944*
Guam, capture and occupation	21 Jul. 1944–15 Aug. 1944*
Tinian, capture and occupation	24 Jul. 1944–10 Aug. 1944*
Peleliu, capture and occupation	15 Sept. 1944–14 Oct. 1944*
Leyte (Philippines) landings	20 Oct. 1944*
Leyte Gulf (air and naval)	24–6 Oct. 1944
Iwo Jima	19 Feb. 1945–16 Mar. 1945*
Okinawa, capture and occupation	01 Apr. 1945–21 Jun. 1945*

* major battle or campaign

CHAPTER THIRTEEN

SOME FAMOUS MARINES

There are many wartime Marines who deserve special mention in this book – heroes who were awarded their country's highest honours, officers who made a major impact on the tactics of amphibious warfare as a whole and the Marine Corps in particular, other senior commanders who led Marine units with great élan. Unfortunately there is not room here for them all, so I have chosen a representative selection from the war years.

JOHN BASILONE

'Manila John', as he was known in the Marine Corps, was of Italian descent, and had lived in New Jersey, selling vegetables and working in a laundry before joining the Army in the 1930s. Stationed in Manila, he became a Golden Gloves boxing champion at light heavyweight. After completing his time with the Army, he went home, wanting to settle down. However, he missed the military life, so enlisted in the Marine Corps in 1940. On Guadalcanal, Basilone was a machine-gunner in 'Chesty' Puller's battalion (see later), defending Lunga Ridge near Henderson Field. The Japanese were determined to take the airfield and drive off the Marines. On the second night of the battle, there was a torrential rainstorm and the enemy managed to reach the barbed-wire defenses less than 40yd from his position, while many infiltrated behind the

Guadalcanal heroes. From left to right, these four Congressional Medal of Honor holders are MajGen Alexander A. Vandegrift, then commanding 1st Marine Division; Col Merritt 'Red Mike' Edson, CO of 1st Raider Battalion; 2/Lt Mitchell Paige; and Sgt John Basilone. The last two were both machine-gunners on Guadalcanal and have just been awarded with their medals. *(USMC 56749 via Do You Graphics, USA)*

244

Marine lines through gaps in the wire. Basilone kept his machine guns firing, despite having to go back through the jungle to the company command post in order to obtain spare parts and more belts of ammunition, fighting his way through the infiltrators with just his .45 automatic. After one such trip, he was told that the Japanese had overrun a section of machine guns on his right, killing two of the Marines and wounding three more. The Japanese had then tried to turn the machine guns on to other Marine slit trenches, but fortunately the guns had jammed. Sgt Basilone did not hesitate; he rushed immediately to the position, killed all the Japanese gun crews – eight in all – and then got the guns firing again. He achieved a highly successful pattern of crossfire with his other gun position across the gaps in the barbed wire. After the battle, it was found that there were over 800 enemy dead in front of his position. 'Manila John' was awarded the Congressional Medal of Honor for his bravery over the period 24–5 October 1942, the first enlisted Marine to be so honoured in the war.

Sent home a hero, in September 1944 he joined 27th Marine Regiment as they were training to invade Iwo Jima, 'hitting the beach' with them on 19 February 1945 with his machine-gun platoon. Despite being up to their knees in volcanic ash and under heavy enemy fire, his platoon managed to reach the end of the beach, where they were held up by an enemy blockhouse on top of which was a heavy machine gun. Basilone ordered his men to dig in, then circled behind the blockhouse and put it out of action with grenades. Moments later, he was killed by a mortar bomb, along with four of his platoon. He was posthumously awarded the Navy Cross and his statue now stands in Raritan, New Jersey.

GREGORY BOYINGTON

Growing up in Tacoma, Washington State, Gregory Boyington attended the University of Washington during the Depression, studying aeronautical science. He was a member of the ROTC there and an intercollegiate wrestling champion. He enlisted in the Marine Corps Reserve in 1936, was appointed an aviation cadet, then,

Maj Gregory 'Pappy' Boyington, skipper of VMF-214, the 'Black Sheep' Squadron, and USMC 'ace', climbs aboard his Vought F4U Corsair on Guadalcanal. Later, he was shot down, wounded and taken prisoner, but survived and was awarded the Medal of Honor. *(USN N-24894 via Real War Photos)*

after being awarded his wings, became a flight instructor. However, he craved action and so resigned his commission and went to China to join the legendary 'Flying Tigers'. Before they were disbanded he had logged over 300 flying hours and had shot down six enemy planes.

In 1942, he was recommissioned as a first lieutenant, sent to the Pacific and given command of VMF-214, a squadron of fledgling pilots, known as the 'Black Sheep' squadron. Boyington, now 31 years old, was nicknamed 'Pappy'. In its first month of combat on Guadalcanal, the squadron shot down 57 enemy aircraft; before they had completed their tour, the figure was 127, of which 'Pappy' had a personal tally of 22, making him one of the leading Marine 'aces'. During one sweep over Rabaul in which he had shot down three enemy planes, he then saw more enemy planes just below him. Before he could engage them, however, his plane was hit and the fuel tank exploded. Seriously wounded, he bailed out, landed in the sea and was taken prisoner. He was subsequently put into a special POW camp that was kept a secret by the Japanese from the Red Cross and the Americans, as they were special prisoners from whom they hoped to extract valuable information; needless to say, they got nothing out of 'Pappy'. However, this meant that his family did not know that he had survived until he was liberated at the end of the war, some twenty months after his capture. On his return home, he was promoted to lieutenant-colonel and awarded the Medal of Honor by President Harry S. Truman.

Visiting Guadalcanal, Adm Chester W. Nimitz decorates Lt Col Evans C. Carlson, CO 2nd Raider Battalion. Gen Vandegrift is in the rear, while behind Carlson are Brig Gen Rupertus, Col Edson, Lt Col Pollock and Maj Smith. *(USMC 50883)*

EVANS CARLSON

Son of a Congregationalist minister, Brig Gen Evans Fordyce Carlson grew up in Vermont, and served as an Army captain in the First World War. He enjoyed Army life very much, but decided to enlist as a Marine in 1922. He was later commissioned and sent to fight rebels in Nicaragua. It was here that he adopted the rebel tactics of travelling at night and ambushing by day, but improved on them by doing both during the night. With a small mounted detachment of 15th Marine Regiment, he once routed over a hundred rebels and chased them back across the border into Honduras, being awarded the Navy Cross for this exploit. He went to China, observing the Sino-Japanese war and becoming very impressed by the tough, mobile, self-reliant outlook of the Chinese Red Army; this was the foundation of his later 'gung-ho' ('pull together') way of training his raider battalion. When he came back to the USA he got into trouble for expressing his views in public, saying that the USA were undermining the Chinese communists by selling scrap metal and oil to Japan. This led to his resigning his commission in 1930 and returning to China as a civilian to study Red Army tactics further. The intense, young officer had, however, made a favourable impression upon President Roosevelt, to whom he sent back personal reports on a weekly basis. This visit confirmed his conviction that Japan was going to attack the USA; he returned home, told the authorities what he had seen, and was recommissioned as a lieutenant-colonel and given command of 2nd Raider Battalion. Carlson organised and ran his battalion very differently from 'Red Mike' Edson's 1st Battalion (see later), and his assault on Makin in August 1944 did not go entirely to plan. However, Carlson was awarded a Navy Cross for this operation, and another for his next, much more successful operation, spearheading a landing on Guadalcanal to capture Henderson Field. 'Lean, leathery, hawk-nosed, bushy-browed and brave' is how one of his contemporaries described this complex man, who had to retire early from injuries sustained on Saipan while trying to rescue a wounded man. He died just a year later, in 1947.

ANTHONY CASAMENTO

Although he was awarded the Congressional Medal of Honor for bravery during the action on Guadalcanal, he did not receive the actual award until 22 August 1980. At the time of the battle he was recommended for the Navy Cross, but eventually it was decided that he deserved the higher award and it was presented to him by President Jimmy Carter in person at the White House. The citation read:

For conspicuous gallantry and intrepidity at the risk of his life, above and beyond the call of duty while serving with Company D, First Battalion, Fifth Marines, 1st Marine Division on Guadalcanal on 1 November 1942. Serving as a leader of a machine gun section, Corporal Casamento directed his unit to advance along a ridge near the Matanikau River where they were engaged by the enemy. He positioned his section to provide direct support for the main force of his company which was behind him.

During the course of this engagement, all members of his section were either killed or severely wounded and he himself suffered multiple, grievous wounds. None the less, Corporal Casamento continued to provide critical supporting fire for the attack and in defense of his position. Following the loss of all effective personnel, he set up, loaded and manned his unit's machine gun, tenaciously holding the enemy forces at bay. Corporal Casamento single-handedly engaged and destroyed one machine gun emplacement to his front and took under fire the other emplacement on the flank. Despite the heat and ferocity of the engagement, he continued to man his weapon and repeatedly repulsed multiple assaults by the enemy forces, thereby protecting the flanks of the adjoining companies and holding his position until the arrival of the main attacking force. Corporal Casamento's courageous fighting spirit, heroic conduct and unwavering dedication to duty reflected great credit upon himself and were in the highest traditions of the Marine Corps and the United States Naval Service.

(Quoted in Westwell, *1st Marine Division*)

CLIFTON CATES

MajGen Clifton B. Cates had served with the USMC for twenty-eight years when he took command of 4th Marine Division at Tinian. At 51, he was one of the few Marine Corps general officers who had held combat command at platoon, company, battalion, regiment and divisional levels. Born in Tiptonville, Tennessee, he had served as a junior officer with 6th Marine Regiment at Belleau Wood, Soissons, St Mihiel and Blanc Mont, being awarded the Navy Cross, two Silver Stars and two Purple Hearts. He had commanded 1st Marine Regiment at Guadalcanal and, three years after Iwo Jima, became the nineteenth Commandant of the USMC.

MERRIT EDSON

'Red Mike' Edson began his military career with the Vermont National Guard on the Mexican border in 1914. Then, when the USA entered the First World War, he dropped out of college and joined the Marines, serving in France. By 1920, he, like Carlson, was a captain, serving in Nicaragua, where he won a Navy Cross for capturing the rebel leader's camp; unfortunately Sandino escaped, but it was nevertheless a highly successful operation. Like Carlson, he also learned the art of guerrilla tactics, travelling light and making the most of light, personal weapons, with high fire-power.

A lieutenant-colonel when the war started, he was appointed to command 1st Raider Battalion, leading them ashore at Tulagi and winning a second Navy Cross. This was followed by Guadalcanal, where the 'Battle of Edson's Ridge' was the decisive contest in the defense of Henderson Field. Despite a severe head-wound he led his men in hand-to-hand fighting and held their position on the ridge, being awarded the Medal of Honor for his bravery and leadership. At Tarawa he was Chief of Staff, 2nd Marine Division, landing on the second day and taking command of the fiercest fighting. Promoted to brigadier-general, he led 8th Marine Regiment in the final mopping-up on Tinian. When war ended, he had served for forty-four months in the Pacific theatre – longer than any other Marine officer.

EARL ELLIS

As a young officer at the Naval Academy before the First World War, Lt Col Earl Hancock 'Pete' Ellis developed a considerable interest in Japanese militarism, being convinced that they would become America's main opponents in the Pacific area. He was also a student of amphibious warfare and expounded his theories in a lecture at the Naval War College as early as 1913. He went on to become adjutant of 4th Marine Brigade, which served so successfully in France during the First World War. After the war, he again continued his work into Plan Orange (for war against the Japanese) and produced a paper on advanced base operations in Micronesia that would become the basis of Operational Plan 712D, the major USMC contribution to Plan Orange. Ellis later became even more obsessed by the Japanese threat and, in 1923, took a leave of absence in order to make a year-long un-official (but with HQ Marine Corps approv-al) tour of Japanese islands in the Pacific. Posing as an American businessman, during this tour he became ill and died in mys-terious circumstances in Kator, one of the Palau Islands, before completing his mission.

GRAVES ERSKINE

One of the youngest major-generals in the USMC at the time of Iwo Jima, Graves B. Erskine had served for twenty-eight years on active duty at that time. A graduate of Louisiana State University, he had received a commission and was immediately deployed with the American Expeditionary Force, as a platoon commander with 6th Marine Regiment at Belleau Wood. Twice wounded in France, he was awarded the Silver Star. In the interwar years he served in Haiti, Santo Domingo, Nicaragua, Cuba and China. Chief of Staff to 'Howlin' Mad' Smith during the campaigns in the Aleutians, Gilberts, Marshalls and Marianas, he assumed com-mand of 3rd Marine Division in October 1944 from MajGen Hal Turnage.

ROY GEIGER

Gen Roy Stanley Geiger was born in Florida in 1885, graduating from Stetson University and enlisting in the USMC in 1907. Two years later, he was commissioned, and then

This group photograph was taken during a visit to Guadalcanal by the then Marine Commandant MajGen Thomas Holcomb, who is standing fourth from the left, next to MajGen Roy Geiger (with helmet). *(USMC 513191)*

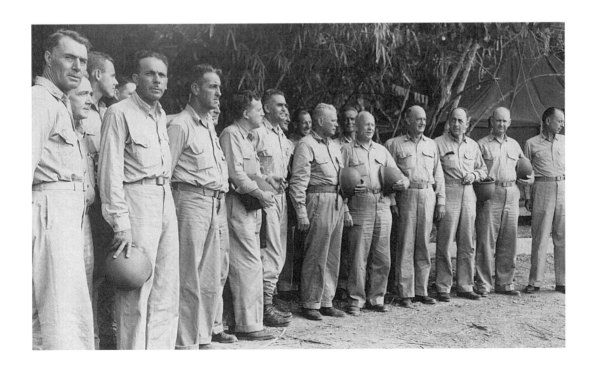

trained as a pilot. In the First World War, he commanded a squadron in France and won the Navy Cross. In early September 1942, he was promoted to brigadier-general and sent to Guadalcanal to command 1st Marine Aircraft Wing. Two months of continual action followed, for which he was awarded another Navy Cross. The following year, in May, he returned to the USA and was given command of all Marine Corps aviation as a major-general. November 1943 saw him taking over command of the I MAC from Gen Vandegrift (see later). The Marines had landed some eight days earlier on Bougainville, then, on 15 December, with their mission virtually completed and the beachhead secure, they handed over to the Army.

In April 1944, Geiger's command was redesignated III AC and he planned the liberation of Guam and Peleliu, before leading his corps on Okinawa. Briefly, he also commanded Tenth US Army after Gen Buckner was killed and before Stillwell arrived. A month later, Geiger took over the Fleet Marine Force, Pacific. After the war he served as an observer at the 1946 atomic bomb tests in Bikini Lagoon. His sombre warnings about the vulnerability of surface ships during ship-to-shore operations, when atomic demolitions were used, led directly to the development of the transport helicopter. He died in 1947.

THOMAS HOLCOMB

MajGen (later Gen) Thomas Holcomb became the US Marine Corps's seventeenth Commandant on 1 December 1936 and would remain in that vital post until 31 December 1943. In his early career (he had joined the USMC in 1900) he was an expert marksman and had headed the first Marine team ever to compete in national shooting matches, becoming the world champion in long-range shooting. He commanded first a battalion, then a regiment in the American Expeditionary Force in France. A genial, easy-going Marine officer who was born in 1879, he was promoted to brigadier-general in 1935 and made Commandant of the Marine Corps Schools. In November 1936, he was promoted over other more-senior officers to take over the post of Commandant USMC from Gen John H. Russell, and was reappointed four years later, in 1940. Holcomb fought long and hard to obtain the increases necessary to preserve the Fleet Marine Force and the concept of amphibious warfare that would become the main *raison d'être* of the USMC in the Second World War. Roosevelt trusted him, and in early 1942 gave him everything he needed – enough men to enlarge the Corps to four (then to six) divisions and two (then four) air wings. Holcomb would continue to fight for his Corps against both Navy and Army interference. One of the most highly decorated US officers (holder of the Navy Cross, four Silver Stars and the Purple Heart), he was the first Marine officer to be promoted to lieutenant-general. Believing that a younger man should take over the job of Command-ant, he retired, handed over to Vandegrift (see later) and was promoted to full general. In April 1944, he became Minister to South Africa, and he died in 1965.

JOHN LEJEUNE

Of French ancestry, MajGen John A. Lejeune's family had migrated to Louisiana from Canada. His farmer father, who had fought for the Confederacy, had always wanted him to join the Army, but as there were no vacancies at West Point, he had gone to Annapolis and been commissioned into the Marine Corps. He would command the Marine detachment that landed in

Panama in 1903 in support of the rebellion there that would create the new country of Panama and allow the canal to be built. Further service followed in Panama, Washington, the Philippines and Cuba. In 1914, he commanded the Marines who occupied Vera Cruz, Mexico, then returned to Washington to take up the post of Assistant to the Marine Corps Commandant. John Lejeune went to France in 1918, in command of 4th Marine Brigade, which fought so valiantly at Belleau Wood. Later, he commanded 2nd Division, which contained both Marines and Army troops (another first for a Marine officer). He was awarded the Distinguished Service Medal, the Légion d'Honneur and the Croix de Guerre for his service in France.

On 1 July 1920, he was made Commandant, a post that he would hold for the next eight years, before handing over to Gen Wendell Neville. Although he was thus long retired before the Second World War began, his development of Plan Orange, and of the part that the Marine Corps would play when it all became a frightening reality on the eruption of war with Japan, was vitally important. Lejeune's major role in the formulation of the revolutionary new concept that would turn the Marine Corps into the world's experts in amphibious warfare, puts this popular, forward-looking Marine officer into a very special place in Marine Corps history.

RANDOLPH PATE

Gen Randolph McCall Pate was born in 1898 and, after a short spell in the US Army, attended the Virginia Military Institute. He graduated in 1921 and was awarded a commission in the USMC. He saw active service in the Dominican Republic and China before the war, joining 1st Marine Division as assistant chief of supply in 1939. After serving with distinction in Guadalcanal, he was promoted to colonel and made deputy chief of staff, V AC. There, he was responsible for the planning and conduct of the battles for Iwo Jima and Okinawa. After the war he held a number of senior administrative posts before becoming director of the Division of Reserve at HQ MC. He was promoted to major-general and became CG 2nd Marine Division; later he took over 1st Marine Division and held that command until May 1954. He was appointed assistant commandant as a lieutenant-general, then, on 1 January 1956, took over from Gen Shepherd as Commandant, remaining in the post until his

A famous Marine Corps daughter. In November 1943 the Hon. Frank Knox, Secretary of the Navy (far left), congratulates 2/Lt Eugenia Lejeune, daughter of the late Lt Gen John A. Lejeune, on receiving her commission. The two USMC officers are MajGen Henry Larsen (right), CG Camp Lejeune, and Lt Gen Thomas Holcomb, Commandant, USMC. *(USMC 6014 via Do You Graphics, USA)*

retirement in 1959. He died after an illness some eighteen months later.

LEWIS PULLER

One of the most decorated and well-known officers in 1st Marine Division, 'Chesty' Puller was born in 1898 and attended the Virginia Military Institute before joining the USMC in 1918. He was commissioned in June 1919, but was rapidly put on inactive duty because the First World War had ended. Puller rejoined as an enlisted man and served against the rebels in Haiti until March 1924. Promoted to second lieutenant, he had a variety of postings, including two years at Pearl Harbor; then, in December 1928, he joined the Nicaraguan guard detachment and, in two tours of duty there, won two Navy Crosses. Next, he went to serve with the US Asiatic Fleet until 1936. After various tours as an instructor and on board USS *Augusta*, he returned to the USA in August 1941 and was given command of 1st Battalion, 7th Marine Regiment, 1st Marine Division. He took part in the battle for Guadalcanal and was awarded his third Navy Cross. Promoted to executive officer of 7th Marine Regiment, he served in that post, winning his fourth Navy Cross during the Cape Gloucester campaign on New Britain in January 1944. A month later he took command of 1st Marines Regiment and led that regiment on Peleliu in September and October of that year. That would be his final operational command of the war; soon afterwards, he returned to the USA and was made executive officer of the Infantry Training Regiment at Camp Lejeune. In August 1946, he became director of 8th Marine Corps Reserve based in New Orleans District. He later commanded the Marine Barracks in Pearl Harbor and then, in August 1950 at the start of the Korean War, he went back to 1st Marine Regiment for

active duty. Leading the regiment ashore at Inchon in September 1950, he was in command until January 1951 and was then made assistant divisional commander in the rank of brigadier-general. In January 1952, he was appointed CG of 3rd Marine Division until ordered to take charge of the Troop Training Unit, Pacific. Command of 2nd Marine Division followed, after promotion to major-general. Despite growing ill health, he tried to return to active service in Vietnam, but was refused. He died in 1971.

KELLER ROCKEY

Born in Columbia City, Indiana, Keller Rockey graduated from Gettysberg College and studied at Yale. He was 56 at Iwo Jima, and a veteran of thirty-one years' service with the Marine Corps. He served with the American Expeditionary Force in France and was awarded the Navy Cross as a junior officer in 5th Marine Regiment at Chateau Thierry. A second Navy Cross followed, for heroic service in Nicaragua. He also served in Haiti and spent two years at sea. After attending the Field Officers' Course at Quantico, and the Army Command and General Staff Course, he became Director of Plans and Policies at HQ USMC, and then Assistant Commandant. In February 1944, he became CG of 5th Marine Division and would lead them in their last great battle of the war.

WILLIAM RUPERTUS

Born in 1889, Gen William Henry Rupertus was commissioned into the US Marine Corps in November 1913, then graduated top of his class two years later at the Marine Officers' School. During the First World War, he commanded a Marine ship detachment on the USS *Florida* as part of the naval squadron serving with the British.

Gen Douglas MacArthur discusses the New Britain operation with MajGen William Rupertus (hands on hips), CG 1st Marine Division, whose troops would lead the assault. *(USMC 75882)*

After the war he served in Haiti, and attended both the Field Officers' School and the Army Command and General Staff School at Fort Leavenworth. Just prior to the Second World War, he served in China, then was Chief of Staff of the FMF.

On the eve of the war, Rupertus was in charge of Marine barracks in Washington, Cuba and San Diego, but was then made Assistant CG of 1st Marine Division, taking over command when Vandegrift left (see later). He was awarded the Navy Cross after the Guadalcanal campaign, overseeing successful landings on neighbouring islands of Tulagi, Gavutu and Tanambogo. He then led the New Britain landings, for which he was awarded the Distinguished Service Medal. After the assault on Peleliu, he returned to the USA and was made Commandant of the Marine Corps Schools at Quantico. He died of a heart attack on 25 March 1945, just a few months later.

HARRY SCHMIDT

Gen Harry Schmidt was the CG of V Amphibious Corps during the assault on Iwo Jima. A native of Holdrege, Nebraska, the 58-year-old had served in the Marine Corps for thirty-six years and had seen service in Guam, China, the Philippines, Mexico, Cuba and Nicaragua that had prevented him from serving with the American Expeditionary Force in France. During the Second World War he had commanded 4th Marine Division at Roi–Namur and Saipan, then assumed command of V AC for the Tinian landings. In the Iwo Jima assault he would command the largest force of Marines ever

committed to a single battle – 'it was the greatest honour of my life,' he said later.

LEMUEL SHEPHERD

MajGen Lemuel C. Shepherd, Jr, was the commander of 6th Marine Division from September 1944 onwards. A native of Norfolk, Virginia, the 49-year-old CG had served with great distinction during the First World War with 5th Marine Regiment in France, being wounded three times and awarded the Navy Cross. He was one of the few officers to have commanded every unit from platoon up to division. Earlier in the Pacific war, he had commanded 9th Marine Regiment and served as Assistant CG of 1st Marine Division at Cape Gloucester, and of 1st Provisional Marine Brigade at Guam. He commanded the newly formed 6th Marine Division and continued to do so with great valour in Okinawa. After the war ended he served as CG FMF, Pacific during the first

Above: MajGen Lemuel Shepherd, CG of 6th Marine Division, studies his map, with Naha, capital of Okinawa, in the background, in June 1945. Later, he was CG FMF during the Korean War and the twentieth Marine Commandant. *(USMC 127-GR-122119/SI 1230 via Compendium Publishing)*

Below: A good action shot of Lt Col David Shoup's command post on Okinawa, November 1943. Sitting in the foreground is Col Evans Carlson of the raiders. Shoup is carrying the obvious mapcase and talking to one of his commanders close by. *(USMC 63505 via Do You Graphics, USA)*

two years of the Korean War, then became the twentieth Commandant. He died in 1990.

DAVID SHOUP

MajGen David M. Shoup was a former farmboy from Battle Ground, Indiana, who would be awarded the Medal of Honor in 1943, after Tarawa. After the war, he became the Marine Corps Commandant (1960–3). 'An interesting character,' wrote Robert Sherrod after first meeting him: 'a squat red-faced man with a bull neck, a hard boiled, profane shouter of orders, he would carry the biggest burden on Tarawa.' Someone else described him as a 'Marine's Marine, a leader the troops could go to the well with'. This extract from his Medal of Honor citation reflects his strength of character: 'Upon arrival at the shore [Tarawa], he assumed command of all landed troops and working without rest under constant withering enemy fire during the next two days, conducted smashing attacks against unbelievably strong and fanatically defended Japanese positions despite innumerable obstacles and heavy casualties.' 'The brainiest, nerviest, best soldiering Marine I ever met' was high praise indeed from First Sgt Edward Doughman, who served with Shoup in China. Shoup died on 13 January 1983, aged 78, and was buried in Arlington National Cemetery.

HOLLAND SMITH

Gen Holland McTyeire 'Howlin' Mad' Smith was born in Seale, Alabama, in April 1882. After attending the Alabama Polytechnic Institute, he decided to become a career officer and joined the Marines, being commissioned in March 1905. He fought with the American Expeditionary Force in

France, winning the Croix de Guerre with Palm. After the war he was director of operations and training at Marine Corps HQ, being responsible in the main for developing amphibious warfare. In September 1939, he took command of 1st Marine Brigade. Moving to Cuba, he was promoted to major-general and commanded 1st Marine Division, formed from the expanded 1st Marine Brigade, until June 1941. Returning to the USA, he took command of the Amphibious Force, Atlantic Fleet.

Short, heavy-set with glasses and a moustache, he looked more like a business tycoon than a fighting general, but his reputation was legendary. In September 1941, he went to the west coast to oversee the organisation of the Pacific Fleet Amphibious Force. He was 60 years old and serving at Quantico in 1942 when he was wrongly found, by a medical board, to be suffering from severe diabetes; however, he managed to prove them wrong. ('The events set me wondering', he wrote later, 'about a conspiracy that could deprive a man from an opportunity to fight for his country by killing him with a medical certificate.') Increasingly depressed at being unable to get 'into the action', he was eventually made CG Fleet Marine Force, Pacific and led some of the most critical Pacific landings – at Kwajalein, Eniwetok, Saipan, Guam and Tinian. During the Saipan operation he was forced to relieve Army general Ralph Smith for lack of aggressiveness. 'Howlin' Mad' Smith oversaw the 1945 landings on Iwo Jima and Okinawa, then, in July 1945, returned to Camp Pendleton to direct training until May 1946, when he retired as a full general after forty-one years' service. He died in January 1967.

JULIAN SMITH

Graduating from the University of Delaware, Lt Gen Julian C. Smith, who had been born in Elkton, Maryland, in 1885, also graduated from the Naval War College in 1917, then spent the duration of the war at Quantico with numerous other frustrated Marine officers. His overseas service after the First World War included Panama, Mexico, Haiti, Santo Domingo, Cuba and Nicaragua, where he won the Navy Cross. A distinguished marksman and rifle team coach, he commanded 5th Marine Regiment and later the FMF Training School before joining 2nd Marine Division in May 1943. Unassuming and self-effacing, he was genuinely loved by his soldiers, who would follow him anywhere. He was awarded the Distinguished Service Medal after Tarawa, retiring as a lieutenant-general in 1946. He died in 1975, aged 90.

Talking about the tactical situation on Saipan with Lt Gen 'Howlin' Mad' Smith (helmet under arm) are MajGen Thomas Watson, CG 2nd Marine Division, and Adm Raymond A. Spruance. *(USMC M-127 via Real War Photos)*

Above: The two Gen Smiths pictured on Betio: MajGen Julian C. Smith, then CG 2nd Marine Division, with hand on chest, and MajGen Holland M. 'Howlin' Mad' Smith, then commanding V Amphibious Corps. *(USMC 70729)*

Below: Taking the salute at a WR review at Camp Lejeune in 1945 is Col Ruth Cheney Streeter, first director of the Marine Corps Women's Reserve. *(USMC via Do You Graphics, USA)*

RUTH STREETER

First woman to be appointed as Director of the Marine Corps Women's Reserves was Col Ruth Cheney Streeter, who took the post on 13 February 1943, having been sworn in by the Secretary of State for the Navy on 29 January 1943, in the rank of major. She was promoted to the rank of colonel when the directors of the other women's services were similarly promoted. At the time she was 47 and had been president of her class at Bryn Mawr. Wife of a prominent business-man, mother of four, including three sons in the services, actively involved in twenty years of work in New Jersey health and welfare, she had been chosen from twelve outstanding women. She was described as being 'confi-dent, spirited, fiercely patriotic and highly principled'. She retired in December 1945 and died in September 1990.

PEDRO DEL VALLE

MajGen Pedro A. del Valle was born in San Juan, Puerto Rico, and graduated from the Naval Academy in 1915. He commanded the Marine detachment on board USS *Texas* in the North Atlantic during the First World War. Between the wars he took part in the capture of San Domingo and in the campaign in the Dominican Republic. In 1931, he was, as a major, appointed to the Landing Operations Text Board in Quantico and wrote a challenging essay, 'Ship to Shore in Amphibious Operations', which urged his contemporaries to think seriously about opposed landings. A decade later, now a veteran artilleryman, he commanded 11th Marine Regiment with distinction during the Guadalcanal campaign. He later commanded the III AC corps artillery at Guam, being awarded a Gold Star, before assuming command of the 'Old Breed' for Okinawa. He was later awarded a Disting-

MajGen Pedro A. del Valle, who commanded
11th Marine Regiment with distinction during the
Guadalcanal operations and went on to command
1st Marine Division on Okinawa. He was later
awarded the Distinguished Service Medal. *(USMC)*

uished Service Medal for his leadership. Gen del Valle died in 1978.

ALEXANDER VANDEGRIFT

'Sunny Jim', as he was nicknamed, was a modest, quiet man, whose many abilities, such as tenacity, courage and resourcefulness, were never immediately apparent. He was also the first officer to lead a US Marine division in combat since the First World War. He became the eighteenth Commandant of the USMC in January 1944 and was the first Marine ever to hold four-star rank. He was born in Charlottesville, Virginia, in 1887; his grandfather was a captain in Pickett's charge at Gettysberg. Commissioned into the

Marines in 1909 after spending two years at Virginia Military Academy, he saw action in Nicaragua and later in Haiti against the Cocos, then in China, where he served under Gen Smedley D. 'Old Gimlet Eye' Butler. In 1936, after further service in China, he was appointed Assistant Commandant to Gen Holcomb, then, just before the attack on Pearl Harbor, he became Assistant CG of 1st Marine Division. In March 1942, he took over the division and was promoted to major-general. He was in command during the landings on Guadalcanal and, despite the fact that there was no time for rehearsals, this first amphibious assault of the war went extremely well, thanks in no small way to his ability. Vandegrift won the Navy Cross and was later awarded the Medal of Honor. 'Sunny Jim' was expecting to return to the USA after this exhausting campaign, but instead remained in theatre because of the sudden

President Franklin D. Roosevelt presents Gen Vandegrift with his Medal of Honor, assisted by Mrs Vandegrift and watched by the General's son, Maj Alexander Vandegrift, USMC. *(National Archives 208-PU-209V-4)*

[Browning] automatic [rifle] at point-blank range into a depression housing Japanese troops, killing eight of the enemy and enabling the greater part of his platoon to take cover. During his platoon's withdrawal for consolidation of lines, he remained to safeguard a severely wounded comrade, courageously returning the enemy's fire until the arrival of stretcher bearers, and then covered the evacuation by sustained fire as he moved backwards toward his own lines. With his platoon again pinned down by a hostile machine gun, Pfc Witek, on his own initiative moved forward boldly to the reinforcing tanks and infantry, alternately throwing hand grenades and firing as he advanced to within 5 to 10 yards of the enemy position, and destroying the hostile machine gun emplacement and an additional eight Japanese before he himself was struck down by an enemy rifleman. His valiant and inspiring action effectively reduced the enemy's firepower, thereby enabling his platoon to attain its objective and reflects the highest credit upon Pfc Witek and the US naval service. He gallantly gave his life for his country.

death of the commander of I Marine Corps, taking charge of the corps during the landings at Empress Augusta Bay, Bougainville, on 11 November 1943.

Subsequently he did go home, taking over as Commandant from Gen Holcomb and overseeing the massive wartime expansion of the USMC. He gained his fourth star on 4 April 1945, the first Marine officer to do so. He retired on 31 December 1947 and died on 8 May 1973.

FRANK WITEK

Pfc Frank Peter Witek's Medal of Honor citation reads:

For conspicuous gallantry and intrepidity at the risk of his life and beyond the call of duty while serving with the 1st Battalion, 9th Marines, 3rd Marine Division, during the Battle of Finegayen at Guam, Marianas Islands on 3 August 1944. When his rifle platoon was halted by heavy surprise fire from well camouflaged enemy positions Pfc Witek daringly remained standing to fire a full magazine from his

FAMOUS MARINES ON POSTAGE STAMPS

In 2005, the United States Postal Service (USPS) issued stamps saluting four distinguished Marines: Gunnery Sgt John Basilone, Sgt Maj Dan Daly, Lt Gen John A. Lejeune and Lt Gen Lewis B. Puller. Details of those relevant to this book have already been mentioned above, Sgt Maj Dan Daly was a double Medal of Honor winner from the 1915–18 era. More information can be obtained (including purchasing the stamps) at www.usps.com.

CHRONOLOGY OF THE WAR IN THE FAR EAST AND PACIFIC THEATRE

1941

22 June	1st Marine Brigade (Provisional) departs USA
7 July	1st Marine Brigade (Provisional) arrives Iceland
7 December	Japan attacks Pearl Harbor; USA declares war against Japan
8 December	Japan attacks the Philippines, Hong Kong, Malaya and Wake Island
24 December	Japan captures Wake Island
25 December	Hong Kong surrenders
31 December	Japanese advance on Manila (capital of the Philippines)

1942

16 January	Japanese invade Burma
February–March	1st Marine Brigade (Provisional) relieved by Army Task Force 4 and returns to USA
15 February	Singapore surrenders
12 March	Gen MacArthur leaves the Philippines
25 March	1st Marine Brigade (Provisional) disbanded in New York City and units rejoin 2nd Marine Division in San Diego
18 April	The Doolittle raid on Japan
30 April	Japanese capture Burma
6 May	Last US troops in Philippines surrender
4–7 June	Naval battle of Midway (turning point of Pacific war)
7 June	Japanese invade Aleutians
7 August	USMC land on Guadalcanal (Solomons)
17 August	USMC raiders attack Makin (Gilberts)
15 November	Large Japanese transport convoy destroyed off Guadalcanal
18 December	US and Australian troops in heavy fighting against the Japanese in Papua New Guinea

1943

4 January	Japanese begin to withdraw from Guadalcanal
1 February	Japanese withdrawal from Guadalcanal complete
2–5 March	Japanese transport convoy sunk off Lae, New Guinea
18 April	Adm Yamamoto shot down and killed by US fighter aircraft over Bougainville
20 June	Japanese launch major attack in New Guinea
30 June	US amphibious attack on Japanese in the Solomon Islands (Operation 'Cartwheel')
1 July	US troops capture Viru Harbour, New Georgia, and consolidate their positions in New Guinea
28 August	Japanese evacuate New Georgia and other islands in the Solomons, so as to consolidate their positions on Bougainville and New Britain
5 September	US and Australian forces land east of Lae, New Guinea
11 September	US and Australian forces take Salamaua, New Guinea
15 September	Capture of Lae by US and Australian forces
6 October	USMC land on Kolombangara, New Georgia
20–3 November	Battle for Tarawa
25 December	USMC land on New Britain
29 December	USMC capture Cape Gloucester airfield, New Britain

1944

31 January– 5 February	US troops land on the Marshall Islands
18 February	US Task Force 58 attacks Truk
21 February	Gen Tojo appointed Chief of Staff, Japanese Army
29 February	US troops land on Admiralty Islands
9 March	Japanese offensive on Bougainville
29 March	US task force attacks Caroline Islands
22 April	US troops land in Holpandia, New Guinea
17 May	US troops land on Wadke Island, New Guinea
27 May	USMC attack Biak Island in Wadke Bay
15 June	US troops invade Saipan in the Marianas
13 July	Saipan secured
21 July	US troops land on Guam in the Marianas
24 July	US troops land on Tinian in the Marianas
25–7 July	Task Force 58 assaults Palau Islands
1 August	Tinian secured
8 August	Guam secured
31 August	Task Force 58 assault Bonin Islands
15 September	US troops land on Peleliu
17 September	US troops land on Angaur Island
10–21 October	US troops raid Formosa, Luzon and Ryukyus

12 October	Peleliu secured
20 October	US troops land on Leyte, central Philippines
23 October	Anguar secured
25 November	First B-29 (Superfortress) raid on mainland Japan (from the Marianas)
26–7 December	Heavy Japanese counter-attacks on Leyte

1945

1 January	US troops begin mopping up on Leyte
23 January	Sixth US Army approaches Clark Field on Luzon
1 February	Sixth US Army drives towards Manila
16 February	Task Force 58 raids Tokyo and Yokohama
19 February	US troops land on Iwo Jima
24 February	US troops secure Manila
8 March	US troops land on Mindanao, southern Philippines
26 March	US troops secure Iwo Jima
1 April	US troops land on Okinawa
12 April	Death of President Roosevelt (Harry S. Truman replaces him)
19 May	US troops secure Luzon, Philippines
22 June	US troops secure Okinawa, Ryuku Islands
6 August	First atomic bomb dropped on Hiroshima
9 August	Second atomic bomb dropped on Nagasaki
14 August	Japanese agree to an unconditional surrender
2 September	Surrender signed on board USS *Missouri* in Tokyo Bay

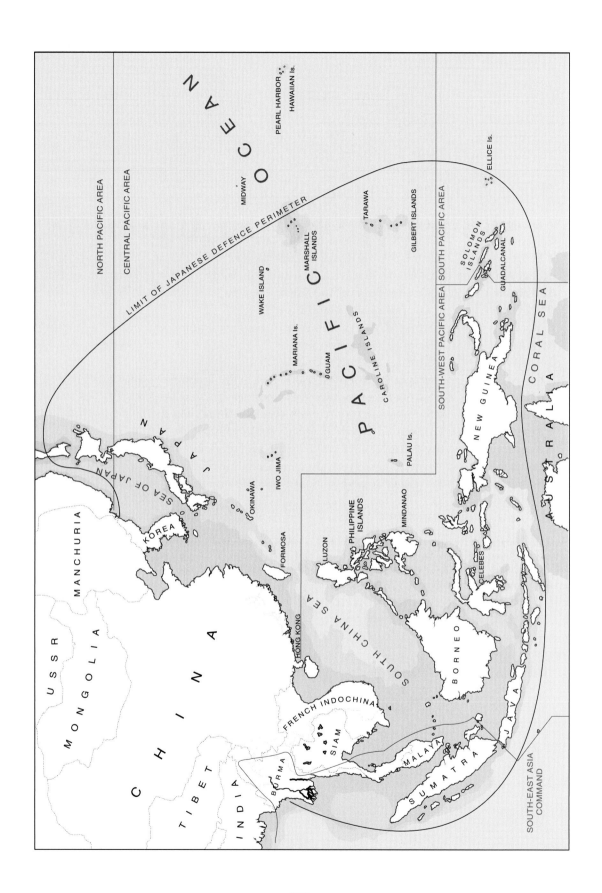

NORTH PACIFIC AREA

CENTRAL PACIFIC AREA

PACIFIC OCEAN

PEARL HARBOR

HAWAIIAN Is.

MIDWAY

LIMIT OF JAPANESE DEFENCE PERIMETER

TARAWA

GILBERT ISLANDS

ELLICE Is.

SOUTH PACIFIC AREA

WAKE ISLAND

MARSHALL ISLANDS

SOLOMON ISLANDS

GUADALCANAL

MARIANA Is.

GUAM

CAROLINE ISLANDS

SOUTH-WEST PACIFIC AREA

SEA OF JAPAN

JAPAN

PALAU Is.

NEW GUINEA

CORAL SEA

AUSTRALIA

IWO JIMA

OKINAWA

FORMOSA

LUZON

PHILIPPINE ISLANDS

MINDANAO

CELEBES

HONG KONG

SOUTH CHINA SEA

BORNEO

USSR

MONGOLIA

MANCHURIA

KOREA

CHINA

FRENCH INDOCHINA

SIAM

JAVA

TIBET

INDIA

BURMA

MALAYA

SUMATRA

SOUTH-EAST ASIA COMMAND

262

ABBREVIATIONS AND ACRONYMS

British equivalents, where different, are shown in brackets with 'Br'.

AA	anti-aircraft	**BAD**	Base Air Detachment
AAA	anti-aircraft artillery	**BAR**	Browning automatic rifle
AAWS	Assault Air Warning Squadron	**BB**	battleship
ABG	Air Base Group	**BGen**	Brigadier-General (Br: Brig)
ACIO	Air Combat Intelligence Office(r)	**Bhp**	brake horse power
Acorn	construction unit (amphibious)	**Blip**	echo on radar screen
ADC	Air Defense Command	**Bln**	balloon
ADCC	Air Defense Control Centre	**Bn**	Battalion
AES	Aircraft Engineering Squadron	**Bogey**	unidentified plane
AGC	amphibious force flagship	**Brig**	Brigade (Br: Bde)
AI	airborne intercept (radar)	**BuAer**	Bureau of Aeronautics
AirFMFPac	Aircraft, Fleet Marine Force, Pacific		
AK	cargo vessel	**CA**	heavy cruiser
ALP	Air Liaison Party	**CAM**	Composite Army–Marine Division
amtrac	amphibian tractor	**CAP**	combat air patrol
A/N	Army/Navy (joint equipment designation system)	**CAS**	close air support
		CASD	Carrier Aircraft Service Detachment
AO	oiler	**CB**	Construction Battalion (Seabees)
AP, APA	troop transport	**CG**	Commanding General
APD	troop transport (high speed)	**CINCPAC/**	Commander in Chief Pacific Fleet/
APO	Army Post Office	**POA**	Pacific Ocean Area
Argus	Naval Air Warning Squadron	**CL**	light cruiser
Arty	artillery	**CMC**	Commandant of the Marine Corps
ASP	anti-submarine patrol	**CMCS**	Commandant of the Marine Corps Schools
AT	anti-tank (Br: A tk)	**CO**	commanding officer
ATC	Air Transport Command (Army)	**Co**	Company (Br: Coy)
ATIS	Allied Translation and Interrogation Service	**Col**	Colonel
		Cp	camp
AWRS	Aviation Women's Reserve Squadron	**CV**	aircraft carrier
AWS	Air Warning Squadron		

CVE	aircraft carrier escort		(tri-service, responsible for comms for air coordinators, naval gunfire spotters and shore party commanders)
CVG	naval carrier air group		
CVL	aircraft carrier small		
CVS	carrier squadron		
		JCS	Joint Chiefs of Staff
DD	destroyer	**JICPOA**	Joint Intelligence Centre/Pacific Ocean Area
DE	destroyer escort		
Deact	deactivate(d)		
Det	Detachment	**KIA**	killed in action
DUC	Distinguished Unit Citation (Army)	**kts**	knots (i.e. nautical miles per hour)
Dumbo	air-sea rescue plane		
		LantFlt	US Atlantic Fleet
Engr	engineer	**LCC(1)**	Landing Craft Control (Mk 1) (also called a 'Control boat')
ETO	European Theatre of Operations		
		LCI	Landing Craft Infantry
Flex	fleet landing exercise	**LCI(G)**	Landing Craft Infantry (Gun)
FM	Field Manual (Army)	**LCI(L)**	Landing Craft Infantry (Large) (also called an 'Elsie Item')
FMF	Fleet Marine Force		
FMFLant	Fleet Marine Force, Atlantic	**LCI(M)**	Landing Craft Infantry (Mortar)
FMFPac	Fleet Marine Force, Pacific	**LCI(R)**	Landing Craft Infantry (Rocket)
FPO NY	Fleet Post Office, New York	**LCM**	Landing Craft Mechanised
FPO SF	Fleet Post Office, San Francisco	**LCP**	Landing Craft Personnel (also called 'Papa boat')
FSCC	Fire Support Coordination Centre		
Ft	fort	**LCP(L)**	Landing Craft Personnel, Large (also called a 'Eureka boat')
GCI	ground control intercept (radar)	**LCP(R)**	Landing Craft Personnel (Ramp) (also called a 'Higgins boat')
Gen	General		
		LCR(L)	Landing Craft Rubber (Large)
Hedron	HQ Squadron	**LCR(S)**	Landing Craft Rubber (Small)
HMG	heavy machine gun	**LCS(S)**	Landing Craft Support (Small)
How	howitzer	**LCT**	Landing Craft Tank
HQ	headquarters	**LCV**	Landing Craft Vehicle (also called a 'Higgins boat')
HQMC	Headquarters, Marine Corps		
HqSq	HQ Squadron	**LCVP**	Landing Craft Vehicle or Personnel (also called a 'Papa boat' or a 'Higgins boat')
IFF	identification, friend or foe (radar)		
III AC	III Amphibious Corps	**LFASCU**	Landing Force Air Support Control Unit
IJA	Imperial Japanese Army		
IJN	Imperial Japanese Navy	**LMG**	light machine gun
I MAC	I Marine Amphibious Corps	**Loran**	Long-range Radio Aid to Navigation
Inf	infantry	**LSD**	Landing Ship, Dock
		LSM	Landing Ship, Medium
JANAC	Joint Army–Navy Assessment Committee	**LSM(R)**	Landing Ship Medium (Rocket)
		LST	Landing Ship, Tank
JASCo	Joint Assault Signal Company	**LSV**	Landing Ship Vehicle

LT	Landing Team (Battalion)	**ND**	Naval District
Lt Col	Lieutenant-Colonel	**NGF**	Naval Gunfire Section
Lt Gen	Lieutenant-General	**nm**	nautical miles (1nm = 1.151 statute miles)
LVT	Landing Vehicle Tracked (amtrac)		
		NOB	Naval Operating Base
MAD	Marine Aviation or Air Detachment	**NTLF**	Northern Troops and Landing Force
MAG	Marine Aircraft Group	**NUC**	Navy Unit Citation
MAGS	Marine Air Task Force (2–3 MAGs)		
MAHA	Marine Aircraft Hawaiian Area	**PacFlt**	US Pacific Fleet
MajGen	Major-General	**Phib Corps LantFlt**	Amphibious Corps Atlantic Fleet
MAR	Marine Air Reserve		
Mar Admin Comd	Marine Administrative Command	**PhibCorps PacFlt**	Amphibious Corps Pacific Fleet
MarAir SoPac	Marine Aircraft South Pacific	**Plat**	Platoon (Br: Pl)
		Prcht	Parachute (Br: Para)
MarAir West	Marine Air, West Coast	**Prov**	Provisional
		PUS	Presidential Unit Citation
MarDiv	Marine Division		
MarFAir West	Marine Fleet Air West Coast	**RCT**	Regimental Combat Team (USA)
		React	Reactivated
MarFor	Department of the Pacific, USMC	**Redes**	Redesignated
MASG	Marine Air Support Group	**Regt**	Regiment
MASP	Marine Aircraft South Pacific	**Reinf** or **(+)**	Reinforced ('-' = Less, i.e. elements detached from parent unit)
MAW	Marine Aircraft Wing		
MAWC	Marine Air, West Coast	**RIB**	Rigid Inflatable Boat
MAWPac FMF	Marine Aircraft Wings, Pacific Fleet Marine Force	**RL**	rocket launcher
		RLT	Regimental Landing Team
MB	Marine Barracks		
MBDAG	Marine Base Defense Aircraft Group	**S&S**	Service and Supply
MCAAF	Marine Corps Auxiliary Air Facility	**SCAT**	South Pacific Combat Air Transport
MCAB	Marine Corps Air Base	**SCR**	set, complete radio (later Signal Corps radio)
MCAS	Marine Corps Air Station		
MCBSD	Marine Corps Base San Diego	**SerGrp-(Prov)**	Service Group (Provisional) – aviation ground unit
MCS	Marine Corps Schools		
MD	Marine Detachment	**SoPacMar ProvCorps**	South Pacific Marine Provisional Corps
MFAWC	Marine Fleet Air West Coast		
MIA	missing in action	**SP**	self-propelled
MOG	Marine Observation Group	**Spt**	Support
Mort	mortar	**Sqdn**	Squadron (Br: Sqn)
Motor-T	motor transport	**STLF**	Southern Troops and Landing Force
MP	Military Police		
MT	motor transport	**TAG**	Tactical Air Group
MTD	Marine Training Detachment	**TF**	Task Force
NAS	Naval Air Station	**TIC**	Target Information Centre
NCB	Naval Construction Battalion ('Seabees')	**Tng**	Training (Br: Trg)

T/O	Table of Organisation		**VMF**	Marine Fighting Squadron
			VMF(N)	Marine Night Fighting Squadron
UDT	Underwater Demolition Team		**VMJ**	Marine Utility Squadron (before
USA	United States Army			Jun. 1944)
USAAF	United States Army Air Force		**VML**	Marine Glider Squadron
USMC	United States Marine Corps		**VMO**	Marine Observation Squadron
USMCR	United States Marine Corps Reserve		**VMR**	Marine Transport Squadron
USMCWR	United States Marine Corps Women's			(after Jun. 1944)
	Reserve		**VMS**	Marine Scouting Squadron
USN	United States Navy		**VMSB**	Marine Scout-Bombing Squadron
USS	United States Ship		**VMTB**	Marine Torpedo-Bombing Squadron
VAC	V Amphibious Corps		**WIA**	wounded in action
VMB	Marine Bombing Squadron		**WTLF**	Western Troops and Landing Force
VMBF	Marine Fighter-Bombing Squadron			
VMD	Marine Photographic Squadron		**ZMQ**	Marine Barrage Balloon Squadron

APPENDIX III

THE PHONETIC ALPHABET

Used to ensure that words/letters were clearly understood on the radio or telephone. First used in 1938 and revised slightly in 1941 – old words are shown in brackets. The British armed forces had similar systems but they were not standardised between the Allies until after the war (then based upon the in-service US alphabet).

A	ABLE (AFIRM)	N	NAN (NEGAT)
B	BAKER	O	OBOE
C	CHARLIE (CAST)	P	PETER
D	DOG	Q	QUEEN
E	EASY	R	ROGER
F	FOX	S	SUGAR (SAIL)
G	GEORGE	T	TARE
H	HOW (HYPO)	U	UNCLE (UNIT)
I	ITEM (INT)	V	VICTOR
J	JIG	W	WILLIAM
K	KING	X	XRAY
L	LOVE	Y	YOKE
M	MIKE	Z	ZEBRA (ZED)

APPENDIX IV

SOME EXAMPLES OF NICKNAMES

Alligator	LVT (also 'Large Vulnerable Target')
Beach Buster	LVT(3)
Betty	Marmon-Harrington light tank (after Adm 'Betty' Stark)
Blowtorch	flame-thrower
Buck Rogers Gun	Reising sub-machine gun
Corkscrew	demolition
Duck	DUKW amphibian
Elsie Item gunboat	Landing Craft Infantry (Gun)
Mighty Midget	Landing Craft Support (Large) Mk III
Sandy Andy	4.5in Mk 7 self-propelled rocket-launcher
Seabees	Naval Construction Battalion
Water Buffalo	LVT(2)
Weasel	M29C amphibious carrier
Whoofus	Landing Ship, Medium (Rocket)

APPENDIX V

SOME EXAMPLES OF OPERATIONAL CODEWORDS FOR ASSAULTS ON ISLANDS

BACKHANDER Cape Gloucester
BREWER Admiralty Islands
CARTWHEEL Two-axis operation in south and south-west Pacific areas to seize central Solomons; main focus was Imperial Japanese Navy base at Rabaul, New Britain
CATARACT Marshall Islands
CATCHPOLE Eniwetok and Ujelang Atolls
CLEANSLATE Russell Islands
DETACHMENT Iwo Jima
DEXTERITY New Britain
DIPPER Bougainville
DOWNFALL Overall plan for invasion of Japan
FLINTLOCK Marshall Islands
FORAGER Mariana Islands (Saipan, Tinian, Guam)
GALVANIC Gilbert Islands (including Tarawa and Nauru Islands)
ICEBERG Okinawa Group and Ryukyu Island
LONGSUIT Tarawa Atoll assault
OLYMPIC Japan – original codeword for November 1945 invasion, but was compromised in August 1945 and changed to MAJESTIC
STALEMATE Peleliu and Angaur in the Palau Islands
WATCHTOWER Guadalcanal and Tulagi landings

In addition, all the islands, atolls and island groups where the USMC operated were given codewords, e.g. **BALSA** – Midway; **BULLY** – Marshalls; **INCREDIBLE** – Tarawa; **KOURBASH** – Makin; **ROARING** – Hawaii.

BIBLIOGRAPHY AND SOURCES

Adcock, Al, *WW II US Landing Craft in Action*, Warships No. 17, Squadron/Signal Publications, 2003

Alexander, Col Joseph H., *Across the Reef: The Marine Assault of Tarawa*, Marines in World War II Commemorative Series, 1993

——, *Closing In: Marines in the Seizure of Iwo Jima*, Marines in World War II Commemorative Series, 1994

——, *The Final Campaign: Marines in the Victory on Okinawa*, Marines in World War II Commemorative Series, 1996

Bailey, Maj Alfred Dunlop, *Alligators, Buffaloes and Bushmasters: The History of the Development of the LVT through WW II*, History and Museums Division, HQ USMC, 1986

Boatner, Mark M. III, *Biographical Dictionary of World War II*, Presidio Press, 1996

Bradley, John H. and Dice, Jack W., *The Second World War: Asia and the Pacific*, Avery Publishing Group Inc., 1984

Chapin, Capt John C., *Breaching the Marianas: The Battle for Saipan*, Marines in World War II Commemorative Series, 1994

——, *Breaking the Outer Ring: Marine Landings in the Marshall Islands*, Marines in World War II Commemorative Series, 1994

——, *Top of the Ladder: Marine Operations in the Northern Solomons*, Marines in World War II Commemorative Series, 1997

——, *And a Few Marines: Marines in the Liberation of the Philippines*, Marines in World War II Commemorative Series, 1997

Clifford, Lt Col Kenneth J., *Progress and Purpose: A Developmental History of the USMC 1900–1970*, History and Museums Division HQ USMC, 1973

Cole, Maj Merle T., 'The Paramarines', *Journal of the American Aviation Historical Society*, winter 1989

Cressman, Robert J. and Wenger, J. Michael, *Infamous Day: Marines at Pearl Harbor 7 December 1941*, Marines in World War II Commemorative Series, 1992

Cross, Robin, *History of the United States Marine Corps*, Chevprime Ltd, 1988

Donovan, Col James A., *Outpost in the North Atlantic: Marines in the Defense of Iceland*, Marines in World War II Commemorative Series, 1992

Edwards, Lt Col Harry W., *A Different War: Marines in Europe and North Africa*, Marines in World War II Commemorative Series, 1994

Estes, Kenneth W., *Marines under Armour: The Marine Corps and the AFV 1916–2000*, Naval Institute Press, 2000

Forty, George, *United States Tanks of World War II*, Blandford Press, 1983

——, *US Army Handbook 1939–1945*, Sutton Publishing, 1995

Forty, George and Forty, Anne, *Women War Heroines*, Arms and Armour, 1997

Gayle, Brig Gen Gordon D., *Bloody Beaches: The Marines at Peleliu*, Marines in World War II Commemorative Series, 1996

Harwood, Richard, *A Close Encounter: The Marine*

Landing on Tinian, Marines in World War II Commemorative Series, 1994

Hearn, Chester G., *An Illustrated History of the United States Marine Corps*, Salamander Books Ltd, 2002

——, *The Illustrated Directory of the United States Marine Corps*, Salamander Books Ltd, 2003

Hoffman, Lt Col Jon T., *Silk Chutes and Hard Fighting: USMC Parachute Units in WWII*, Marines in World War II Commemorative Series, 1999

——, *From Makin to Bougainville: Marine Raiders in the Pacific War*, Marines in World War II Commemorative Series, 1995

Hogg, Ian V., *The American Arsenal*, Greenhill Books, 1996

Hough, F.O. *et al.*, *History of the US Marine Corps Operations in World War II*, US Government Printing Office, 1958–68, vols 1–5

Isely, Jeter A. and Crowl, Philip A., *The US Marines and Amphibious Warfare: Its Theory and its Practice in the Pacific*, Princeton University Press, 1951

Lawliss, Chuck, *The Marine Book*, Guild Publishing, 1988

McMillan, George, Zurlinden Jr, C. Peter, Josephy Jr, Alvin M., Dempsey, David, Beech, Keyes and Kogan, Herman, *Uncommon Valor: Marine Divisions in Action*, Infantry Journal Press, 1946 and Battery Press, 1986

Melson, Maj Charles D., *Up the Slot: Marines in the Central Solomons*, Marines in World War II Commemorative Series, 1993

——, *Marine Recon 1940–90*, Osprey Military, 1994

——, *Condition Red: Marine Defense Battalions in World War II*, Marines in World War II Commemorative Series, 1996

Mersky, Cdr Peter B., *Time of the Aces: Marine Pilots in the Solomons 1942–1944*, Marines in World War II Commemorative Series, 1993

Miller, J. Michael, *From Shanghai to Corregidor, Marines in Defense of the Philippines*, Marines in World War II Commemorative Series, 1997

Millett, Alan R., *Semper Fidelis: The History of the United States Marine Corps*, Macmillan Publishing Co., Inc, 1980

Mondey, David, *The Concise Guide to American Aircraft of World War II*, Hamlyn, 1982

——, *American Aircraft of World War II*, Chancellor Press, 1996

Moran, Jim, *US Marine Corps Uniforms and Equipment in World War 2*, Windrow & Greene, 1992

——, *Peleliu 1944: The Forgotten Corner of Hell*, Campaign 110, Osprey, 2002

Nalty, Bernard C., *Cape Gloucester: The Green Inferno*, Marines in World War II Commemorative Series, 1994

——, *The Right to Fight: African American Marines in WWII*, Marines in World War II Commemorative Series, 1995

O'Brien, Cyril J., *Liberation: Marines in the Recapture of Guam*, Marines in World War II Commemorative Series, 1994

Rottman, Gordon L., *US Marine Corps 1941–45*, Elite 59, Osprey, 1995

——, *Okinawa 1945: The Last Battle*, Campaign 96, Osprey, 2002

——, *US Marine Corps World War II Order of Battle*, Greenwood Publishing, Westport, Conn., 2002

——, *World War II Pacific Island Guide: A Geo-Military Study*, Greenwood Publishing, Westport, Conn., 2002

——, *Guam 1941 & 1944: Loss and Reconquest*, Campaign 139, Osprey, 2004

——, *The Marshall Islands 1944: Operation Flintlock, the Capture of Kwajalein and Eniwetok*, Campaign 146, Osprey, 2004

——, *Saipan & Tinian 1944: Piercing the Japanese Empire*, Campaign 137, Osprey, 2004

——, *US Marine Corps Pacific Theater of Operations 1941–43*, Battle Orders 1, Osprey, 2004

——, *US Marine Corps Pacific Theater of Operations 1943–44*, Battle Orders 7, Osprey, 2004

——, *US Marine Corps Pacific Theater of Operations 1944–45*, Battle Orders 8, Osprey, 2004

——, *US World War II Amphibious Tactics: Army & Marine Corps, Pacific Theater*, Elite 117, Osprey, 2004

——, *US Special Warfare Units in the Pacific Theater 1941–45: Scouts, Raiders, Rangers and Reconnaissance Units*, Battle Orders 12, Osprey, 2005

Shaw, Henry I. Jr, *Opening Moves. Marines Gear Up for War*, Marines in World War II Commemorative Series, 1991

——, *First Offensive. The Marine Campaign for Guadalcanal*, Marines in World War II Commemorative Series, 1992

Sherrod, Robert, *History of Marine Corps Aviation in World War II*, Presidio Press, 1952 and 1980

Smith, Charles R., *Securing the Surrender: Marines in the Occupation of Japan*, Marines in World War II Commemorative Series, 1997

Stremlow, Col Mary V., *Free a Marine to Fight: Women Marines in World War II*, Marines in World War II Commemorative Series, 1994

Suermont, Jan, *Infantry Weapons of World War II*, Iola, Wisc., Compendium Publishing, 2004

Tulkoff, Alec S., *'Grunt Gear': USMC Combat Infantry Equipment of World War II*, R. James Bender Publishing, 2003

Tyson, Carolyn A., *A Chronology of the United States Marine Corps, 1935–1946*, USMC, 1971

Updegraph, Charles L. Jr, *US Marine Corps Special Units of World War II*, History and Museums Division, HQ USMC, 1972

Westwell, Ian, *1st Marine Division 'The Old Breed'*, Spearhead 8, Ian Allan, 2002

Wright, Derrick, *Pacific Victory*, Sutton Publishing, 2005

PERIODICALS

Marine Corps Gazette, ISSN 0025-3170, published monthly by the Marine Corps Association, Box 1775, Quantico, Va. 22134.

INTERNET RESOURCES

HQ USMC   www.hqmc.usmc.mil
Marine Link   www.usmc.mil

Marine Corps   www.mca-marines.org/gazette.
  Gazette

MUSEUMS

The Marine Corps History Division
3079 Moreell Avenue, Quantico, Virginia 22134, USA.

The Marine Corps Museum Division
Currently located at 2014 Anderson Avenue, Quantico, Virginia 22134, USA.

Marine Corps Historical Center
The Chief Historian, Charles D. Melson, can be contacted at melsoncd@hqmc.usmc.mil. There is a library with extensive archives, including personal papers, available to researchers.

The Marine Corps Museum, the National Museum of the Marine Corps
Currently under construction and is scheduled to open in November 2006.

USMC Air/Ground Museum
Brown Field, Quantico, Va. 22134, USA. Tel: 703 784 2606.

US Marine Raider Museum
Raider Hall, US Marine Base, Quantico, Va., USA.
The Curator of the Marine Raider Museum is George MacRae.

Marine Corps Recruit Depot Museum
1600 Henderson Avenue, San Diego, CA 92140, USA. Tel: 619 524 6038.

There is also a Research Centre at the Marine Corps Quantico Base, containing a large collection of private papers of officers and enlisted men.

INDEX

The numbers in italic refer to illustrations.